BOMBS BEARDS AND BARRICADES

BOMBS BEARDS AND BARRICADES

150 Years of Youth in Revolt

ANTHONY ESLER

STEIN AND DAY/*Publishers*/New York

First published in 1971

Library of Congress Catalog Card No. 71-163351

Published simultaneously in Canada by Saunders of Toronto, Ltd.

Designed by David Miller

Manufactured in the United States of America

Stein and Day/*Publishers*/7 East 48 Street, New York, N.Y. 10017

ISBN 0-8128-1403-7

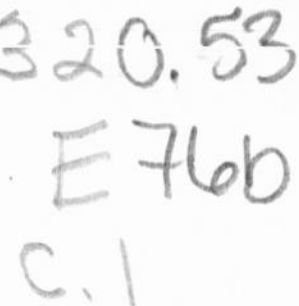

Contents

PART III: THE GROWTH OF THE YOUTH REVOLUTION

PART IV: WHERE DO WE GO FROM HERE?

Preface

This is a book about the history of the Youth Revolution.

For many, the very coupling of these two concepts—"history" and "the Youth Revolution"—will appear to be a glaring contradiction in terms. The upsurge of youthful dissent that has become such a disturbing part of all our lives often seems (especially to participants) much too recent and short-lived a phenomenon to *have* a history. Even for those older citizens who recognize that "the Movement" does go back at least a dozen years, to a flashpoint somewhere around 1960, the revolt of the younger generation usually seems somehow *sui generis,* a unique, almost a-historical explosion of youthful insurgency with only the flimsiest parallels in the past. To suggest that generational rebellion has been a significant part of the history of the Western World for at least 150 years is likely to earn the historian an irritable shrug of disbelief from today's young rebels—and from their outraged elders too.

Such, nevertheless, is the thesis of this book.

The special significance of the turbulent 1960's and early '70's does *not* lie in any startling originality manifested by the long-haired young Bohemians and revolutionaries of these colorful, crusading, violent years. Unaware though most of the young rebels may have been of past precedents for their revolts, such precedents do in fact exist. Practically everything our insurrectionary youth have tried—from New-Left militance to hippie-style withdrawal from society, from the campus revolt to the commune movement—has been tried before.

The crucial importance of the Youth Revolution of our times lies not in its alleged uniqueness, but in that very continuity with history which the Movement itself—and most of its critics—have so vehemently rejected. The prime significance of the generation gap, in America and beyond the seas, lies precisely in the fact that generational rebellion *is* a continuing and growing part of Modern History. The Youth Revolution is no nine-days' wonder, no baffling anomaly of the past decade or so. It is a vital, if badly neglected, element in the history of the past two centuries, and one which will almost certainly loom even larger in the chronicles of the future. The continuing Youth Revolution, its colorful history and its vital thrust into the future, comprise the subject of this book.

The writing of even so brief a volume on so sweeping a subject has inevitably put the present author deeply in debt to many authorities on nineteenth- and twentieth-century history, politics, social life and intellectual developments. I have tried to acknowledge some at least of this debt in the appended notes. It would be downright churlish, however, not to express special appreciation here to a few of the many individuals and institutions without whom this book would never have been written at all.

I should like to express my gratitude to the American Council of Learned Societies, whose generous financial help enabled me to devote full time to research for this book, and to the College of William and Mary for dispensing with my services for two consecutive years. Thanks also to the student-run Williamsburg Free College, where I had the opportunity to offer an abbreviated version of what follows as a course in "Rebellious Youth in Modern History," and to the students at Northwestern University for a similar opportunity.

I should particularly like to express my appreciation to the friends and colleagues who have lent me their expertise in the various specialty areas dealt with here. Thanks again to Professors Dietrich Orlow, Bob Bezucha, George Strong, Gil McArthur, and Ed Crapol for many shrewd criticisms and helpful suggestions. Thanks to Bill Williams for criticisms, suggestions, and good company in the streets. My gratitude also to Miss Jutta Hans for her imaginative help with the Russian sources, and for her translations of them. And thanks to my wife, Carol, for pitching in heroically whenever help was needed.

All surviving wrongheaded interpretations and other *gaffes* are, of course, strictly the responsibility of the author.

Thanks, finally, to a man I have never met, but whose eminently sensible strictures on books about the Youth Revolution have been devoutly taken to heart in the pages that follow. I quote from Mr. Michael Rossmann's review article on the Berkeley Free Speech Movement of 1964:

> In these books taken together, FSM appears in reverse: the absent dimensions are revealing. There is no humor, no poetry, no community, no contact with the real, no collective sense of value, no sense of the strange. The atmosphere is one of analytical structures . . . that refuse to become relevant, to function properly.[1]

The present book contains a minimum of "analytical structures." It represents a serious effort to recapture some of the "absent dimensions" Mr. Rossmann emphasizes—the reality, the community, the sense of value, the flashes of poetry and humor. Without these subjective but crucial elements, no account of the continuing revolt of the younger generation is likely to make any sense at all.

A. E.
30 July 1971

Part I

THAT GAP

1

The Other Side of the Barricades

No one who was young then will ever forget the first week of May, 1970. No one, at least, who was young and in college and even remotely concerned about the way the world wagged. For in May of 1970, they finally started shooting college kids—white, middle-class college kids in America. And the universities blew their tops.

The "youth revolt" had been making headlines and influencing policies and politics in America for a decade by then. For millions of college and university students, however, their own much-discussed revolt acquired a new and painfully personal dimension that sunny week in the spring. Suddenly, on May 4, 1970, the perspectives changed radically for America's concerned college youth. The battle cry that brought the hair and beads and bell bottoms swarming into the streets was no longer Selma or Saigon or "the ghetto," or someplace equally far off and romantically unreal. The name of the revolution that spring of 1970 was *Kent State*. It was a cry that convulsed the campuses as nothing else had in the whole insurgent decade of the sixties.

1. *REMEMBER KENT STATE?*

Neither Columbia nor Berkeley

Americans like to fight for causes. They particularly like to take up arms in a fine fury of indignation at some perfidious act of treachery on the part of their adversaries. "Remember the Alamo!" "Remember the 'Maine'!" "Remember Pearl Harbor!"—the ringing calls to arms echo down our history. The insurgent youth of

1970 were simply following in their elders' footsteps when they raised their own, new battle cry that May: "Remember Kent State!"

Kent State University was not the sort of place you would pick as the trigger for the explosion that would bring to a climax ten wild years of youthful crusading and insurgency. It was a state school located at Kent, Ohio, "in the middle of the country," as a subsequent volume of student reminiscences would describe it.[1] A corn-fed campus in the great middle-American heartland, far from the New York radical crowd or the freaked-out weirdos of the West Coast; a far cry from such riot-scarred institutions as Berkeley or Columbia. Who could imagine the Free Speech Movement or the Columbia occupation in Kent, Ohio?

But the new fashions and new values of the hippie counterculture had spread even to America's heartland. And by the later 1960's, the more militant strain of social concern and radical activism had also reached as far into the interior as Kent. Opposition to the Vietnam War in particular seems to have grown on the campus from 1967 on. Terry Robbins, a leading student organizer at Kent State, went on to die in the famous Greenwich Village townhouse explosion in March, 1970, one of the first casualties of the Weatherman Underground. By that dark winter of 1969–70 the Movement was clearly a real, if somewhat shaky force at KSU.

At the end of April, President Nixon formally announced the American invasion of Cambodia. At Kent, as elsewhere, student reaction was strongly negative. The badly fragmented local chapter of the SDS (Students for a Democratic Society) once again found an audience for its radical rhetoric. The resulting confrontation escalated rapidly from angry words to angry deeds.

Friday, May 1, marked the beginning of three nights of street and campus violence—trashing and burning by the SDS and a few hundred followers, tear gassing and arrests by the local police. Scores of windows were shattered by demonstrators; scores of students were arrested by police. On Saturday night, rampaging youths burned the ROTC building—an old frame Army barracks—to the ground, and the National Guard was dispatched to Kent by the Governor of Ohio.

It was a familiar pattern, an almost ritualistic exchange of thrust and counterthrust, challenge and response. Then the scenario veered suddenly from disturbing reality to nightmare.

At high noon on Monday, May 4, an unauthorized rally was called on a grassy hill on the Kent State campus. Guardsmen with rifles and gas masks drove the students off the hill with barrages of tear gas. The demonstrators, resentful of the presence of the Guard on campus and convinced that they had a right to rally there, hurled insults and rocks at the Guardsmen. The troopers, weary from long hours on duty and apparently feeling themselves hemmed in by hostile students, suddenly knelt and fired. The brief, ragged volley wounded ten Kent State students—some demonstrators, some mere bystanders—and killed four.

The result was the most massive student rebellion of the decade, and quite possibly the greatest single such upheaval in American history.

Trashing Pig Amerika

The stunning pictures flashed across the country. A single, long-haired protester confronting a kneeling line of Guardsmen, defiantly flourishing the black flag of anarchy as the troopers level their rifles. The contorted corpse of one of the dead students, sprawling at the end of a smear of blood that stretched halfway across the street on which he lay. The horrified face of a girl crouching over the body of a young man, staring in disbelief.

Across the country, the campuses rose. The National Guard had to be called out in half a dozen states. Dozens of universities were rocked by riots. Hundreds of campuses were swept up in a nation-wide student strike. A hundred thousand young people surged onto the well-worn path to Washington for yet another monster demonstration of the outrage of the younger generation. In all, perhaps half the student population of the country was affected by what one news magazine called "the most turbulent week on the campus since the protest era began." [2]

Students in New York and Los Angeles poured off the campuses to close down major highways leading into the cities. Radicals at the University of Wisconsin fought the police for days, trashing windows and flinging rocks and fire bombs. In California, Governor Reagan, who seldom flinched before campus revolutionaries, prudently shut down the entire state-university system for four days. The more liberal presidents of Princeton, Oberlin, and some other prestigious institutions simply closed down for the rest of the semester.

Everywhere there were rallies, marches, demonstrations, memorial services, demands for change. All the slogans of the sixties, reformist and revolutionary, rose once more from hundreds of campuses: End the war now! End racism, poverty, and pollution! Reform the university! Revolutionize America! The more moderately inclined trooped to Washington to see their Congressmen. The more radical disrupted traffic, destroyed property, and hurled the tear gas back in the teeth of the police.

On campus after campus across the country, the same neat row of four white crosses bloomed. Students came, often in couples, to stand a moment in silence and read the names: Jeff Miller—Allison Krause—William Schroeder—Sandy Scheuer. Those who stood before the primitive cenotaph seldom said anything or stayed long. More often than not, they were serious, straight-looking young people, the kind who would never dream of picking up a brick or calling a policeman "pig."

The radicals seldom paused before the crosses of the Kent State four. They had done their mourning already—for Ho Chi Minh, dead the previous summer. For Che Guevara, killed with the guerrillas in Bolivia. For Fred Hampton, the young Black Panther leader shot to death the previous winter by the Chicago police. These self-styled revolutionaries had no time now for paying silent tributes. They were too busy organizing—and fighting.

On Strike—SHUT IT DOWN!

The explosion that rocked the Midwestern university where I had been observing and researching the past and present of the youth revolt for two years was not atypical.

Northwestern University in Evanston, Illinois, on the plushy North Shore side of Chicago was far from a hotbed of radicalism. Northwestern was a Big Ten school, more famous for its pretty girls than for its football team. Sororities and fraternities had always been strong there, though recently they seemed to have lost some of their appeal. But the leafy, beach-fringed campus still stretched lovely and green along the shore of Lake Michigan, to all intents and purposes as much a bastion of the establishment as ever.

The students, mostly bright and prosperous children of the well-to-do, had recently begun to show some concern over issues like the war, or perhaps dormitory visiting hours. The faculty was liberal, the administration willing to compromise—up to a point. There had been a black sit-in a couple of years before—settled peacefully—and a few radical "incidents" since. The small SDS cadre could sometimes rally fifty or a hundred stalwarts (plus of course a few hundred gawkers) for a demonstration against the presence of Dow Chemical or the ROTC on campus. By and large, however, apathy still seemed to be the mood of the majority at NU.

The morning after the Kent State killings, I saw the first black arm bands, and a few red ones. *The usual SDS types,* I noted, as I retired to my library carrel and my note cards.

When I took my coffee break at ten, I found a roughly scrawled handbill in the lounge. No tortured radical rhetoric this time, no statistics carefully culled from *The New York Times.* It was simple and to the point, not a dozen words long:

VIETNAM
LAOS
CAMBODIA
KENT STATE
FUCK IT!
STRIKE!!

By noon, the first lines of marchers were moving across the campus. Red flags, black flags, arm bands, leg bands, headbands. "Peace Now! Peace Now! Peace Now!" The old Moratorium chant from the preceding fall. And then: "On Strike—SHUT IT DOWN! On Strike—SHUT IT DOWN! On Strike—"

They shut it down.

By evening, the few dozen SDSers had found thousands of allies at Northwestern University; basically straight young people still, many of them uneasy at the company they were keeping, but ready now to move with the radical front: to drape red flags from their dormitory windows and tie red headbands around their hair; to picket and leaflet, to buttonhole citizens on the street, to go from door to door; to acquiesce, albeit a bit nervously, when the SDS responded to a comparatively mild police gesture by flinging up a makeshift barricade across a main commuter artery flowing past the university into Chicago.

A barricade, in the streets of 1970 America! I watched the thing go up—the wooden sawhorses, the hunks of paving from a nearby street-repair project, the huge metal garbage containers, yards of iron fencing, and the wrought-iron gates of the university itself. I saw the red flag of revolution and the black flag of anarchy planted defiantly on the jagged ramparts.

I had taught it all often enough to college history classes—I had never dreamed of seeing it. In Paris, in the Revolution of 1830, or 1848, or 1871. Or 1968, for that matter: barricades were somehow *natural* in Paris. But in Evanston, Illinois—*now?*

It was all there. The wild costumes, the wilder bravado, the fraternity of the barricades. The symbols and the *-isms.* And the youth.

Revolution—ideology—and youth. The history book I had been writing for years was standing right there in front of me, a living reality in 1970 America.

2. *THE VIEW FROM THE CAMPUS*

Spring, 1970: Frisbees and Ecology

For most Americans, it all came on with bewildering suddenness.

That spring had seemed to many to bring an easing of tensions. There was a new mood of moderation and responsibility among the nation's turned-on young. Even a certain resurgence of apathy here and there, around the edges.

There was a quieter tone to the crowds of kids who gathered on green campuses or in sunny parks for the annual rites of spring. They tossed their frisbees or dug rock concerts, smoked a little dope, made love. Or they just lay there on the grass, smiling up at the warm blue sky. If it hadn't been for the marijuana and the throbbing volume of the music, for the long hair of the boys and the bra-lessness of the girls, it might easily have been some idyllic musical-comedy campus out of the 1920's.

It was a mood that made their elders hope, at least, that the worst was over. There was much talk about the "Woodstock spirit."

Granted, it had been a tumultuous autumn and a sporadically violent winter. There had been the big anti-war "Moratorium" marches of October and November. Women's Lib was a hot issue, in the magazines at least, and Gay Lib was beginning to organize. There had been the noisily disruptive courtroom tactics at the trials of the New York Twenty-One (Black Panthers) and the Chicago Eight (charged with plotting the Democratic National Convention riots of the year before). There had been rioting here and there, especially over the Chicago trial: youthful demonstrators had burned a bank as far west as Santa Barbara, California. There had been many Weatherman-style bombings, and some Panther shoot-outs with police.

But more Panthers had been killed than policemen. The Weathermen had made their biggest headlines by blowing up some of their own people in a Greenwich Village townhouse. Most encouraging of all, the clean-cut kids who had flocked in astonishing numbers to the Moratoria the preceding fall seemed now to have turned their celebrated crusading energies in a far less disturbing direction. The ecology movement was big this spring.

Up with the environment—down with pollution! The cockles of their elders' hearts warmed to see the younger generation take up such public-spirited, nonviolent, safely co-optable concerns as poisoned air and dirty water. Politicians and the press fell all over each other offering congratulations, encouragement and support.

In April, the Moratorium committee closed down its offices in Washington. The youthful anti-war movement and all the agony it had brought to the national conscience seemed to be dead. As dead as the anti-poverty and civil-rights crusades that had preceded it. The turbulent 1960's were laid to rest at last. And about time too, many people over thirty muttered disgustedly. The country was pretty sick of its kids—but at least the younger generation was beginning to see sense.

Z *and* Easy Rider

The picture looked rather different from inside the manicured putting-green campuses that had once seemed like such safe havens of the American way of life. There was a new tranquillity, all right, but it was that "eerie tranquillity" that Kingman Brewster, the president of Yale, would note a year later, in the stunned and silent aftermath of Kent State. It was, in the spring of 1970, the sudden nervous paralysis that comes with the dawning realization that society at large has had enough of crusades.

In the eyes of the radicalized young, at least, the great crusades of the sixties, to which young people had contributed so much, had clearly failed.

Laws against racial discrimination had piled up on the statute books. But blacks were still last hired, first fired; still ghettoized and sharecropping; still—God help us—going to segregated schools, North and South, a decade and a half after the Supreme Court had ordered desegregation to be accomplished with all deliberate speed. The nation had been publicly committed to a War on Poverty. Yet those "pockets of poverty"—forty million strong—were still there, almost ten years after Michael Harrington had discovered the Other America and the SDS had gone in to organize. The President himself had announced his decision to wind down the Vietnam War, and the Peace Movement had put millions of marchers into the streets to urge him on with his task. And yet the war dragged on, year after sanguinary year. Six months after the first horrifying disclosures, nobody much seemed to care about the women and children of My Lai.

To this suffocating sense of failure was added a growing conviction that repression was loose in the land.

Tough-talking administrators like S. I. Hayakawa at San Francisco State and Father Hesburgh at Notre Dame had shown the way the year before. By 1970, student militants at many schools were facing academic suspension or expulsion, if not arrest and trial by the civil authorities. Countless otherwise straight students across the country felt the fear of the prowling narc and the pot bust. Countless others brooded over splitting for Canada to escape the draft.

Recent history was taking on a shape and a direction, not only for the dissenters, but for many otherwise apolitical youths as well. It was a typically generational point of view—typical, at least, for this stage of the youth revolt. We shall come across many like it in the pages that follow.

Everyone seemed to know someone who had been clubbed at

the Democratic Convention in 1968, or gassed at the People's Park in 1969. Abbie Hoffman, Jerry Rubin, and the other flamboyant defendants in the Chicago conspiracy trial, as well as their emotional attorney, William Kunstler, fanned out across the nation that winter of 1969–70, telling college audiences how the establishment was railroading them to prison. Students flocked to movies like *Z,* to see how the generals had crushed dissent in Greece, or to *Easy Rider,* with its hippie heroes gunned down by jeering, sneering middle America. "Pig Amerika," the omnipresent underground press called it. The homeland of racism, imperialism, the military-industrial complex, and the lengthening shadow of the riot-helmeted, club-wielding cop.

The Battle of Algiers was going around the art houses again—a gripping, documentary-style account of urban guerrillas in action. It was obviously relevant for revolutionaries in an urban nation like the United States. It was also a very moving experience for many deeply disturbed young people who were never likely to take up the gun themselves. "After I saw *Algiers,*" a girl told me over coffee one morning, "I just wanted to go out and blow something up. You know? I mean, I was just so mad—" I remember young girls coming out of *Easy Rider* with tears on their cheeks.

These were people who would never join the Weathermachine themselves. But would they turn a bomber over to the FBI? Turn a freedom fighter over to the fascists?

James Rector Died for You

If you asked them what historic events during their lifetimes had had the greatest impact on them, the youth of 1970 did not point with pride to America's conquest of the moon. Time after time, classes full of students wrote on the little informal polls I used to take: "the assassinations of the Kennedy brothers," or "the murder of Martin Luther King." Young radicals, reaching back to their earliest political memories and beyond, wrote: "the murder of Che . . . of Malcolm X . . . of Patrice Lumumba . . ."

Why is it always our side that gets killed? asked a young radical in *Z*. "They been killing blacks for years," a visiting Panther warned an intent college audience that spring, "and now it's yellow people over there in Veet-nam. One of these days, if you all don't get your shit together, they gonna come up here to your nice safe college campus and blow *you* away too."

This was the way the world looked to the college activist, and to increasing numbers of straight youth, that spring of 1970.

They still spun their colored plastic frisbees across the lawns in front of the library. They dug the touring rock groups on starry spring nights. But the uneasiness was there, brooding beneath the surface. A haunting anxiety was there, over the draft and the narcs and the college "disciplinary proceedings" against last term's disrupters; and over the haunting image, nationally circulated by the press, of Panther leader Bobby Seale, gagged and bound to his chair in Judge Hoffman's seething courtroom.

A sign scrawled with spray paint on a campus sidewalk many months before was still dimly visible that May. It said: *James Rector Died for You.* James Rector was a young man who had been shot to death by a squad of shotgun-armed deputy sheriffs at the People's Park bust in California the preceding spring. A number of others had been injured in the confrontation.

Tom Hayden, one of the Chicago conspiracy defendants, had tried to rouse some indignation over the People's Park shootings in a speech he made at Northwestern in the fall. "They've already started killing people," he said in his flat, emotionless, professional-revolutionary voice. "Sure," said somebody impatiently in the back row, "but that was Berkeley. This is Northwestern. . . ." Things like that just didn't happen at places like Northwestern.

When it happened at Kent, the kids remembered Tom Hayden and Bobby Seale, *Z* and *Easy Rider.*

3. *MARX OR WEATHERMAN—THE NEED FOR IDEOLOGY*

What Would Lenin Say?

It was a wild, weird, surrealistic experience, that first week in May, 1970. Standing behind the Northwestern barricade with a hairy, denim-clad crew of would-be revolutionaries one chilly midnight, I tried to make sense out of it.

The tangled barrier of wood and stone and metal gleamed garishly unreal in the flickering light of fires burning in trash cans. Its young defenders moved restlessly about, warming themselves at the fires, talking, laughing. The red flag fluttered above them in the darkness. "Go, New Red Guard!" somebody sang out. There was a ragged, half-serious effort at the "Internationale."

The police cars were parked a block away, an invisible presence in the darkness. They had announced that the barricade would have to come down before morning, when commuters from the wealthy North Shore suburbs would stream down this street into Chicago. The New Red Guard—an impromptu alliance of SDS cadre and visiting street people—said they were going to fight.

"What would Lenin say?" I asked a red-bearded graduate student. "Even Lenin had no use for petty plots and street fighting. And what the hell has all this got to do with class struggle, after all?" The red-bearded young man was a Marxist of sorts, and very bright. We had had a number of casual arguments over the validity of a class analysis of what was happening in America.

"All the causes this is about," he said, "are basically *proletarian* causes. Poverty is a proletarian thing. And race because the ghettos are black. And the war because that's where the draftees are coming from. The blacks are most of what's left of the internal proletariat, and the Vietnamese people are the external proletariat of the American Empire. And the enemy of all of us is the same class enemy: the same capitalists that pollute Lake Michigan are defoliating Vietnam."

"I still don't see," I said, "how the Movement—this Movement here in the streets—" I nodded at the young rebels milling around us "—relates to that situation. How is this barricade, built and staffed by the sons and daughters of the bourgeoisie, a class thing?"

The long-haired girl who stood beside him shrugged irritably at my obtuseness. He went on speaking, evenly but firmly.

"A worker-student alliance can't really grow, of course, until the proletariat becomes conscious of its situation. Nobody ever said class consciousness was easy to build. But it's growing. The blacks are beginning to dig it, and the welfare mothers, some of them. And the high school kids. Some of the blue-collar kid gangs on the South Side have stopped bopping with the blacks and begun to realize who the common class enemy is. . . ."

A worker-student alliance! Long-haired freaks and Wallace

people marching shoulder to shoulder together into the sun! I remembered a march on Fountain Square in downtown Evanston some months before. I remembered how the hard hats, clustered high in the girders of the new bank building on one side of the square, had given the kids the finger as they passed.

Venceremos!

"The Third World," another young radical was saying. "The nonwhite masses of the globe are going to do it, man. They'll isolate America like the cities in a peasant sea—and then they'll swamp it. The yellow peoples, the brown peoples, the black peoples, the red peoples of the world—they're the ones that are going to off Pig Amerika!"

He was a square-jawed, not overly intelligent young man who had been suspended for disrupting classes the preceding spring. He was just back from several months of chopping cane in Cuba with the *Venceremos* Brigade.

"I know," I said. "Two, three, many Vietnams. And the ghettos are going up at home, to make a second front." I sounded skeptical and I felt it. The uncritical idolatry of colored skin—*any* color—seemed as naive to me as the other sort of racism I had carried signs against in the South.

". . . all those black Nam veterans," the tanned young man was telling me, "you bet your ass they learned something over there. They're organizing, man. When the blacks start burning the cities down again next time, they're going to be led by a bunch of fucking black Green Berets!"

It was the Weatherman line, and I had heard rumors that this radical drop-out was hanging around with alleged local Weatherpeople. I had seen Weatherman charge too—into the Chicago Loop at high noon, chanting the magic names of Che and Ho, echoing the ululating Algerian war cry, invisible Cong loping up the street beside them. But their allies beyond the seas had done them little good, and most of them were in jail or underground now. As for the ghetto fifth column, the blacks, they had their own problems to worry about and remained notoriously absent from white actions these days.

It was the old apocalyptic vision of the World Revolution, I thought, color-based instead of class-based. The Third World rising as one man, instead of the Workers of the World united.

"Well," I said, "I don't see it. But I'd like to talk it over some time."

"Yes," the young revolutionary said. His eyes shifted back to the barricade, squinted into the darkness beyond. "I'd like to do that some time. After all this is over."

The red flag fluttered gustily in the breeze, the fires in the garbage cans blazed and twisted. "Hey, New Red Guard!" There was a rush to help two or three alert vandals who had discovered that the huge metal sign that broadcast the name of the university to passing motorists could, with a little heaving and hauling, be ripped off and added to the barricade.

"You really think they'll fight?" I asked the red-haired graduate student I had spoken to before. "You really think they'll stay if the police come to tear this thing down?"

"Sure," he said. "Some of them will. The spirit is very high."

"Yeah," I said, "it always is."

This was a graduate student, after all. Older than the kids around us; soon to become a fullfledged member of the historical fraternity himself. A weary, bone-chilled professor who was beginning to feel a little old for street research could let down a bit with a future colleague, surely. Let a little of the cynical "realism" that comes from poring over too many lost utopias peep out.

"The spirit was high in 1848 too," I said. "The Springtime of the Peoples." Smashed to flinders in 1849.

The bearded young man in his middle twenties shrugged and turned away. "Bullshit," I heard the long-haired girl at his elbow breathe, very softly. The two of them walked off toward the barricade.

2

"Everyone Believes in His Youth That the World Began with Him" * *—and It Did!*

He is not a new figure in history, this bearded young man on his way to the barricades. Despite the present-centeredness of most accounts of him, and of most attempts to explain his behavior, the young ideological rebel has been around for some time. For a hundred and fifty years at least, according to those who have traced him and his antecedents back to their beginnings.

This book is the story of the young man on the barricades, from his first appearance in history to his most recent—and most disturbing—incarnation.

1. *BUMS AND SNOBS AND CONSCIOUSNESS III*

Marching on to Glory

The archetypal rebel is above all young, in his late 'teens or early twenties. His hair quite often hangs lank and dirty to his shoulders. His clothing is usually unconventional, outlandish enough to make people stop and stare. Sometimes he looks—and smells—as if soap and water seldom touched his skin. Sometimes he is sallow-faced, undernourished, even unhealthy. The look in his young eyes ranges from fawnlike innocence to sullen rebelliousness, from the most exalted idealism to the rankest forms of fanaticism.

His ideas and his values are usually quite as unconventional as his appearance. By his parents' standards, at least, his notions are

* Johann Peter Eckermann, *Conversations with Goethe* (London and New York, 1930), p. 333.

generally immoral, often radical, and sometimes revolutionary. But for the judgment of his elders, as for all their works, the hairy rebel has only impatience or indifference. He speaks with the arrogant contempt of the young for the blows he has not suffered, the problems he has not yet had to face. His is the serene certainty of the root-and-branch revolutionary, busy building his brave new world, with only pity or disgust for the half-measures, the compromises, and the failures of the past.

We have all come across him one way or another, these past turbulent years. We have seen him panhandling in Haight-Ashbury, or sprawling stoned at the fountain in Central Park. We have heard his war cry as he surges up Pennsylvania Avenue beneath a sea of signs and banners, demanding peace and freedom now. We have seen his picture in the papers or on the television news, occupying universities, smashing windows, hurling the tear gas canisters back at the police.

The young militant at war with the world he lives in—or the young Bohemian withdrawing from it—is as familiar to us all as tomorrow's headlines.

But the hairy revolutionary described above is by no means exclusively the child of the second half of the twentieth century. He might be a flower child, a black-power militant, or a New-Left revolutionary of the 1960's and 1970's. But he might almost as easily be a rebellious youth of a century or a century and a half ago. For this description, despite its contemporary ring, would also fit a German student radical of the years after Waterloo, noisily demonstrating for a liberal and united postwar Germany. Or a French Bohemian of the 1830's, passionately defying bourgeois morality at the very moment of middle-class triumph in France. Or a Russian nihilist of the 1860's, who rejected as inadequate all the reforms of Alexander II, the tsar emancipator, and set Russia firmly on the road to revolution. Or even a young Nazi of the 1930's, marching on to certain glory in the vanguard of the Hitler Youth.

This arrogantly insurrectionary, totally committed young man is the quintessential rebel of the past hundred and fifty years. He is dedicated to a cause—or at least embittered against the world he lives in. He is sometimes naively idealistic, sometimes pragmatically, even ruthlessly practical. He may launch an assault against the society of his day, or he may simply withdraw from that society into a Bohemian subculture of his own. But always, generation after generation, he is a young man up in arms against the *status quo,* against the only world his fathers have to offer him.

God Help America

Many efforts have been made to explain him. He has been analyzed, categorized, eulogized and damned. A vast and often contradictory literature has grown up around the young ideological rebel, especially in recent years.[1]

The revolt of the younger generation is explained by Spockian "permissiveness" in child-rearing, for instance; or by the computerized anonymity of mass education in what Clark Kerr has called the "multiversity"; or simply by the dehumanizing experience of "growing up absurd" in modern American society.

Sociologically speaking, the younger generation is analyzed in terms of the unique pressures of life in the "technetronic society," the happy hunting ground of Marcuse's "one-dimensional man." Psychologically, such concepts as alienation, the Eriksonian identity crisis, and various darkly Freudian drives involving hostility to the father are brought into play to help us understand the youth.

From a purely political point of view, some simple souls have even suggested that the issues and avowed objectives of the youth movements themselves provide sufficient cause for the present generational upheaval: that significant segments of the youth are genuinely disturbed by racism, poverty, and war. Or conversely, that some of the young agitators actually are what they increasingly claim to be—agents of the international forces of revolution.

Interpretations have clearly varied. But they have had one thing in common: most of the interpreters have tended to pass judgment —often quite emotionally—on the young.

A surprising number of establishment analysts have praised the younger generation for its "commitment" and "idealism," for "telling it like it is" and for being willing to *act* on its beliefs. Militants are hailed as a "prophetic minority." The Bohemian flower children of the 1960's and '70's are described as the nation's greatest hope for spiritual revival, for a new "greening of America."

Others equally rooted in the establishment, by contrast, have condemned the young dissenters as "bums" or "effete snobs." Even more passionate critics have responded like the middle-aged man who stood watching a motley horde of bearded, long-haired, bell-bottomed peace marchers surging up the main street of a great city one afternoon in the late sixties. "There goes the youth of America," this square-jawed citizen of the republic muttered grimly. "God help America!"

This tendency to take sides for or against the revolting youth has penetrated even the most scientific efforts to understand the phenomenon. One has only to compare the analyses of such authorities as Kenneth Keniston and Lewis Feuer—the one empathetically admiring, the other unhappily opposed—to detect strong emotional responses to the Youth Revolution even in impeccably scholarly circles.

Outside such circles, strong opinions have been even more vigorously expressed. Many a cocktail-party argument in recent years has turned on such issues as the viability of "Consciousness III," such questions as whether Dr. Spock has *really* ruined all our children.

One thing that has generally been lacking in such disputes, however—and in many more learned disquisitions—is a sense of history. Neither admirers nor enemies of the dissenting youth of our day seem to have much of a feel for the historical dimension of the Youth Revolution. Beyond an occasional hazy reference to the 1930's, or perhaps to the Revolutions of 1848, few seem to think of "the Movement" as having a past. Fewer still have looked at all objectively at the actual contributions of the youth revolt to human history.[2]

A sense of history could do wonders for our understanding of the situation with which we are confronted. A little historical perspective might at the very least help to calm the passions of the past few years. This in itself might be a signal service: we would all be better off if we could face the next generational upheaval with drier eyes and fewer heartburnings. And if a knowledge of the mechanics of the Youth Revolution—its causes, development, and consequences—can help us to formulate a more logical response, the pattern of the past may be of real help in our continuing efforts to deal justly and effectively with the revolt of the younger generation.

2. *THE YOUNG MEN HEAR THE WORD*

History and Youth

In the following exploration of the 150-year history of the Youth Revolution, an interpretive concept oddly neglected by historians has proved to be of inestimable value: the notion of "social generations." [3] The theory of social generations, properly utilized, may provide us with an invaluable tool for measuring the impact of history on youth—and the impact of youth on history. It has been utilized to that end throughout this book.

It is usually a good idea for the historian, who claims to deal in hard facts—is he not, after all, the official keeper of "the record"? —to get his underlying assumptions and presuppositions clearly out upon the table. There follows, then, a brief excursion into the theory of social generations.

We read a great deal about the younger generation and the older generation, generational conflict and the generation gap. But what exactly is a *social generation?*

Basically, of course, it is an age group. It is a group of people with a common birthday—or, to be more accurate, of people born within a few years of each other. How many years? The theorists have not yet reached a consensus on this crucial point—the length of a social generation. What historical evidence there is, however, would seem to indicate a span of perhaps ten or fifteen years in earlier, comparatively slow-moving centuries, five years or even less in our own fast-moving epoch. It is the pace of social change that determines how frequently new socially-conditioned generations emerge upon the scene. As history speeds up, the generational turnover also accelerates—a process which will be dealt with in more detail presently.

A social generation, then, is an age group. But it is more than that. Members of the same generation, born within a few years of each other, advance together through life. In so doing, they are psychologically and sociologically conditioned by common institutions and social circumstance. Perhaps most important of all, they grow up through the same brief span of history.

A word or two on each of these shaping forces in the life of a social generation will be useful here.

As the German sociologist Karl Mannheim—one of the founding fathers of modern generational theory—pointed out some forty years ago, members of the same social generation are usually products of the same sociological environment. They are all urban, or they are all rural. They are members of the same social class—the bourgeoisie or the aristocracy, the peasantry or the proletariat. The importance of this common sociological background can hardly be exaggerated.

There are crucial psychological determinants of generationhood as well. Members of a given social generation have typically been raised according to the same child-rearing practices. They have been conditioned by the same family structures, the same parental and sibling relationships. They have been exposed to the same pattern of education, formal and informal. They have been indoctrinated, more or less successfully, in the same psychologically weighted views of the world at large and of their own place in it.

Many of these psychological and sociological factors have been explored in some detail by specialists in these areas. But there are other forces involved in the molding of a generation—forces that are essentially historical in character. It is with these special pressures exerted by a society on the move through time that this book will be primarily concerned.

Almost any sort of historical trend or traumatic event may leave its imprint on a social generation. Political or military events, economic developments, even the hazier challenges of change in world views or value systems may have a profound effect. This seems to be particularly so when such major historical changes occur in the tender, early years of generational development. A cataclysm in the 'teens or early twenties can mark a generation for life, inculcating basic ideas and attitudes that no amount of subsequent experience will efface.

In a very real sense, then, the feeling of each new generation that "the world began with them"—as Goethe put it a century and a half ago—reflects a profound historical truth. Each generation *is* unique in that no other has ever grown up through the particular span of history that encompasses the younger years of this precise birth cohort. *That* world, the world that shapes this cohort into a social generation, *is* new. In times of accelerated social change especially, the historically conditioned life experience that shapes each birth cohort may be almost unrecognizably different from that which shaped the older generation currently in power. Conflict is almost inevitable. The conflict of generations is thus no mere matter of individual, often transitory issues: it is a case of whole worlds in collision.

Youth and History

The result of the convergence of all these influences—psychological, sociological, and historical—on the developing psyches of a single age group is to produce a singular harmony of outlook which we may almost designate as a "group mind." Generational contemporaries, shaped by the same events impacting on all their lives at the same stage of psycho-social development, tend naturally to think and feel alike about many things. They share the same general ideas about history (past, present, and to come) and about society (as it is and as it ought to be). They share certain ethical and aesthetic values, certain life styles, certain patterns of action and reaction.

Even where they disagree, they tend at least to operate within the same categories of thought and feeling. They are characteristically moderate in their views, for instance, or typically extremist in their patterns of response. They are all hard-boiled realists, or all exalted idealists, despite specific differences of ideology.

The power of this common outlook, the pull of generational loyalties, is especially strong when a social generation is still young. For reasons which psychologists like Erik Erikson and Kenneth Keniston have convincingly outlined, an age group usually seems to be most self-conscious and most cohesive in its youth. To this I might add that a generation is likely to be most historically influential—as a group, at least—when it is still young. The seventeenth-century preacher had a shrewd insight when he said: "The young men hear the word!" [4] He might also have said: *The young men act upon it.*

The actions that they take are more than likely to be insurrectionary. The main historical function of the ideologically motivated younger generation has been, quite simply: the fostering of social change through generational rebellion. Let me outline the pattern briefly, as we will presently observe it, not only in the present, but over a dozen rebellious younger generations of the past.

The characteristic conflict of generations in history seems to develop along the following lines:

A generation of educated young people is stimulated intellectually and emotionally by an unusual twist of history. A war, a depression, a major reform movement launched by their elders—almost any sort of historic upheaval may provide the spark. Whatever the precipitating cause, the effect is the same: a young generation in the grip of an idea is propelled into open revolt against their parents' world.

Only a minority of any given birth cohort, of course, is likely to follow this insurrectionary path to the end. Society typically lavishes considerable energy and ingenuity on the effort to turn the young into carbon copies of their parents, fit guardians of the ideals and institutions their elders hold dear. The surprising thing is that any sizable percentage of the young are sufficiently perceptive of the realities of social change—or psychologically alienated enough—to accept the revolutionary logic of their situation. But the revolutionaries have historically found increasing tacit support among their age mates, enough support to transform the vigorous activism of what is often stigmatized as "a small minority" into a genuine expression of the values and world view of an entire generation.

This insurrection of the youth may also be encouraged by the more liberal among their elders—for a time. Sooner or later, however, the young extremists inevitably escalate the level of struggle beyond the range of even the most benign parental toleration. The predictable result is sharp repression. All the power of organized society is mobilized to suppress this startling challenge to the established order. The revolt of the younger generation is crushed.

But that is not necessarily the end of the story. In the long run, the insurgency of a generation of young true believers may have crucial consequences for the society that has destroyed them. For the young rebels, before they go down to present defeat, not infrequently sow the seeds of their own future victory.

It is a simple pattern—too simple to warrant further theoretical development here. The following pages should flesh out these bare bones and give the social generation some approximation of its true place in modern history.

3. *150 YEARS OF YOUTH IN REVOLT*

Seeds of the Holy War

This revolt of the youth is clearly older than our time. It is not, however, so old as history.

Historical accounts of earlier ages seldom lay much stress on the influence of age groups, young or old, on the march of events. There are exceptions, of course. It is hard to study the Reformation era, for instance, without noticing the importance of zealous youth in spreading the new gospel. The youthfulness of the men who made the American Revolution, who in 1776 were by no means the stately patriarchs of their official portraits, is also sometimes remarked upon.[5] And there are other examples. By and large, however, the social generation seems infinitely less important throughout most of our history than, for example, the social class, the religious sect, the national or ethnic group.

Beyond the confines of Western society, furthermore, the revolt of the young against their elders has been even less common. "In other cultures," an eminent social scientist points out, "the outstanding fact is generally not the rebelliousness of youth, but its docility. There is practically no custom, no matter how tedious or painful, to which youth in primitive tribes or archaic civilizations will not willingly submit." [6] In other societies, as in other times, the younger generation seems to have accepted with little friction the social niche and the pattern of life prescribed for it. Whatever tensions may have existed within individual families, between biological fathers and sons, rebellious youth does not seem to have been a social problem in most other times and places than our own.

The trouble seems to have begun with the nineteenth century, when the transforming influences of the Democratic and Industrial Revolutions were first felt in the Western World. The unprecedented upheavals that swept over our society in the decades around 1800 set in motion forces that have been radically altering every aspect of our lives ever since, forces that have impacted with particular violence upon the lives of the young.

The Industrial Revolution began it. Human life has never been the same since the first clanking, puffing steam engines began the unheard-of process of making human labor obsolete. From the Age of Steam to the Age of the Computer, the amazing transformation has gone on. This most important of all human revolutions deluged modern man with goods and services, doubled his life span, multiplied his comforts beyond the dreams of ancient kings. But the application of science to society also created the oppressed proletariat and the middle-class mastery of the world, made possible Western imperial hegemony of the entire globe, and led to the ecological rape of the earth itself by entrepreneurs and technicians drunk with their own unprecedented power. Successive phases of the rise of technology spawned big business, big labor, and big government, total war and totalitarianism. From the beginning, finally, the continuing Industrial Revolution did astonishing things to one of the immemorial human rhythms—the sequence of social generations.

Alvin Toffler, in *Future Shock,* has documented in detail perhaps the most important consequences of this continuing technological transformation of the globe—the fantastic acceleration of the pace of social change itself. As Toffler points out, this "roaring current of change" has become "so powerful today that it overturns institutions, shifts our values, and shrivels our roots." [7] It is this "roaring current of change" which has produced for each new generation a world vastly different from that of its ancestors. It is precisely due to this unending Industrial Revolution, then, that each generation is so totally cut off from its predecessors by a widening chasm of differing influences and divergent experiences. Here is the first cause of the generation gap that bedevils our times.

The Industrial Revolution made generational conflict inevitable. But the Democratic Revolution and the flood of our revolutionary *'isms* that followed between 1776 and 1848 transformed the struggle between young and old into a holy war.

The two centuries that began with the flowering of the Enlightenment in the later eighteenth century have seen an unparalleled outpouring of ideologies. New views of human society have appeared on all sides, accompanied by new theories of God and man and of the nature of the universe itself. Liberalism and conservatism, several forms of socialism and many nationalisms, romanticism and materialism, positivism, pragmatism, belief in progress, in evolution, and in revolution, existentialism, irrationalism—there is literally no end to the new *'isms* of the past two centuries.

Even more phenomenal has been the massive dissemination of these new ideas among the citizenry at large. No longer is the traffic in ideas a luxury trade, confined to a handful of the well-born, well-educated, and wealthy. The spread of public schools and universities, of a comparatively uncensored periodical press, cheaping books and lending libraries, and in our own times of radios, phonograph records, television and moving pictures have seen to that.

Younger generations cut off from a recognized place in an increasingly complex industrial society have thus been crammed together in the gilded ghettos of school and university, exiled to the private world of fun-and-games known as the "youth culture." Even more important, youth deprived of firm roots in the world views and value systems of their elders by the pell-mell pace of change have been presented with a steady stream of alternative ideologies. In the penny press or the poetry of the Romantics, in the *avant-garde* theater, the paperback guru, or each year's new recording star, the young have found ideas and ideals that *do* seem relevant to the strange new world that is perpetually taking shape around them. Vague discontents thus gain form and substance and a cutting edge of revolutionary ideas. Disaffection acquires a crusading fervor. The holy war is on.

Byron and Blanqui

It was apparently around 1815, the year of Waterloo, that the great revolt of the youth began. The first gaudy, young, ideologically driven rebels of the modern stripe were perhaps the romantic youth who thronged the revolutionary secret societies of those years after the French Revolution and the Napoleonic Wars. The first wave of this nineteenth-century youth revolt dedicated itself to the overthrow of the kings and priests and aristocracies of Restoration Europe. Their successors crusaded just as passionately against the bourgeois businessman's establishment that soon succeeded the regime of throne and altar in many parts of Europe.

The rebellious younger generations of that vanished century found many causes worthy of their dedication. They fought for liberalism, for socialism, for many nationalisms. They fought beneath the banners of Mazzini, the founder of Young Italy and Young Europe, of Blanqui, the first of the professional revolutionaries, and of Lenin, the most successful of them. They fought behind the barricades of 1830 and 1848 and 1871 and many a less heralded political upheaval. They took to the streets with a regularity that made the idealistic young conspirator-*cum*-barricade-builder one of the clichés of nineteenth-century political history.

The revolt of the younger generation took other forms in that century as well. The great Romantic revolution in the arts, for example, was the work of young men, and the Romantic image has always, quite legitimately, been one of youth: the image of Goethe's *Young Werther,* dreamy and impractical, rejecting success in the establishment for an unsanctioned love—and rejecting life itself when the hopelessness of his love became apparent; the dashing image of Lord Byron, as colorfully unconventional in his private life as in his poetry, dying for freedom in revolutionary Greece. Nor were these isolated instances. Both the fictional Werther, who died for love, and the vividly real Lord Byron, who died for liberty, were idols for whole generations of Romantic youth.

Bohemian withdrawal in all its forms was also a creation of the insurgent youth of the nineteenth century. By the time the gay nineties rolled around, the garrets of Paris were filling up with young poets and painters, all vociferously rebelling against the Victorian prudery and money-grubbing materialism of the age. Beyond the Rhine, the "wandering birds" (*Wandervögel*), nature-loving flower children of Wilhelmine Germany, tramped the hills and forests with guitars across their backs. In cities, from Soho to Greenwich Village, Bohemia, the last refuge of alienated youth, was in full swing.

Guns and bombs and street riots, ideologies and plots, revolutions in the arts, Bohemian amorality and freedom—all were common preoccupations of the youth before the century turned. There was really very little left for our own highly touted century to originate.

Is Modern Youth Going to the Devil?

The first half of the twentieth century did, however, see an amazing expansion of the youthful malaise that had begun in the nineteenth. The disenchantment of the Bohemian garrets spread broadcast among the sons and daughters of the bourgeoisie. The revolutionary political and social doctrines nurtured by radical European youth spread beyond the confines of Europe, to find new generations of converts in Asia and Africa and the Americas. In the twentieth century, in short, the youth movement became a mass movement.

The voice of Dada nihilism still speaks to us with a familiar ring from the hectic early years of the flaming twenties:

> . . . dissolution was the ultimate in everything that Dada represented, philosophically and morally; everything must be pulled apart, not a screw left in its customary place, the screw-holes wrenched out of shape, the screw, like man himself, set on its way towards new functions which could only be known after the total negation of everything that had existed before. Until then: riot, destruction, defiance, confusion . . . dissolution and anarchy.[8]

The notorious lost generation of the 1920's plunged with febrile eagerness into a wild new world of jazz music and bathtub gin, of bobbed hair, short skirts, and the back seats of automobiles. No wonder the parents of such insubordinate offspring turned desperately to magazine articles like "Is Modern Youth Going to the Devil?", "The Destructive Younger Generation," "The Unspanked Generation," and "Keeping Up with Susannah" by "the mother of a radical daughter." [9]

The younger generations of the jazz age shocked their elders with their hedonistic escapism and their moral anarchism. The youth of the 1930's turned once more to social and political commitment—and horrified their parents even more.

In the West, the thirties were the red decade. Faced with the Great Depression and the ominous rise of fascism, young liberal idealists easily fell under the spell of Stalinist statistics and the humane eloquence of Litvinov. Some of the most dedicated youths of the decade experienced spiritual conversions over the *Communist Manifesto*. The Spanish Civil War, the great crusade of their generation, drew thousands of them to offer their bloody homage to Catalonia, or to die in Madrid.

In the totalitarian states, the longing of the younger generation for involvement and commitment to a cause was channeled into the Komsomol or the Young Octobrists, the Hitler Youth or Mussolini's Sons of the Wolf. "Youth Rules Itself," said Hitler, and many of his young acolytes believed it. The Italian fascist hymn was "La Giovanezza"—"Youth." All these totalitarian youth groups were, in fact, institutionalized youth revolts, paradoxically channeling the passion of the young to build a bright new world into the service of the state.

On the surface of it, Hitler's Condor Legion—the bombers of Guernica—seemed very different from Malraux's tattered volunteer airmen, who fought for the Republic. Yet the dedicated youth of many lands who met on the battlefields of Spain had much in common after all.

A Detestation of All Existing Governments

The second postwar period of this century, like the first, produced a sharp acceleration in the spread of the youth culture—and of the youth problem that seems to be its inevitable concomitant. There is no need to trace the familiar story here. A few gaudy images, which the reader himself may readily supplement from his own memory, will suffice to round out the picture of a century and a half of youth in revolt.

The fifties: bobby sox and hula hoops, cheap wine and *haiku* poetry, cool jazz and bop and early rock, Elvis the Pelvis, Screaming Lord Sutch, and *les chats sauvages*. The existentialist youth of postwar Paris, long-haired café loungers, worshiping at the shrine of Sartre and Camus. The angry young men of England and the American beat generation. Juvenile delinquents, motorcycle gangs, teddy boys, *stilyagi*. James Dean as the Rebel without a Cause; Brando as the Wild One. The palmy, peaceful years when youthful street fighters were only to be found in far-off totalitarian places like Warsaw or Budapest.

And then the sixties, the violent decade just past. A decade that began, symbolically enough, with the vigorous young Kennedy clan descending upon America—the Kennedys, with their rumpled hair, their touch football, and their ringing declaration that the torch was about to pass to a new generation of Americans. Then the civil-rights demonstrators, the poverty organizers, the peace marchers—the committed youth of the nation on the move. The hippies and the flower children following hard upon: hard rock and acid rock, pot and LSD, Haight-Ashbury, Woodstock, communal living and sexual anarchy. Gay Lib, Women's Lib, black power, Black Panthers, SDS, and Weatherman. The bitter road from Selma to Watts, from Berkeley to Chicago to Kent State.

A youth revolt that swept across the world. Students "liberating" universities from Columbia to the London School of Economics to half the colleges of Italy. Young martyrs burning themselves alive in New York and Saigon and briefly liberated Prague. Red Rudi Dutschke filling the streets of Berlin with mobs that reminded older Germans of the days of Hitler's rise to power. Daniel Cohn-Bendit defying de Gaulle's geriatric tyranny in the flamboyant "May days" in Paris, with their echoes of so many revolutions of an earlier century. The stick-wielding Zengakuren in Tokyo. The astonishing Red Guard, dragging Mao's totalitarian China to the brink of anarchy. Fidel and Che, the battle of Algiers and the Viet Cong image—the haunting vision of the young guerrilla, challenging the old order in all lands to do battle for its life.

It has been a long and violent road, from the generational rebellions and withdrawals of the early nineteenth century to those of the later twentieth. But the spirit of the youth revolt—and much of its mechanics as well—remains much the same today as yesterday. The Romantic Bohemians of that century worshiped love and freedom as passionately as the hippie of our own time. The bombs are more efficient in our day, but the fanatical young bomb throwers remain much the same. "I have simplified my politics," wrote Lord Byron, the sometime freedom fighter, "into a detestation of all existing governments." [10] No nihilist of today could have said it better.

Not to understand the past, historians have been warning ever since Cicero's day, is to be doomed to repeat it. Whether the converse is true—whether an understanding of the past will actually help us to avoid its follies and brutalities—may be a more dubious proposition. Nevertheless, it is in this hope that the present book has been written. For we are surely in need of all the help we can get if we are to deal even halfway adequately with what is perhaps the most disturbing of all the revolutions of our times—the revolt of our own children against the modern world.

Part II

THE BIRTH OF THE YOUTH REVOLUTION

3

"The Noble Freedom of the Youth" * *The First Student Revolt* *Germany, 1815*

Student militance is one of the mainstreams of the youth revolt. It is not the only one, despite the all too common tendency to equate the two. Yet students have been an important part of the picture since the earliest years of the continuing revolt of the younger generation. The schools and colleges which have multiplied like rabbits in the West these last two centuries have certainly been a prime source of the young rebel's special passion for ideology. And that aggressive militance which is so essential to the modern Youth Revolution has flowered perhaps most frequently among student elites.

The history of the Youth Revolution in fact begins with a student revolt. A rebellion that, for ideological commitment and snowballing militance, can scarcely be bettered even in our own distracted time.

The Germany of a century and a half ago was in many ways a thoroughly backward region. For one thing, German-speaking Central Europe was entirely lacking in political unity. There was no German nation—only dozens of separate and sovereign principalities. Austria and Prussia, the most important of them, were great European powers; but the others ranged down to the Free State of Bremen, three square miles in area.

Economically too, "the Germanies" were not marching in the van of European progress. The Industrial Revolution was well under way in Britain by 1815, and it was beginning to be felt in

* Massmann on the Wartburg, in Frederick Bülau, *Geschichte Deutschlands von 1806–1830* (Hamburg, 1842), p. 436.

France and Belgium as well. But it had hardly touched Central Europe as yet. Outside of a scattering of cities, Europe east of the Rhine remained a land of rustic Junkers and illiterate peasants, of stagecoaches and candlelight.

Ideologically also, Germany remained in many ways behind the times. The new liberal ideas spawned by the Enlightenment and the French Revolution had reached the German states by the end of the preceding century. But democracy had been disgraced by the excesses of the Revolution, and radical notions like liberty, equality, and fraternity were no longer welcome in the Germanies. The Europe-wide reaction against such subversive ideas had, in fact, found its most implacable champion in the Austrian foreign minister, Prince Metternich, who accurately described himself as a "rock of order" in a troubled sea of ideologies.[1]

In one way, however, this fragmented, underdeveloped, illiberal corner of the continent was well ahead of the times. The three dozen German states boasted among them a score of the best universities in Europe.

Every petty princeling who could afford one supported an institution of higher learning. Nor was all this merely a matter of prestige. There were said to be more books in the single German principality of Hanover than in all the public libraries in the United States.[2] Students flocked from all over Europe to sit in the lecture halls of celebrated German professors whose learning was as legendary as their abstruse language. Hegel would soon be taking up his duties at the University of Berlin; Fichte had recently retired from Jena.

German students were famous drudges in the classroom—the sort of indefatigable note takers who really *do* write down the jokes. They were also copious beer drinkers, notorious duelists—the saber scar on the cheek was already *de rigueur*—and noisy rowdies of a Saturday night. The aristocratic, regionally based fraternity system laid down the life style of almost all the universities.

Then in that year of grace 1815—the year of Bonaparte's defeat, the year that Metternich began his lifelong campaign to maintain law and order on the continent—the little college towns of the Germanies were suddenly transformed.

1. A NEW SPIRIT AMONG THE STUDENTS

A New Age Was About to Begin

The rector of the University of Göttingen noticed something strikingly different about the students who reported for classes that fall of 1815, three months after the battle of Waterloo. "Recent events have made a deep impression on the students," he reported solemnly. "Their active participation in the struggles for liberation, their susceptibility to the ideas stirred up by great world events have bred an entirely new spirit in them . . ." It was a spirit, he opined, "which brings forward salutary questions, but also can easily become the source of turbulent excesses." [3] Just the sort of evaluation one might expect of an academic administrator, judicious without passing judgment. But the rector had his finger on a great and glaring truth.

The students themselves remembered that new spirit of high hope and infinite possibility all their lives. "A new age," one recalled nostalgically, "was about to begin." "It is impossible for anyone who went to school earlier or later to understand university life during the years 1816 to '20," another wrote. There was "a whole new impetus . . ." [4] There was indeed—and the students themselves were the source of it.

Those German student militants of a century and a half ago would probably have caused a few heads to turn if a contingent of them had appeared on the streets of 1970 America. The long hair, the bristling mustaches, the rough clothing, and the unwashed skin would be familiar enough. Their stout cudgels might pass for crude versions of the long street-fighting staves wielded by the Japanese Zengakuren of our own day. The black, red, and gold sash, or the long dagger hanging at the hip might puzzle us mildly; but we have become used to such flights of fancy on the Yippie left.

Their explanation for it all—that this was the costume of the real *Volk*—would probably sound reassuringly familiar. At least until we realized that they were spelling *Volk* with a *V*.

The *Burschenschaft* or "Student Union" movement of 1815–19 has been described as the first student revolt in Western history. It was, in fact, something more than that. The Student Unions of the years after Waterloo clearly constituted a *generational rebellion* in the technical sense outlined in the preceding chapter. It is only as such that the behavior of these young men—and the nature of their ultimate contribution to modern history—can be understood and appreciated.

It was more than a matter of long hair and unbleached linen—that was clear even to contemporaries.

There was the strenuous Christian revival for one thing, an almost puritanical passion for morality and vigorous hymn singing. There was an odd cult of physical fitness among the young too, with newfangled "gymnastics clubs" spreading from town to town across the Germanies. The new student associations were springing up at many universities, and the old fraternity system was under heavy attack.

Even more disturbing, the subversive liberal doctrines of the eighteenth century—which for thoughtful Germans had long since perished under the guillotines of the French Revolution—were in vogue with the young again. There was talk of social contracts and written constitutions. Radical notions of universal equality and individual freedom were bandied about the student beer halls.

But the heart of the matter, the ideological core of the youth revolt, was a bizarre idea that was finding astonishing numbers of young converts in the postwar years—German nationalism, or *Teutomania,* as Prince Metternich contemptuously dismissed this youthful enthusiasm for all things Teutonic.

Nationalism was a new and exotic flower in the three dozen Germanies of 150 years ago. Particularistic local loyalties were still strong in all the German states, and regional differences seemed insurmountable. To many good burghers of the older generation, youthful talk of a "united Germany" smacked of treason to the local prince, to the ancient dynasty that had ruled them and their ancestors sometimes for centuries. These older Germans, staunch Bavarians or Saxons, Austrians or Prussians, could only mutter or shake their heads at this youthful passion for a larger national identity. To anyone who had grown up before the turn of the century, when there had been over three hundred separate states in Central Europe, the idea of German unity seemed bizarre beyond belief.

Roots of Rebellion

A number of explanations have been offered for this yawning generation gap. They range from the evil machinations of the international Jacobin conspiracy—Prince Metternich's informed opinion—to the irrational force of the "melange of terrorism, suicide, elitism, juvenocracy, and idealism" suggested by a more recent commentator.[5] The most common historical explanation is to point to the German Wars of Liberation against Napoleon (1813–15). Young Germans who volunteered for this epic national struggle were allowed to believe that they were fighting for a new and greater German union—a dream that was quickly extinguished by the conservative statesmen of the Congress of Vienna.

The complex constellation of causal factors behind the revolt of these hairy, loudmouthed young liberal nationalists can, however, only be grasped in terms of their total generational experience. Perhaps the simplest way of getting at this is through a "group biography" of the generation of 1815. For certainly the life of this young generation, the birth cohort of 1795, was very different from that of any of their elders.

The typical young *Burschenschaft* recruit had been born into a middle-class Protestant family in North Germany. He had been raised by an autocratic but unconvincing father, and by a devoutly pietistic mother. Such "heavy fathers" produced rebellious sons throughout the century. Such emotionally pious mothers may well have planted the seeds of crusading zeal in this particular German generation at least.

The long-haired, roughly clad youth who turned twenty in 1815 had been ten years old in 1805, the black year of Napoleon's victory at Austerlitz. His faith in the existing system of German states had thus been early undermined. His childish eyes had seen the greatest of them—Austria and Prussia—humiliated by the little Corsican Emperor of the French. Before he was old enough to feel the scope of the catastrophe, he had heard his troubled elders tell how uncounted lesser German principalities had been wiped off the map by the simple fiat of Napoleon.

Even as the old state system of Central Europe crumbled around him, however, the future Student Unionist had grown up with a gathering wave of literary enthusiasm for his larger German *cultural* heritage.

A man's books may tell us much about him. Certainly the bookshelves of a future nationalist crusader of this first generation would have been revealing. There were the anti-French pamphlets and the slender volumes of Romantic verse which had taught the youth to revere the heroic traditions of the German *Volk.* There were the colorful folk tales collected by the industrious brothers Grimm, and the recently rediscovered legends of Siegfried and Teutonic chivalry. There surely were the militant works of Martin Luther, Germany's greatest young rebel with a cause. From all of these, the youth of 1815 had early imbibed a vague but emotion-laden sense of the unique importance of his *Germanness.*

But the mind of the youth had been shaped by more than books. The future *Burschenschafter* had been stirred also by exciting events in the real world—especially by the talk of a "national rebirth" that had accompanied the Prussian Regeneration after 1806, and the comparable Austrian effort at reform after 1809.

In the wake of their repeated defeats by Napoleon, the two great powers of Central Europe had launched major campaigns to modernize their antiquated institutions. Particularly in Prussia, vigorous administrative reformers like Stein and Hardenberg had embarked upon sweeping drives for social betterment. The serfs were freed at last; townsmen were granted self-government; soldiers were no longer to be flogged. Even the young were to have something: a new system of public education was to be established, subsidized by the state.

When, in 1813, the Wars of Liberation had finally broken out, the young volunteer had been well prepared to take at face value all the florid official rhetoric urging him to go forth and do battle for "the fatherland." And the fatherland he had in mind was more than likely to be that larger Germandom whose cultural achievement had been such a signal part of his growing up.

It is hardly surprising, then, that the great unifying experience of the war, in which young men of all the Germanies fought shoulder to shoulder for that common fatherland, seared and molded the souls of the youth in ways totally incomprehensible to their war-weary elders. Nor is it astonishing that the younger generation should be correspondingly outraged when Metternich and the other statesmen who gathered at Vienna to impose a peace on Europe simply shrugged off "national feeling" as irrelevant to the serious business of diplomacy. This betrayal of their high hopes for German unity certainly played a part in the shaping of this generation. But it only finished what a lifetime's experience had begun—the welding of this militant young cohort into a crusading band of brothers.

The process was thoroughly completed at their universities during the first year or two after the war.

The young veterans returned to the small college towns of the German states as instant heroes after their service with the victorious armies of the Germanies. Students still younger than they, who had missed the holy war, gathered around them admiringly. They became the natural leaders of the new student radicalism.

The new youth—both those who had fought and those who hadn't—quickly found prophets to their liking. They turned, in particular, to the scattered disciples of Herder, the eighteenth-century apostle of German cultural nationalism who had been so isolated in his own time. They marched with generational culture heroes like "Father" Jahn, the long-haired, militant founder of the gymnastics movement, who was also an exuberant preacher of the new gospel of German political unification. They devoured every issue of the new liberal nationalist journals: the *Nemesis,* the *People's Friend,* the *Opposition Sheet.* They sat at the feet of youngish liberal professors, especially at the University of Jena, the Berkeley of that first student revolt.

Out of all these converging influences were forged the Student Unions, the militant vanguard of this ideologically driven generation.

The first *Burschenschaft* was set up in 1815 at the prestigious University of Jena, in the comparatively liberal central-German state of Weimar. The principles of this and subsequent Student Unions were liberal and nationalistic. Their purposes were campus reform first of all, with a larger national regeneration in the hazy middle distance. Within two years, there were *Burschenschaften* at three-quarters of the universities in Germany.

The German student associations—like SDS and so many other youth groups of our time—transformed the life of the German universities. Fraternity dueling and brawling were widely replaced by gymnastics exercises and reverent study of the greater German heritage. Father Jahn's muscular young gymnasts—many of them students—tramped back and forth across the countryside, bellowing out marching songs full of radical rhetoric:

> We fight for the day when the fatherland
> Shall have her liberty!
> For we shall have an empire free!
> In rank and class all equals be!
> An empire free!
> Equality!
> Hurrah! Hurray! [6]

The German youth of 1815, like the American civil rights marchers of the early 1960's, were singing revolutionaries.

God and the Fatherland

The movement did not march to instant triumph everywhere, however. In some universities, the Student Unions met stiff resistance from the entrenched establishment. Where this happened, a new and far more militant breed of *Burschenschafter* was likely to be generated. It is a familiar pattern: every activist soon learns that nothing radicalizes the youth so quickly as repression.

The radical wing of the German Student Union movement was known as "the Unconditionals." They sprang up first at the little provincial university of Giessen, in the Rhineland principality of Hesse-Darmstadt. And the guiding spirit of the Unconditionals, as it happened, was a young man whose career as a student leader provides a paradigm case of radicalization through repression. His name was Karl Follen.

Personally, Karl Follen was a familiar type—the radical son of a liberal father. Old Judge Follen, a respected magistrate in the town of Giessen, was an eighteenth-century liberal. He believed in the rights of the individual, in freedom of speech and the press, and in German cultural unity as much as his son did. But young Karl went further. He demanded a written constitution *guaranteeing* those rights and freedoms. He insisted on *political* as well as cultural unity for the fatherland. Their differences were those of their respective generations—and of many generations of old liberals and young radicals since.

Karl Follen, as he himself recalled it, was not a happy child. His mother died when he was only three. He was physically feeble as a boy, fearful of heights and ghosts and many other things. He grew up in his father's study, clearly intelligent but sober-sided and abnormally religious. His playmates teased him for his eccentricities, often driving him into fits of childish melancholy.

Karl solved his problems by cultivating the quality he was to epitomize in the minds of his later followers—will power. He overcame his fears by facing them. He built up his feeble body by vigorous gymnastic exercises till his stocky, powerful frame was a match for many taller youths. Still in his teens, he evolved a simple but rigid code of conduct for himself: "to live and die for the common weal," to "serve God and the fatherland." [7] At seventeen, he acted on his beliefs. He and his brothers enlisted to fight in the Wars of Liberation.

On his return from the wars, he enrolled in the University of Giessen, where he soon became the center of the youth movement. He was intelligent, dedicated, indefatigable. He was even rather good-looking, with his longish blond hair and mustache, his broad forehead and blue eyes full of what they called "soul" in those Romantic days. He and his brother Adolf quickly rallied young kinspirits around them—boys committed like themselves to union, liberty, and the will of God.

But Giessen was a far cry from liberal Weimar. Follen and the Giessen Student Unionists met a solid wall of hostility to their proposed reforms. The aristocratic dueling fraternities, the rather timid faculty, the fundamentally conservative Hessian Grand Duke and his equally illiberal subjects, all stood foursquare against any significant change at Giessen. The result was the extremist sect that came to be known as "the Unconditionals."

Demagogues and Preachers of Freedom

Follen and his followers first organized a university "Reading Society" to study their precious legacy of German culture. Internal rivalries, student apathy, and an unpopular campaign against dueling soon led to the group's dissolution.

Next the small group of radicals set up an association called the *Germania,* dedicated to university reform. Attacks by the fraternities and administration pressure destroyed the *Germania* in its turn.

By the beginning of 1817, however, the arrogance and bullying tactics of the fraternities had alienated so many students that support began to grow for the radicals. A Student Union was actually organized at Giessen. For a few heady months, Karl Follen and the Unconditionals rode a wave of enthusiasm for campus democracy and a "student commonwealth."

But wild rumors of Jacobin plots and subversive activities—many of them apparently originating with the frustrated fraternity leaders—spread rapidly through the town and province. Follen and his black-clad comrades, resplendent in their long hair and Old German coats, were hissed on the streets as "traitors" and "bandits." [8] Parents began to withdraw their sons from this hotbed of anti-Hessian agitation.

Once more, the university moved against the *Burschenschaft.* A faculty investigation was launched, pushed vigorously by a reactionary rector. Weeks of probing and testimony provided no evidence that the Student Union was—as its enemies alleged—a training camp for "demagogues and preachers of freedom," part of a larger plot "to overthrow all existing institutions." [9] But the radical student organization was clearly doing the university no good. Once again, Follen and his friends were ordered to disband.

By his senior year at Giessen, Karl Follen was a very different sort of person from the intense young idealist who had enrolled in the university three years before. Repeated failure at reform on the university level, for instance, had caused him, not to give up, but to raise his sights to the larger goal of national unification and liberation. More important, abrasive conflict with the system had transformed him from a committed youth into something resembling a fanatic.

In three years, he had become an extremist. He demanded "unconditional" allegiance to the exalted imperatives of freedom and nationality. He sneered at moderates: "They would not hesitate to defend themselves against a highway robber by shooting him down, but they are afraid to draw the dagger against the great robbers and murderers of popular freedom!" He meant it metaphorically, of course, but it had a pleasingly militant ring.

Revolution was now Karl Follen's extravagant dream, and he indulged in the violent rhetoric of young would-be revolutionaries the world over. "The tyrants," he would say intently, "must learn to tremble before our daggers." [10] His hairy, rather scruffy disciples would purse their lips or narrow their eyes and look far away, as though something very serious had been said.

The Unconditionals were still a tiny minority in the Student Union movement. There were perhaps ten thousand students in all the German universities, out of a Central European population of more than thirty million solidly traditional and fundamentally conservative souls. Revolution, to put it mildly, was not imminent.

But the youth movement rolled on, oblivious.

2. *THE WARTBURG FESTIVAL*

The Hall of the Minnesingers

Sooner or later, developed youth movements are likely to feel the need to flex their muscles, en masse, in public. They need to rally, to march, to gather in large numbers so as to encourage each other and astound the state. The first student revolt set the pattern in this as in so many other things.

The occasion for an all-German youth festival was ready to hand, as close as the nearest calendar. The year 1817 marked three hundred years since Martin Luther, the prototype of all German ideological rebels, had nailed up his Theses and challenged the world to debate. In 1817, there also fell the fourth anniversary of the Battle of the Nations, Napoleon's most catastrophic defeat on German soil. To commemorate these two great German liberations of the past, then, the youth who hoped to save the fatherland once again gathered for a solemn festival. To hail Blücher, the liberator of the German land; to honor Luther, the emancipator of the German soul.

They met in mid-October, harvest time and a time for thanksgiving. They met at the Wartburg Castle near Eisenach, where Luther had once found refuge from his enemies. Perhaps not altogether incidentally, they thus came together under the jurisdiction of Grand Duke Karl August of Weimar, the last of the enlightened despots and the students' strongest bastion against their conservative enemies.

The great stone foundations of the Wartburg had been laid far back in those misty Middle Ages when, as Romantic nationalists saw it, Germany had been truly great. The celebrated Hermann I, Landgrave of Thuringia, had made his feudal court there in the twelfth century and filled its vaulted halls with the music of Walther von der Vogelweide and other famous minnesingers. The lyrical Battle of the Minstrels had been held in the great hall of the Wartburg in the thirteenth century. The Elector Frederick the Wise of Saxony had hidden Luther there for almost a year, in 1521 and 1522, and the father of the Reformation had written some of his most moving prose beneath its roof.

Since those days of music and poetry, Scripture and inspired prose, the hilltop castle had sunk into decay. Vines curled over crumbling walls. Leafy compost heaps rose imperceptibly about the moldering foundations. But there was history in every stone; more German greatness and true German freedom in this medieval ruin, so the students swore, than in all the baroque splendor of Vienna.

The marchers gathered at Eisenach, an old town in the valley below the Wartburg. By nightfall on October 17, there were almost five hundred young men milling in the narrow cobblestoned streets —youths from Jena, Berlin, Heidelberg, Leipzig, Halle, Tübingen, and other famous universities. More than half the colleges in Germany were represented.

The young *Burschenschafter* met old friends, made new ones, and were repeatedly astonished by their own numbers and variety. They no doubt exchanged the usual somewhat exaggerated accounts of how "the movement" fared in their own town or university. They certainly discussed the next day's doings; and perhaps, much later, over beer, the Meaning of the great event.

The townsmen of Eisenach stared at the odd costumes, the hair and the handlebar mustaches, the long daggers on the hip. They listened to the babble of high German and low, of crude and cultured voices. Older, countrified, conservative by nature, they could not fathom all this talk of "Germanness." But the brains of the young men were giddy, their stomachs knotted with the excitement and the joy of it. They had not shared this sense of their own oneness, this surge of confidence in their cause, since the Wars of Liberation.

To Show Our People What They Have to Hope for from Their Youth

Next morning, the sun shone brightly, the air exhilarated young bodies that had had little rest the night before. About nine o'clock, the procession formed in the market square. Crowds of townsfolk and visitors from Jena and Weimar and even farther away thronged the square to watch. There was a milling, bustling confusion as individuals and university contingents found their places in the line. There was shouting and laughter, the glitter of autumn sunlight on band instruments and accouterments, a sharp tingle of excitement in the air.

The march moved out. At the head of the procession a young man named Scheidler, one of the founders of the Jena Student Union, proudly bore the official "Sword of the *Burschen.*" After him came a four-man honor guard, shoulders square and chins held high, conscious of their place. Then came the black, red, and gold banner of the *Burschenschaft* itself, followed by a color guard of four. After that, the drummers and the trumpeters, with martial music blaring over the crowded square. And then came the youth of Germany, marching two by two, an endless stream of them unwinding out the village gate and turning up the forest path that led to the castle on the hill.

An old picture shows the long procession winding upward through the trees. Most wear the heavy Old German coat and carry the student's staff, though none have any need to lean upon it. There are rough beards in evidence, and shoulder-hanging hair. A scattering of spectators watch from beneath the trees. A dog frisks and barks on the scanty grass beside the path. Above them, the forest thins as the Wartburg heaves into view.

They poured into the great banqueting hall of the castle. The lofty chamber where minnesingers had once sung the glory of German chivalry was decorated with wreaths and garlands, courtesy of old Duke Karl August. The youth spilled into their seats. Excited talk died down, scraped, and muttered into silence. Then the high arched hall echoed again to young voices singing, as it had so many hundred years before:

A mighty fortress is our God,
A bulwark and a weapon:
He helps us in our ev'ry need,
'Gainst mortal ills that threaten . . .

And though this world, with devils filled,
Should threaten to undo us,
We will not fear, for God hath willed
His truth to triumph through us . . .[11]

The ancient Lutheran hymn had an oddly barbaric sound: weapons clashed behind the martial words, the clear voices of the long-haired young crusaders.

One of their own authentic heroes rose then to welcome them—a young war veteran and wearer of the Iron Cross named Riemann, another of the founders of the first *Burschenschaft*. He spoke ardently of Luther and of the Wars of Liberation. He spoke of the betrayal of that holy war:

> Four long years have flowed away since that battle; the German people had built up beautiful hopes—but they are shattered now; it all came out so differently from what we expected. . . . Now I ask you, you who are gathered here in the bloom of your youth . . . you who have once already—with the will and for the welfare of the fatherland—fought with weapons in your hands—I ask you, will you accept this situation? No—now and forevermore! [12]

More singing after that, and more flamboyant oratory. Everyone was confident that he knew the will of "the German people," and that the younger generation was the destined standard bearer of the nation. They met here, concluded one young speaker, not only to celebrate the past victories of Luther and Blücher, but "to show our people what they have to hope for from their youth!" "Dear brothers!" cried another, "our people are absolutely confident that the youth, who struck down the foreign foe, will labor also to uproot the pernicious internal enemy. . . . We must stand the test, as Germany's reborn sons, as the outlawed bearers of the new, pure German spirit—" [13] And so on, with many a flourish, much moral earnestness, and more than a touch of the youthful arrogance that particularly alienated their elders.

Presently a trumpet sounded to announce a ceremonial dinner. There was food and wine; there were many florid toasts. It was well into the afternoon before they all trooped down to Eisenach once more for a special church service, with a dazzling display of gymnastics afterward. The day closed on a note of harmony and enthusiasm.

The Burning of the Books

Darkness fell, but the celebration was not ended. Torches flared against the night, and shadows waved grotesquely across the tall, narrow house fronts of the town. The untiring young people were off again, back to the Wartburg in a long torchlight parade.

It was a gorgeous sight, a river of orange fire flowing upward through the trees; particularly moving for these students, at the end of this intoxicating day. The tense excitement of the morning, the march, the drums and trumpets and the singing, orations that had brought tears to many eyes, wine that had warmed the belly and the heart at once, the solemn service of the Lord, gymnastics before a gaping crowd—it had all keyed them to a pitch unparalleled in their young lives. Now the flaring, hissing torches near at hand, the endless numbers of them sparkling far-off through the shadowy trees were one last touch of madness. And there were those among them who had come prepared for just this moment.

On the hilltop, more than one huge bonfire already blazed. Citizen spectators in the hats and frock coats of nineteenth-century burghers stood clustered before the castle buildings to watch. Some sat on broken walls or peered from vantage points in the castle windows up above. There were even a few ladies present, twittering in excited counterpoint to their husbands' uncommitted gravity or open disapproval. A child or two was held up to see, by some emotional liberal of the older generation.

Through most of the evening's celebrations, it was all innocuous enough. Only at the end, when the last song had been sung and the last speech cheered, did things take a new and more disturbing turn.

It began when a handful of burly gymnasts from Berlin, the

special protégés of the exuberant but generally harmless Father Jahn, shouldered their way through the crowd to the largest bonfire still burning. They were lugging mysterious packages—old books apparently—and other things in sacks. And one of them, a hot-eyed young gymnast named Massmann, began to speak.

He talked about Martin Luther, in whose honor they were gathered here, and about Luther's superb act of defiance—the burning of the papal bull of excommunication launched against him by the establishment of his day. A noble precedent, said Massmann, for free-souled youth confronted by corrupt authority in any age. Was there not a book or two in their own nineteenth century, for instance, a few lying tracts spawned by the Vienna conspirators and the Restoration system, that would profit from a cleansing bath of flame?

Like this, for instance! He waved a sheaf of newspapers on high, the arch-conservative *Alemannia,* and flung the bundle into the fire. Sparks scattered in the night, the flames blazed up. So much for "newspapers which disgrace and dishonor the fatherland!"

Or these! He waved some tattered old volumes with large new titles crudely lettered on them. There was Haller's *Restoration,* that disgusting attempt at philosophic justification of the postwar return of the old order. There was the *German History* of August von Kotzebue—that old libertine, that toady of the princes, what did he know of the true history of the fatherland? Into the crackling flames they went.

The young *Burschenschafter,* their excitement rekindled by this novelty, cheered lustily. Their enthusiasm was undimmed by the fact that very few of them had ever read the weighty tomes in question.

And what better fate for this? the young militant demanded. A gasp and a cheer at the title: Kamptz's *Police Manual.* Even the least politically conscious could remember run-ins with the constabulary, a common enough thing for university *Burschen* of a Saturday night. "In you go," whooped Massmann, "you evil enemy and arch-demon of the noble freedom of the youth!"

And these! A corporal's cane, a guardsman's stays, a wig—symbols of the spit-and-polish drill teams that passed for armies in the German states. Every former volunteer could recall how the Prussian regulars had looked down their noses at the volunteer regiments in the Wars of Liberation. There were enthusiastic cheers as the Berliners consigned these symbols of autocracy and militarism also to the flames.

The young gymnast was wild with his success. "All the world of Germany," he shouted, "can see what we desire; can know what is to be expected of us in the future!" [14] The students gave him three booming cheers, followed by three long groans for the old men who ran the Germanies, before they trooped back down the hill to Eisenach and bed.

Next morning there were more meetings, mostly to discuss student organization and the politics of the Student Unions. Some stayed on as late as supper time, but most had set off homeward before the day was over. Departures were an emotional business in those Romantic days. Many young men's cheeks were streaked with tears as they said good-by to blood brothers who had been strangers not three days before. They turned upon the road for a last glimpse of the Wartburg in the sunset, a lofty, glowing symbol of the fatherland that they would not soon forget.

There were those who swore in later years that the Wartburg Festival had been the highest point, the climax of their youthful lives.

A Jacobin Orgy—Metapolitics— and the First National Student Association

The conservative rulers of the Germanies also saw this first great rally of the new youth as an event of considerable significance, but from a very different point of view. Not a hand had been raised in anger, hardly a seditious phrase had passed any speaker's lips. But from the conservative reaction, one might have thought that a conclave of revolutionaries had met upon the Wartburg to plot the overthrow of the established order. A report from the Austrian minister at Weimar to Metternich described the *Wartburgfest* as a "Jacobin orgy," with speeches full of subversion and radical fanaticism.[15]

More disturbing still, the Wartburg Festival marked the beginning of the open break between the liberals of the older generation and the young radicals. Their journalistic and professorial mentors stuck with them, but other former friends began to turn against them. Duke Karl August felt obliged to reprimand one of the Jena professors who had spoken overboldly at the Wartburg. Hardenberg, the aging Prussian reformer, fearing that his own moderate reforms might be disgraced by association with the new radicalism, now openly attacked the students. The liberal Stein, who had fought for German national unity at Vienna, began to heap scorn on the "metapolitics" of the radical newspapers that catered to the student youth.

At Jena, however, where it all began, things were still happening. There in October, 1818, a year after the Wartburg rally, representatives from fourteen universities gathered once again to take an even more momentous step.

For some time, there had been talk in the movement of a larger organization—a "student commonwealth" it was sometimes called. Plans for such a move had been discussed well in advance by correspondence between student leaders at various universities. At Jena, in 1818, the Universal German Student Union—*Allgemeine deutsche Burschenschaft*—finally took shape. All the individual Unions were invited to become members. It was the first truly national student association in history.

The members had many differences still. There was a fundamental conflict between the essentially nonpolitical majority and a minority of "politicals," who were increasingly militant in their demands for some direct action to further the larger liberal-nationalist goals of the movement. There were increasing objections to the admission of Jews into a Christian organization—objections intensified by the widespread belief that German Jews had made little contribution to the war effort, had perhaps even been French sympathizers.[16] The question of how strong a stand to take against dueling—an unpopular stand to take at any university—remained as insoluble as ever. But all such disputes did not negate the fact that the youth had achieved what seemed beyond their elders—an all-German union. The young *Burschenschaft* leaders returned to their universities exulting.

There was a feeling of progress; things were happening. It was the high tide of the university generation of 1815.

3. *ASSASSINATION!*

The Mind of an Assassin

But the worm, as we have seen, was already well ensconced in the bosom of this first of modern student movements. As so often happens, the violent words and deeds of a small minority were to damn a whole generation in the eyes of their elders. In this particular paradigm case, a single brutal act, inspired by extremist rhetoric and executed by a psychologically disturbed fanatic, brought massive repression down upon the entire German youth movement.

The tangled web of cause and effect that shattered the *Burschenschaft* brought three very different lives into fatal conjunction.

The young man whose words—however unconsciously—nerved the assassin to strike was Karl Follen, the most outspoken leader of the militant, Unconditional wing of the movement.

The youth who struck the fatal blow—and became the most celebrated martyr of his generation—was a neurotic young Jena Student Unionist named Karl Sand.

The victim, whose murder shocked Europe and gave the forces of conservative order the excuse they sought to smash the student revolt in Germany, was a white-haired *littérateur* and right-wing propagandist named August von Kotzebue.

In 1818, Karl Follen graduated from Giessen with a degree in civil laws. That same year, he was invited by the liberal element of the faculty at Jena to come up and give a course of lectures at that famous university. Follen thus spent the winter of 1818–19 as a popular instructor and a new leader of campus radicalism at Jena.

But here, at the very fountainhead of the movement, Karl Follen found only further frustration and disappointment. The basic problem seems to have been that even the Jena *Urburschenschaft* proved too tame for his revolutionary taste.

To spread his own "advanced" views, the young instructor organized a discussion group of the more radical students. Almost at once, he met unexpected opposition. The Jena students were brighter, better trained in debate, and not likely to become abject admirers of the provincial radical from Hesse-Darmstadt. The young teacher responded by trying to force his propositions on the group by sheer assertion of his formidable will. He even hinted broadly that only a secret fear of "total commitment" prevented them from accepting his extremist line. At this, some of the students began to turn away from him altogether.

But one among them listened with feverish intensity. He was a long-haired youth in the heavy Old German coat and flowing collar, rather older than most of the other students. He had anxious eyes and a tight mouth, the forehead somewhat low, the expression often oddly vacuous, inward-looking. Altogether a quiet, rather unimpressive young man, generally on the outskirts of the group.

His name was Karl Ludwig Sand. Outwardly, his life had not differed from the lives of thousands of other Student Unionists and gymnasts. Psychologically, however, Sand was very different from most of the naive, hard-muscled, often impractical idealists he mingled with in gymnastics and debate.

Karl Sand's father had been a bureaucrat, no harsher than most German fathers—but that may have been harsh enough. His mother had raised the boy with a strong sense of his own righteousness, and of the great expectations she had for him. He had grown into an unnaturally pious youth, filled with a sense of his own uniqueness, of a special destiny reserved for him alone.

In his 'teens, he had run away from home to join the Bavarian volunteers, leaving his parents a letter full of religious piety and patriotic zeal. But the war had disappointed him. He had missed out on the fighting, and had resigned in disgust as soon as Napoleon was beaten.

Thereafter, at the universities of Tübingen, Erlangen, and finally Jena, Sand's view of the world had darkened steadily. His closest friend had drowned before his eyes—and the aristocratic student fraternities had refused even to attend the funeral and do proper honor to their fellow student. Sand was bitter about it. He helped to organize the *Burschenschaft* at Erlangen.

"The spirit of the organization," he wrote in his diary, "consists in burning hatred of the internal as well as the external enemies of the fatherland." He already saw the world with pathological clarity, in glaring blacks and whites. It was free-souled youth and high ideals against corrupted age, a death struggle between God and Satan in which there could be no compromise.

The mind of Karl Sand was a strange place. Lurid dreams of heroism and martyrdom mingled in his brain with God, freedom, and the fatherland. "Our life is a hero's course," he wrote in an album on a June day in 1818: "speedy victory; early death! Nothing else matters, if only we are real heroes!" Or he would sit glooming over his beer, listening to the sentimental singing of his comrades:

> From our martyr-crowns of thorns
> Bloom roses for our fatherland . . .

His heart would bound, his eyes would glisten. There was the special destiny reserved for him: he knew it, he longed for it. "O, if only I could die this very moment," he wrote in his diary, "for some noble purpose!" [17]

Now I Have a Belief . . .

Karl Sand first came within the range of Karl Follen's firm voice and dominating personality in October, 1818. The overwrought student was tinder to the young instructor's flame.

By early November, Sand's diary began to reflect the new influence. What was needed, he earnestly explained to its pages, was "unconditional will" to take action in the just cause of the German *Volk*. To his mother he wrote ecstatically of his conversion. Though his faith had faltered in the past, he told her, "now I have a belief, the highest conviction on this earth, and I shall rejoice in it alone." [18] Will power, conviction, unconditionality: the creed of the Giessen Unconditionals had found one convert, at least, in Jena.

The new disciple listened most intently when Follen spoke, as he did with increasing frequency, of violence. He was still talking "daggers and oath"—that is, suggesting that for a great cause unconditionally believed in, even lies and murder were legitimate. The intense young teacher, here as during his last years at Giessen, spoke metaphorically half the time and hypothetically the rest; but his instances were often all too concrete. On one occasion, for example, he detailed a plan to kill Alexander I, the reactionary tsar of Russia. It was merely a bizarre joke, as it turned out, intended to test the resolution of some young waverers. But the impact of such talk on Karl Sand—who as a boy had dreamed of assassinating Napoleon Bonaparte—cannot have been healthy.

Great self-sacrifice would of course be required of the martyr-hero who would take upon himself the Roman task of tyrannicide. The moral sacrifice alone, on the part of the honest youth whose scruples were revolted by such a deed, would be immense. But Follen had an answer for those who hesitated even to consider violence as part of their unconditional duty to the fatherland. "He who resorts to these measures . . . is morally all the nobler, the harder it is for him to overcome his natural aversion to such action." [19] The morose, slow-thinking young man on the outskirts of the Follen circle nodded his own heavy but intense agreement.

By the end of 1818, Karl Sand had fixed upon a target for his pathological need to strike a historic blow for his cause.

August von Kotzebue was a living symbol of all that was wrong with Germany. Student Unionists and gymnasts, liberal professors and journalists alike despised him with a passion normally reserved for policemen or princes or those pillars of reaction, Metternich and Tsar Alexander. There could be no more fitting target for Sand's dagger—the real one he would substitute for Follen's metaphor.

August von Kotzebue was neither a policeman nor a politician: he was a man of letters. An old-fashioned eighteenth-century man of letters, and very successful at it. His comic plays—more than two hundred of them in his long life—had earned him a Europe-wide reputation and had been performed as far away as America. He was a famous wit as well, notorious for his savage diatribes against his literary rivals—and against the political enemies of whatever sovereign he happened to be serving at any given moment.

During the years after the war, Kotzebue had settled in the Rhineland as editor of the *Literary Weekly,* a storm center of aesthetic—and political—debate. A foreign visitor who took tea with him saw the celebrated author as "a lively little man, somewhat of a coxcomb." He had a good-sized family about him in these later years and was "not without . . . domestic feelings . . ." [20]

August von Kotzebue had been a liberal once, as a student at Jena—but that was forty years ago. Then, he had verbally roasted priests and royal despots and social inequality with the best wits of the Enlightenment. But time and disillusioning events had made a very different man of the white-haired editor of the *Literary Weekly.*

He leveled his fire now at would-be reformers and Jacobin revolutionaries. He had no use for talk about constitutions and representative assemblies and freedom of the press. He had nothing but scorn for subversive moonshine about "German unity."

His most withering contempt was reserved for the younger generation and the radical student movement.

Thus for example, commenting in his *Weekly* on liberal pieties about academic freedom, Kotzebue lashed out at the dangerously undisciplined state of the German universities. "We cannot convince ourselves," he wrote in the high-flown invective style for which he was famous, "that the *self-called academical liberty* can be pronounced either noble or liberal!" What do we send our sons to college for, after all? he asked rhetorically. To be seduced into subversive associations like the Student Unions? To be fed radical poisons "even [in] the lecture rooms, where ignorant professors tell him he is born to reform his native land . . . ?"[21] Let the university youth be disciplined and set to their books again, instead of marching and rallying and lecturing their elders on how to run the world!

Perhaps most bitterly of all, however, the younger generation hated this eloquent enemy of the movement for his *attitude*. Kotzebue was not *sincere*. His comedy was trivial, written for paltry gain. His wit was sometimes risqué, the sort of thing the corrupt courts of petty German princes battened on. Above all, he was not dedicated, committed to a cause. In their eyes, he was a vile old man, a sneerer and a jeerer, and the most notorious literary hatchet man for the establishment in all the German states.

Karl Sand had been vaguely aware of him for years. In 1817, Sand had been present on the Wartburg when Kotzebue's *German History* was flung into the fire. The raw-nerved young *Burschenschafter* had recorded his own humiliation at the "new insults" the old man had heaped on the "patriotic students" by way of paying them back.[22] And he had been outraged, with nationalistic youth all over Germany, when in January, 1818, the liberal journal *Nemesis* struck the most telling blow yet in this nasty war of words—by "exposing" August von Kotzebue as a Russian spy!

The celebrated author, it seemed, was sending "secret reports" to Tsar Alexander. These "reports," as it turned out, consisted largely of accounts of public opinion in the Germanies, of educational and literary, financial and political trends of the most general sort. The old, internationally recognized man of letters saw nothing wrong in it. He had grown up in the cosmopolitan eighteenth century and had served a number of sovereigns in his time without worrying about whether their "court French" was spoken with a German or a Russian accent. The new fad for "German nationalism" meant nothing to him.

But the liberal press rang with denunciations, and the patriotic Student Unionists fairly seethed with indignation. In Jena, Karl Sand crouched over the writing desk in his little room, his pen flicking across the pages of his diary: "There ought to be somebody brave enough to stick a sword through the carcass of this Kotzebue . . ."

Sand's diary entries grew wilder, sometimes almost hysterical, as the year 1818 drew to a close. And always now the Follenesque note was there:

> O the momentous hour when I decided to live unconditionally for my country, when I broke the thousand bonds which constrained me from dying for my fatherland. . . . Not to decide to live from conviction, not to die for it, is sinful; it is the sin of millions.

On New Year's Eve, with snow on the ground and sleigh bells jingling outside his window, he wrote with a new calmness, the inner peace of a decision taken:

> I am spending the last day of this year, 1818, in a solemn mood, and I am resolved that the Christmas which I have just celebrated will have been my last. If anything is to come of our efforts; if the cause of humanity is to prevail in our fatherland; if in this momentous time enthusiasm is to revive again in our country and everything is not to be forgotten again, then the traitor and seducer of youth, A. v. K., must fall . . .[23]

The Carcass of This Kotzebue

In the latter half of March, 1819, with a blustery spring coming on, Karl Sand set out for Mannheim, where Kotzebue lived.

Mannheim was a city in the southern Rhineland, several days' journey by foot and coach from Jena. In the old drinking songs of the student subculture, it was "Mannheim with its maidens and champagne."[24] The road west from Heidelberg, along which Sand approached his destination, was straight and poplar-lined, crowded not only with peasants and their beasts, but with carriages, and travelers on horseback. Few of the busy citizens who passed this way can have had a second glance for the hairy student, a common enough sight on the roads of Germany these days.

Karl Sand was trundled into town on a friendly peasant's cart fairly early on the twenty-third of March. He apparently spent some time looking around town. He talked for some hours—quite rationally—with a clergyman he met at the inn where he took a meal. Finally, after some inquiries, he made his way to Kotzebue's unpretentious home. It was late afternoon by this time, after five o'clock.

The long-haired student greeted the elegant, if slightly puzzled, old man. Sand managed a few words of nervous small talk as he crossed the parlor toward his host. The dagger was concealed up the sleeve of his heavy coat. As soon as he was within arm's reach of his victim, he jerked out the knife and lunged wildly, shouting:

"Traitor to the fatherland!"

Sand struck at the old man's face. Under interrogation later, he could not remember how many times he drove the blade into the frail figure before him. He did remember how Kotzebue extended feeble hands to ward off the thrusting point. He remembered that the dying man gave "the merest whimper" as he crumpled to the carpeted floor.[25]

Sand started for the door, inadvertently carrying off a handwritten "Sentence of Death against August von Kotzebue" he had intended to leave beside the corpse. Before he could get out of the house, he found himself confronted by the dead man's little son, rushing futilely to his father's rescue. He dodged past the boy, lurched out into the street, and turned the bloody knife upon himself. Covered with blood and still babbling about fatherland and freedom, he was taken into custody within a few feet of his crime.

Sand did not die. The doctors managed to keep him alive for more than a year, to face his trial and his punishment.

4. *THE UNIVERSITIES MUST BE PURIFIED AT ANY PRICE*

The End of Academical Liberty

Meantime Germany seethed with rumors, fears, and outraged indignation. In those quiet states of Central Europe, the very heartland of the Metternich system, the crime broke like a thunderclap. That "repose" which the Austrian minister had labored so diligently to achieve was shattered more violently by this murder of a literary man than a less conservative society might have been by a royal assassination.

From one end of Germany to the other, fear of a revolutionary conspiracy was rampant. At the secret meetings of the *Burschenschaft* leaders, it was solemnly asserted, plans were being laid to assassinate leading statesmen in all the German states. Jena was the fountainhead, but all the affiliated universities were involved. The student radicals drew lots to see which of them would wield the knife. And of course it was all part of the larger, international Jacobin plot to destroy civilization as we know it. Everyone seemed to know about the ultra-secret "Central Committee" in Paris . . .

Blame for the crime of a single psychopath was heaped not only on the invisible student conspirators, but also on the academic and journalistic radicals who had filled their young minds with poisonous ideas. "Kotzebue had been hated long," declared one judicious observer, "but before the student dared to use his dagger upon him, it was necessary for certain journals to make him contemptible." "The real culprits," another wrote, "are and ever will be Fries, Luden, Oken, Kieser [liberal professors at Jena] of whom the universities must be purified at any price . . ." [26] The radical professors, the inflammatory press, the "international revolutionary conspiracy," and above all, the student militants—these were the sinister forces behind the crime of Karl Sand.

If any confirmatory evidence were needed, it was provided three months later, when the Hessian minister von Ibell—a liberal, unfortunately for the conspiracy theorists—was stabbed and slightly wounded by a young man who claimed that his motive was "to rid his country of a man so injurious to the public weal." Even the most faithful liberals were shaken now. "Murders elevated to the rank of patriotic actions," lamented Stein in real agony of spirit, "crimes caused by the perverse application of noble and venerable principles . . . altogether it is enough to drive to despair those who sincerely desire the welfare of humanity as far as it is possible and attainable in this life." [27]

Conservatives wasted no time lamenting: they took action.

Karl Ludwig Sand was tried, convicted, and publicly executed—by beheading—in a meadow outside the gates of Mannheim on the twentieth of May, 1820. The bloodstained boards of the scaffold were bought and treasured by fellow *Burschenschafter* as relics of their martyred hero. Romantic young ladies fell in love with his picture, which was widely circulated in cheap prints. In time, Karl Sand even became the hero of a popular folk song, often sung in student beer halls to the thumping of steins on beer-wet tables.

Sand's unwitting mentor, Karl Follen, was twice interrogated in an effort to prove his complicity in the crime. His papers were confiscated; he was dismissed from the University of Jena; he was kept under close watch by the police in Giessen. Like Sand, he became a hero to large numbers of students. But when his brother Adolf and another of his former university associates were arrested at the beginning of 1820, Karl Follen slipped quietly across the frontier into France. He spent the rest of his life in exile—most of it in America, where he became a Unitarian minister and an ardent abolitionist.

The net spread wider still. Father Jahn, the liberal gymnast, was bundled off to prison in Berlin. A liberal professor or two was discharged from the University of Jena. Even aging administrative reformers like Stein were watched by the police, and spies sat in Schleiermacher's congregation.

Students were arrested for no greater crime than extravagant remarks in private letters to friends. Prussian judges were instructed that the word was to be taken for the deed: subversive talk was to be punished as a form of treasonous activity. All over the German states, the gymnasts and the Student Unions were harried, pressured, punished as individuals or abolished as organizations.

Prince Metternich, meantime, was moving methodically to institutionalize the reaction. The notorious Karlsbad Decrees were presented to the Diet of the German Confederation in September of 1819. They passed unanimously, after only four hours of debate.

The Karlsbad Decrees were brief and to the point.[28] There was a "Press Law" prescribing pre-publication censorship for all periodicals published in the Germanies, with suppression as the penalty for failure to conform. Radical teaching in the universities was proscribed: professors who were found to "abuse their legitimate influence over youthful minds" by teaching "doctrines hostile to the public order or subversive of existing governmental institutions" were to be discharged.

The students themselves were henceforth to be submitted to "the strictest enforcement of . . . disciplinary regulations . . ." Students expelled from one university were not to be admitted to any other institution of higher learning in the German states. And strong measures were to be taken against all "secret and unauthorized societies in the universities . . . especially . . . that association established some years since under the name *Universal Students' Union* . . ."

From the Wartburg to Versailles

As the slow-moving wheels of German officialdom began sluggishly to grind, it seemed as if the German youth movement was at an end. The young *Burschenschafter*'s dream of a united fatherland, of constitutions and equality, seemed to have been only that—unhealthy, unrealistic dreaming.

But there is another ending to this story: a larger, long-term consequence of this upsurge of generational unrest. For a youth revolt, once ignited, is not so easily extinguished.

The German liberal-nationalist youth revolt of 1815 did not end with the execution of a psychologically disturbed young assassin. Not even the suppression of their Student Unions and their newspapers, the wave of arrests, the harrying of their leaders into exile could kill the movement. One generation of young rebels had been broken; but a tradition had been established, and there would be other rebellious younger generations in German history.

There was the *Jünglingsbund,* or Youth League, of the 1820's. There was the Hambach Festival and the abortive Frankfurt *Putsch* of the early 1830's. There was the vigorous participation of the youth in the Revolution of 1848—Student Unionists fighting on the barricades of Berlin and Vienna, husky gymnasts battling in the streets of Dresden and Kiel. Echoes of the marching, singing youth of 1815 are even to be found in the hippie-style *Wandervögel* and the militant Hitler Youth movements of our own century.

More important, some, at least, of the goals for which this first German generation in revolt took up the cudgels were in fact achieved—half a century later.

Liberalism fell by the wayside in Germany—a casualty of the debacle of 1848, of increasing Prussian predominance, and of the new mood of "blood and iron" realism that loomed so large after mid-century. But nationalism survived. And in 1871, in the Great Hall of Mirrors at Versailles, Otto von Bismarck stood up to announce what was in fact the most radical dream of the *Burschenschaft*—the unification of Germany. Bismarck was no more a nationalist crusader than he was a liberal. And yet—could he have accomplished what he did without the wide currency and increasing acceptance the notion of national unity had found over the preceding five decades?

A utopian idea spread broadcast over the land by the long-haired young radicals of 1815 thus became a reality, through the efforts of a hardheaded statesman as fundamentally conservative as Prince Metternich himself. It is a not uncommon paradox in the checkered history of the ongoing revolt of the younger generation.

4

"The Children Have Surpassed Their Fathers" *
The First Counter Culture
France, 1830

Militance looms large in the history of the Youth Revolution. But militant rebellion is not the only way in which young dissidents have expressed their alienation from their elders' world. Almost as commonly, disaffected youth have simply turned their backs and drifted away into a youthful subculture of their own.[1]

Those who withdraw, or "drop out" of modern society have sought refuge in many alternative ideologies and life styles. Their creeds have varied widely, from the worship of art to rank materialism, from Eastern religions to the ultimate acid trip. All of their counter cultures, however, may legitimately be subsumed under the oldest of all rubrics for this form of youthful protest: what Henry Murger made famous as *la vie de bohème*—the Bohemian life.

The first Bohemia, and the first of modern counter cultures, took shape in France around the revolutionary year 1830.

France had been through a lot over the four or five decades preceding 1830. A senior citizen of that year had lived through more history than most of us will ever see—and more than he himself ever wanted to see again.

The famous names and dates were not dry statistics out of books to him, but living, searing memories. He remembered 1789, the year of the Revolution: a demoralized, bankrupt monarchy—the French Estates General meeting for the first time in almost two centuries—and the howling, sweating mob that brought the Bastille down. He remembered '93, the black year of the Terror: Robespierre the Incorruptible, the unwearying blade of the guillotine, and

* Théodore Jouffroy, *Le cahier vert; Comment les dogmes finissent; Lettres inédites,* Pierre Poux, ed. (Paris, 1924), pp. 73–74.

the blood of ten thousand Frenchmen shed to water the Tree of Liberty.

And then Napoleon, Caesar on a white horse bringing order out of chaos at home, and victory to French arms everywhere. The years of glory, the endless roster of Napoleonic triumphs, till all Europe cowered under the shadow of the eagles. Then Moscow burning, and the long retreat, knee-deep in the snows of Russia; Leipzig and the Battle of the Nations; Waterloo, and an island in the far Atlantic called St. Helena.

And for France, drained, exhausted, the Old Regime restored by the armies of her enemies—fifteen dull years to recover from a quarter-century of Revolutionary dreams, Napoleonic splendor, and all the accompanying disasters. The fifteen unexciting years of the Bourbon Restoration.

The Restoration had its alarums and excursions, of course; but by and large those years between 1815 and 1830 provided a respite for a weary nation. No more crusades for freedom or for glory. No more conscriptions and casualty lists, no more tumbrils rumbling to the guillotine. A little peace and quiet for a man to grow old in.

And then the drums began to beat again. There were speeches and parades, demands for change. For there were young men still in France, new generations with new crusades to fight.

There were young men who muttered that the notorious Republic of '93 had never really had a chance to show what it could do; who said aloud that Napoleon had been betrayed; who preached strange new utopias of their own devising—some called it *socialism.* There were even those who—weirdest and farthest-out of all—offered a whole new set of values, and soon a new style of life as well, in the name of Romanticism.

For the young men of the 1820's, the founding generation of French Romanticism, the new movement was, of course, a revolution in the arts, and not much more. Alexandre Dumas was writing plays in those days, and Balzac was grinding out short pieces for the newspapers. Berlioz was already slashing away at his Symphony Fantastique; Delacroix was covering canvases with swirling shapes and blazing colors. Victor Hugo, whose neat little figure and vast, bulging forehead were already familiar on the streets of Paris, was a poet in search of new literary fields to conquer. For them, Romanticism was "the new art," pure and simple.

For their successors, however, for the *second* Romantic generation, the youth of the 1830's, with whom this chapter is concerned, the Romantic creed and the Romantic life were a great deal more than a new school in the arts. Romanticism for the French generation of 1830 was something in the nature of a revelation, with Victor Hugo for its messiah.

Old men shook their heads and middle-aged ones muttered angrily as they watched the young men preaching their new politics, their new social gospels. They had seen all this before, and what came after it. They could smell revolution in the air.

But when they contemplated the unfathomable new phenomenon that called itself Romanticism, they threw up their hands. They had *never* seen anything like this before.

1. *HAVING A LAUGH AT* HERNANI

An Invasion of Shakespearean Barbarians

The Romantic Bohemians began to gather outside the *Théâtre Français* as early as one o'clock in the afternoon that chilly February day in 1830. They were supposed to be admitted early, at Monsieur Hugo's own request, so that they could seat themselves strategically before the paying—and presumably hostile—audience arrived. They came at one, but they were not actually admitted to the theater until three. For two hours, therefore, a crowd of several hundred of the author's special friends from the Left Bank milled about in the *rue de Richelieu,* blowing on their hands, laughing and joking—and creating a spectacle that was the talk of Paris long before the next day's papers were out.

For two hours that celebrated afternoon, the good burghers of Paris had a look at "those people" from beyond the Seine, the writers and artists of the Latin Quarter. The solid citizen could only stare open-mouthed at this astonishing eruption of the apostles of the new art into the decent parts of the city.

The young Romantics were proud to acknowledge Victor Hugo as the leader of their school, and they came to the premiere of his new play, *Hernani,* dressed to do him honor. At first glance, one might have thought it was a fancy-dress ball—increasingly popular in the 1830's—or perhaps carnival season. These artistic revolutionaries had, of course, no use for the dark, swallow-tailed coat, the somber vest, the top hat, high collar, and cravat that constituted the bourgeois uniform. The bearded, long-haired Bohemians came resplendent in satin and velvet, brightly colored and cut to fantastic patterns out of history, fiction, and art. There were "Robespierre" waistcoats and Renaissance capes, doublets out of Rubens' paintings and Spanish cloaks out of every young Romantic's dreams. Revolutionary themes and the more colorful periods of history predominated.

It was a gaudy crowd that gathered that afternoon for the premiere of *Hernani,* "an invasion of young Shakespearian barbarians" that the middle-class, middle-aged majority of Paris playgoers was not going to like at all.[2] It was to be an almost unique occasion in theatrical history—a first night when the audience upstaged the play.

Victor Hugo had labored long and hard to get this drama on the stage. There had been the usual interminable wrangles with the royal censor. There had been arguments too with the star actress, Mademoiselle Mars, who had objected loudly to some of the "unclassical" lines she was asked to recite. The reason, as she candidly admitted, was the generation gap: she was fifty years old, and she still loved the neoclassical plays she had starred in when she was young.

Hugo, with a shrewd sense of the dramatic (and perhaps of the commercial possibilities), had closed all rehearsals to the press. Public curiosity was thus whetted beyond anything in recent memory. As the last days of February approached, and the ice began to break up on the Seine, all playgoing Paris waited to see if the author of the shocking "Preface" to *Cromwell*—the literary manifesto of the French Romantics—could practice what he preached. Or, more precisely, if he would dare to practice such preachments.

One formality remained: the question of the *claqueurs.* The Paris *claqueurs* were the hired cheering section without which no play dared open. Every dramatist employed them during the first few nights of a play's run, to get the piece off to a good start. Hugo, unconventional as usual, decided not to hire any. Or, more precisely, he refused to make use of the professionals who were readily available. New art, he blandly declared, requires a new audience. He would invite his own claque—the poets, playwrights, novelists, painters, sculptors, architects, composers, and musicians who thronged the cafés, artists' studios, and cheap lodging houses of the Left Bank.

Almost to a man, they were members of the younger generations. Some, like Hugo himself, were almost thirty, mature men soon to put youthful things behind them. Others, like Théophile Gautier, a leading light and contemporary chronicler of the new youth, were barely twenty, members of the budding generation of the 1830's. But whether their young manhood was just ending or just beginning, "in the army of the Romantics," as Gautier nostalgically recalled in later years, "everybody was young." [3]

The Romantic Self-Image Incarnate

At three o'clock, the somewhat distressed management finally let them in. Jostling, cheerful, enthusiastic despite the cold and the inconvenience, the garishly dressed young Bohemians deployed themselves strategically about the theater.

They had hours to wait before curtain time, but they had come prepared. They had their dinner with them, and wine to go with it. They made a noisy, boisterous picnic, there in the cathedral twilight of the empty theater. They talked enthusiastically about the play, which "Victor"—as they casually referred to their most celebrated member—had read aloud to some of them. They sang songs, Hugo's own poems and others perhaps less elevated in tone. One minor problem marred their pleasure: the public toilets were locked, and there was no one around in the afternoon who had a key to open them. Not overly concerned with the lack of such amenities, the young Bohemians relieved themselves in a far corner of the balcony.

With noise and laughter and horseplay, the hours passed. Seven o'clock approached. The gaslights were lit, and the paying customers filed in.

The barbarians from the Left Bank gave them an exuberant welcome. Pretty young women in particular, sweeping down the aisle bejeweled and bare-shouldered, were greeted with enthusiastic applause that flushed the faces of their escorts. Gentlemen and ladies alike rolled up their eyes and turned away shocked noses from the scattered remnants of the picnic lunch, the telltale odor from a corner of the balcony. It was all quite enough, as a frantic manager informed Monsieur Hugo, to ruin the play before the curtain even rose.

Rise it did, however, and the play began. Or rather, it made every effort to begin. But the "Battle of *Hernani*" commenced with the first lines spoken on the stage, and few lines after that were heard through to their conclusion. Few lines, in fact, were ever heard at all.

The play of *Hernani* was a showcase for all the Romantic heresies. It was a historical melodrama, like so many of the famous early Romantic productions. As such, it stressed local color, the brilliant pageantry of the High Renaissance, far more than the eternal verities and conscience crises of French Classical tragedy. The classical unities of time and place were cheerfully ignored: the action spanned several months of time (instead of the traditional twenty-four hours), and leaped from one side of Europe to the other. The structure of the verse—and alert French audiences had ears trained to catch verse rhythms—was loose and free, far too much so by neoclassical standards. Altogether it was a gaudy, freewheeling, and totally unclassical piece, sure to rouse the enthusiasm of the Romantic and the ire of the traditionalist.

Above all, Hernani himself, the Spanish bandit who is the hero of the play, was certain to stir the souls of the younger members of the audience. Hernani was the Romantic self-image incarnate. A man of mystery and passion, a doomed outlaw in a society that refused to recognize his true greatness, he was everything the typical young writer or artist of the Latin Quarter imagined himself to be.

The Bohemians could not help but see themselves reflected in this story of the mysterious Hernani's doomed love for Doña Sol and his desperate feud with the Emperor of Spain. Each long-haired youth saw himself as a similarly proscribed outsider in bourgeois society. Each willingly, fervently confessed to being, like Hernani, the slave of his own dark passions. Each imagined himself to be just such a man of unacknowledged greatness, a genius unrecognized by an unjust world. And many of them felt a perverse pleasure in the notion that they too were damned, doomed souls, victims of forces in themselves they hardly understood. When death comes at last for Hernani—on his wedding night—every young heart pounded with the shock of recognition.

Don't Laugh, Lady—Your Teeth Are Showing

Or would have done, if any significant portion of the play had been heard, by the Bohemians or by anyone else. But with the first words of the first act, pandemonium broke loose:

> Can it be he? 'Tis surely someone on the secret
> Stair . . .[4]

This was rank *enjambement,* the running over of a clause or phrase into the second line, and it was strictly against the rules of classical prosody. It may seem a small thing to the modern ear, but it was as blatant a sin in the theater of those days as, say, sloppy cutting or camera work to a modern moviegoer. It brought snorts of derision from more than one neoclassical partisan in the boxes. This in turn stirred the champions of the new art to vocal defense of the piece. And the battle was on.

"Ridiculous! The man can't write, that's all!"

"Can't write?" a long-haired, garishly clothed youth would swivel in his seat to answer. "Why, any fool can see the author's purpose here—"

Angry disputes broke out all over the house. Other spectators shushed them at first, then were sucked into the arguments. Argument itself broke down, gave way to insult.

One society lady laughed shrilly all through the intensely moving "portrait scene."

"Don't laugh, lady," a young Bohemian shouted with brutal candor, "your teeth are showing!"

"Tattooed savages!" sneered the bald-pated classicists.

"Mummies!" howled the hairy youth.

All communication broke down in the polarized house. There was only the clash of sound, the boos and hisses and jeering laughter of the old and orthodox against the cheers and bravos of the young Romantics.[5]

The premiere had been everything the establishment press could desire, and they emptied the vials of their scorn on the wild men from the wrong side of the river. Victor Hugo, they said, had dragged in "spectators worthy of his play, a kind of bandits, ragged and uncultivated, scraped up from God knows what disgusting slum, who proceeded to turn a respectable hall into a nauseating cellar . . ." The Left Bank claque had sung "obscene" and even "sacrilegious" songs. They had "given themselves up to an orgy" which had "prophaned the temple of Melpomene forever." [6]

Thereafter it became a fad in fashionable circles to go "have a laugh at *Hernani.*" [7] Elegant playgoers sat reading their newspapers ostentatiously throughout the play. Some sat all evening with their backs to the stage, conversing loudly with their friends. Some simply rose in the middle and stomped disgustedly out of the theater, slamming the doors behind them.

The play's supporters, supplied with free tickets, continued to come night after night to answer the Philistines in kind. And if sufficient provocation was not forthcoming, the younger generation was more than willing to take the offensive themselves. "Four of my janissaries offer their services," a friend charged with ticket distribution among the artists' studios wrote Hugo. "I guarantee my men. They are the sort that would chop off heads to get at the periwigs." [8]

Students at the university and even in the secondary schools were excited by the controversy. News of the continuing struggle between Romantic and classic, youth and the establishment, spread even into the provinces. At Toulouse, one young enthusiast fought a duel over *Hernani.*

For many, the "Battle of *Hernani*" was probably no more than a game, and, of course, a chance to bait their enemies in public. But for some, at least, this was a genuine cause, a clash of high ideals. Given the Romantic temper of this artistically inclined band of social drop-outs, Théophile Gautier perhaps did not exaggerate when he called it a "beginning of free, young, and new thought," the rallying point of a whole generation of "young men . . . mad for art and poetry." [9]

2. *CHILDREN OF THE CENTURY*

A Vacuum in the Realm of Values

The French Bohemians of 1830, like the German student militants of 1815, constituted a real generational rebellion. In this case also, therefore, it will be well to begin with a brief generational biography. For these were all what Alfred de Musset called them in his famous *Confession d'un enfant du siècle*—children of the century, children of the age. And the roots of their rebellion, as in all such generational upheavals, lay in the impact of that age upon the developing psyche of childhood and early youth.

The typical young French Romantic of the *Hernani* premiere was nineteen or twenty years old at the time of that epochal confrontation.[10] He had been born into a bourgeois home, in Paris or the provinces, around the year 1810—five years before the Battle of Waterloo.

His upbringing had revealed a disturbing pattern of overindulgence in childhood followed by overdisciplined repression in school. A Rousseauian passion for children and for family "togetherness" dominated the middle-class home at the beginning of the century: the child was petted and coddled, made a prime center of family life. But Napoleonic discipline prevailed in the new system of public education: the growing boy was bustled off to boarding school, where he was birched, drilled, marched about, and confined to a cell-like dormitory throughout his adolescent years. Thus, alternately pampered and treated like some form of felon, he quite likely crossed the threshold of young manhood with a definite feeling of deprival, of a paradise lost somewhere in his childhood; a paradise of freedom and total gratification that was rightfully his whenever he should feel the urge to reach out his hand and take it up again.

He also reached the age of consent with a notable lack of believable ideals to guide him.

The fathers of this generation had seen the clay feet of too many idols of the tribe: they had little faith left to pass on to the youth. Voltaire had laughed religion to scorn. Robespierre had turned the glorious liberal dreams of 1789 into the bloody realities of '93. Napoleon on St. Helena had proved to be mortal after all—and many Frenchmen had grown weary of taxes and conscriptions long before Waterloo. After 1815, finally, France had been ruled by a Restoration regime dedicated to re-establishing the supremacy of throne and altar—a regime discredited a quarter of a century since. The fathers of the generation of 1830 were thus not likely to be passionate believers in anything. Voltairian cynics at worst, prudent men of the world at best, they communicated only a vacuum in the realm of values to their offspring.

One thing only the bourgeois *père de famille* did strive to inculcate in his sons: the middle-class urge to get ahead in the world. With this in mind, he dispatched the boy to Paris as soon as he was out of school. Off to the university, the medical school, the law school, the Polytechnic; off to begin a glorious career in business, government, or the professions. Off to Paris, the city of light.

Sending a boy to Paris in search of success in the later 1820's was like sending him to Babylon in search of salvation. The great city on the Seine swarmed with every sort of temptation to bourgeois industry and thrift: dining and dancing, racing and gambling, prostitutes, confidence men, dance halls, vaudeville houses. . . . What Paris did not abound in was jobs—or jobs sufficiently exalted to meet the high level of expectation inculcated in the birth cohort of 1810.

And so the youth in his late 'teens, or perhaps just turned twenty, found himself trapped in the odorous, jabbering, but undeniably colorful purlieus of the student city on the Left Bank, or the tenements that clustered around the Louvre. Out-at-elbows, vaguely yearning for a lost paradise of self-indulgence, deprived of values and a directing faith, he found himself adrift.

The Three Glorious Days

Then, in the later twenties, there came new stirrings, new excitement in the intellectual life of France. There was the "new liberalism" preached by the young philosopher Théodore Jouffroy. There was the strange new view of society spread in journals and public lectures by the disciples of the technocratic messiah, the late comte de Saint-Simon. And most notorious of all, there was the Romantic revolt in the arts, led by Hugo, Dumas, Balzac, George Sand, Berlioz, Delacroix, and other prophets of the new aesthetic sensibility. A generation set adrift and ripe for ideology turned with quickening enthusiasm to these unorthodox new ways of looking at the world.

The passion of this rising generation for new ideas, their enthusiasm for the new creeds, filled their youngish mentors with admiration. "Already these children have surpassed their fathers," wrote Jouffroy, "and have felt the emptiness of their doctrines. . . . The hope of new days is in them; they are the predestined apostles of those days, and the salvation of the world is in their hands." [11] The younger generation, inspired in their turn, redoubled their zeal and their excitement.

And then, to cap the climax, came the revolution.

Eighteen thirty, the year of *Hernani,* was also the year of the July Revolution, the year that dumped the Bourbon dynasty finally and forever into the dustbin of history, the year that saw the rise to power of Louis Philippe d'Orléans, the amiable autocrat whom history has dubbed the "bourgeois king."

Charles X, the last of the Bourbons, finally went too far in his zeal to turn the calendar back to the eighteenth century. In particular, he pressed too hard on the French middle classes. Energetic businessmen who had done well for themselves under the Revolution and Napoleon, when careers were open to talent and war contracts were plentiful, found themselves shunted to one side under the Restoration. The Bourbons, and Charles X in particular, assigned all the plums to unproductive priests and doddering *émigré* noblemen. After a quarter-century of vigorous social mobility and progress, it was galling, to say the least.

Bourgeois France chafed under this neglect. But the bourgeois liberal—and under such a regime, the bourgeoisie was liberal almost by definition—did hope for better things. He hoped particularly for the implementation of the celebrated Charter of French Liberties. The Charter was a constitutional document of sorts, a concession which the Bourbons had nervously offered the country at the moment of their return to power in 1815, and had been trying to undo ever since. This Charter did provide a parliament after all—if only the Bourbon kings could be brought to recognize its legitimate authority.

By the summer of 1830, however, it was all too obvious that the white-haired, divine-right monarch on the throne had no intention of surrendering to the middle-class dream of a British-style constitutional monarchy in France. In July of that year, in fact, alarmed by recent liberal gains at the polls, Charles X launched what looked suspiciously like a reactionary coup designed to finish off the Charter as a potential instrument of government—and bourgeois power—in France.

The royal coup took the form of the July Ordinances. These autocratic decrees dismissed a newly elected Chamber of Deputies before it ever met, temporarily suppressed the press, and drastically modified the election laws. The result was one of the suddenest and shortest of French revolutions—the "July days" of 1830.

The last three days in July—the "three glorious days," as the victorious revolutionaries promptly labeled them—boiled down to three days of rioting and barricade fighting in the city of Paris. But Paris was the metropolis of the nation; and when the Bourbon troops were driven out of the capital, the regime was doomed. Charles X took ship for England, and the Revolution of 1830 was over.

Bourgeois politicians, journalists, and influential moneymen had been the first to defy the king, and it was they who established the new regime that followed the fall of the last Bourbon. But these portly, middle-class men of business and the professions had done little of the fighting in between. The barricades were left for others, for men inspired by the liberal rhetoric that had filled the speeches and the editorials of the bourgeois opposition for the past fifteen years.

The street fighters were men of many sorts: half-educated guildsmen and unemployed proletarians rendered dangerous by a recent depression; grizzled Napoleonic veterans bitter about their meager pensions; and, perhaps most enthusiastic of all, the new youth of 1830.

Where Is Our Republic, Our Utopia?

New converts to half a dozen ideologies, the rebellious younger generation flung itself with unexampled passion into the fray. Many rushed out into the streets waving muskets they had never used, with no more than the haziest idea what form the new France should take. Most cried *Vive la Charte!* on the first day; before the sun set blood-red on the third, many were shouting *Vive la République!* The ideologically inflamed youth of 1830 were clear on one thing only: from those three glorious days in the streets, an equally splendid new nation must surely eventuate.

Then, as for the German students of 1815, came the great betrayal.

Instead of the millennium, the barricades of July brought only Louis Philippe, the bourgeois king. A middle-class monarch who carried an umbrella and pumped the hands of bankers and shopkeepers with untiring cordiality. We now have, the liberal politicians explained to the nation, a constitutional monarchy in place of an absolutist one—a *juste milieu* between tyranny and anarchy. But where is our Republic, our Utopia? demanded the younger generation? Where is that new France the people died for on the barricades?

Like the failure of the Congress of Vienna to forge a new united Germany, the failure of the Chamber of Deputies to undertake a true transformation of French society triggered a major generational revolt. It is never wise to promise youth the moon—an end to prejudice, poverty, and war, for instance—and then deliver a handful of rocks instead.

The streets of Paris in the 1830's present a familiar spectacle to any veteran of the American 1960's. "The July days," as a contemporary recalled, "had heated the brains, over-excited the youth of France . . ."[12] There were demonstrations and riots, street fighting and police repression. Schools were occupied by outraged students. Street fighting flamed and the barricades went up again, manned by would-be revolutionaries. More than once the moldering working-class ghettos exploded, and troops had to be sent in to restore order.

Some young militants flocked into the radical political clubs, demanding the overthrow of all monarchy and the establishment of a commonwealth modeled on Robespierre's republican dream of the 1790's. Others joined the embryonic socialist groups—the word *socialisme* first became fashionable during this decade—and dreamed of future utopian societies after the masterplans of Fourier or Saint-Simon.

The revolt of the Bohemian artists of the Latin Quarter, however, took a different form. These ill-clad young aesthetes simply turned away in visceral disgust from the whole political scene. Their contemporaries rebelled against a bourgeois world: the young Bohemians withdrew.

3. THE GREENING OF THE LEFT BANK

The Counter Culture of the Latin Quarter

Characters like those who turned the *Hernani* premiere into a riot seemed to swarm everywhere in the Paris of the 1830's. Genteel citizens averted their eyes—and their noses—when they passed them in the street. The press labeled them "Bohemians," an old French word for "gypsy," with all its connotations of shiftiness, vagabondage, and criminal tendencies. The papers also slapped the untranslatable tag of *"bousingo"* on the Left Bank youth, an epithet perhaps best rendered by some such familiar equivalent as "beatnik" or "hippie." By whatever name, they were a blight on the landscape to most of their fellow citizens.

They were certainly not appetizing specimens to look at with their long, greasy hair, dirty beards, filthy fingernails, and swarthy complexions that were supposed to look romantically Eastern. Their everyday clothing was definitely on the shabby side of decency —broken boots, battered old coats, cravats worn sloppily awry.

For first nights, all-night parties, and other special occasions, on the other hand, they sported the wild array of costumes we have already seen at the *Hernani* premiere. Like any American hippie haven of the 1960's, the Left Bank in the 1830's was alive with colorful getups. There were minstrels out of Walter Scott, Renaissance cavaliers derived from Rubens or Van Dyck, Byronic corsairs, and others wearing unlikely costumes inspired by the plays of Hugo and Dumas. Every new production spawned its fads. Assorted imitation Poles and Arabs strolled the narrow streets as well, honoring those oppressed peoples who had fought so heroically (if hopelessly) against Russian tyranny and French imperialism respectively. There were trunk hose and doublets in plenty, Spanish capes and English jockey caps, exotic Kuzzilbash hats and ordinary striped nightcaps—worn by day, naturally. Anything and everything went, so long as it set one off from the common herd.

The popular press found this band of cultural anarchists let loose in the Paris of 1830 an endless source of colorful copy. These hairy pariahs, the *Figaro* informed its readers, were "freaks" in the most literal sense—sideshow curiosities out of some traveling show. Their rooms were full of exotic weapons, their bellies full of indigestible medieval foods. They demanded absolute liberty—meaning license to commit any outrage—opposed all law and order, were disturbers of the peace, night brawlers and window breakers.

There was much distortion, much oversimplification here. One thing was true, however: Bohemia did constitute a separate society of its own, a subculture with its own style of life, its own values, its own view of the world. These "Shakespearean barbarians" comprised, in fact, a genuine counter culture, as Theodore Roszak describes it, "a culture so radically disaffiliated from the main stream assumption of our society that it scarcely looks to many as a culture at all, but takes on the appearance of a barbaric intrusion." [13]

One thing certainly set the new generation off from the rest of society: it was young. Young with a fury and a vengeance. Young with a Peter Pan intensity that shuddered at the thought of joining the ossified ranks of the over-thirties. "At twenty," a contemporary declared, "one was Young France, a handsome young melancholic . . ." At twenty-five, one drifted into Byronism and became a "Childe-Harold type, full of cynical world-weariness." From age twenty-eight on, however, the road was all downhill, from *ci-devant* to "false toupé" to "Etruscan" to "the last stage of decrepitude . . . Academician and Member of the Institute . . ." This last wretched state was usually reached "at about forty or so." [14]

Many of the Bohemians were, or had been, students of one sort or another. Often they were provincial youths, living on minuscule allowances while they attended classes at the Sorbonne, the professional schools, or the ateliers of Paris artists. As students, they learned to drink without vomiting and kept mistresses when they could possibly afford it. When they couldn't afford it, there were always the *grisettes,* the complaisant shopgirls of the *quartier*.

Like students in many times and places, they were generally poor. They ate poorly, usually dressed poorly, and lived in squalor. In the ramshackle rooming houses where they lived, doors waved drunkenly in the breeze, staircases and floors threatened to collapse at a step, and sanitation facilities were minimal. As a rule, however, the Bohemians were not unduly disturbed by their impecunious condition. There was, in fact, a good deal of practical joking and general hilarity in the cheap cafés and cheaper boarding houses where they spent most of their waking hours.

The Bohemians not infrequently lived communally in their garishly decorated tenements. They were given to noisy all-night parties, soaked in wine and other alcoholic beverages, drowned in music provided by the band from a nearby cabaret. At the crumbling quarters of Petrus Borel, a notorious *bousingo* who called himself the "Wolfman" of French letters, the festivities often climaxed with a wild "hellfire gallop"—a popular dance of the thirties—careering through the midnight streets of Paris. On hot summer afternoons, Borel and his friends shocked their neighbors even more by sitting around in their back yard, stark naked in the sun.

The Bohemians had their own private jokes, and a special brand of grisly "sick" or "graveyard" humor that was notorious. They were popularly supposed to spend their spare time in cemeteries and dissection rooms, and to be given to waving human shinbones in their mistresses' faces to remind them of their own mortality. Gérard de Nerval, the poet, drank a famous toast to the human condition out of a human skull.

They even had their own private language. Their arcane jargon, developed partly to express their special enthusiasms in the arts, was also clearly calculated to baffle the bourgeoisie. Sacred words like "artist" and "artistic" meant something very special to them. Such terms as "boxed up," "prettified," "thread," and the untranslatable *"chic"* all had private meanings for the *bousingo.* To describe their own artistic output, their taste ran to mouth-filling adjectives like "phosphorescent," "annihilating," or "transcendental."[15]

Young men, often students, with their own distinctive costume, language, private jokes, customary haunts, group attitudes and mores, the Bohemians of the 1830's were as distinct a subculture as a sociologist could wish for. A subculture of outsiders, of social drop-outs, of the rejected and rejecting. When we add to this their common passion for art and their contempt for the bourgeoisie, we have something even more historically significant—a fully developed counter culture united by bonds of ideological commitment, by values and views of the world totally antithetical to those of their society.

L'Art pour l'Art

Within the narrower context of their own time and generation, the disorderly, happy-go-lucky youth of the Latin Quarter were as committed to the ideals of their counter culture as the most dedicated of their more politically oriented contemporaries—the republicans, the socialists, the Bonapartists, the demonstrators and the barricade builders. They were even as religious, in their way, as the Catholic revivalists who also flourished among the youth of the 1830's. The cause they fought for was simply not a social one. Their values were aesthetic, not ethical, and their God was beauty pure. The creed defiantly inscribed upon their banners was *l'art pour l'art*—"art for art's sake."

The great prophet of *l'art pour l'art,* for this and for several succeeding generations, was Théophile Gautier.

Gautier was a striking character from any point of view. He was only nineteen in 1830, but he was the recognized leader of a "tribe" at the *Hernani* premiere. In fact, with his icy stare, his elegantly coiffed hair, and his bright-red doublet, he was probably the best remembered of all the colorful barbarians there. Unlike too many of his fellows, however, he was a productive artist who became in later years a celebrated critic, journalist, and poet. Charles Baudelaire, one of his disciples in the 1840's, described Gautier enthusiastically as "a spiritual immensity." [16]

He was a physical immensity as well. A photograph taken in later life shows him as a huge man, bearded and long-haired, massively overweight but radiating a sense of physical power. In his younger years, he was quite handsome. He had the requisite olive-tinted complexion and wore his curly hair shoulder length. His physical and mental powers alike awed his young contemporaries. He could memorize reams of poetry at a single glance. He could carry two men around the room at arm's length, one in either hand. His eyes were luminous and dark, and they lit up at the sight of a beautiful book.

His aesthetic creed was summed up in two sweeping phrases:

"exclusive love of beauty" and "innate taste for form." His sensitivity was a byword, and it often made him the victim of bourgeois persecution. His long hair was caricatured by cartoonists and mocked by establishment wits. "Since [Gautier] is so philosophically enamored of . . . beautiful form," suggested the *Charivari,* "he really ought to change the form of his coiffure." [17] He was arrested more than once for shirking his compulsory military training—or for showing up in a more "aesthetic" uniform than that provided by the state. Once, for instance, he reported for service in a blue-flowered yellow waistcoat, a green dress coat, and a rose-colored cravat, with a gendarme's hat perched on his flowing locks and an elegant, antique musket on his shoulder.

Théophile Gautier was the prophet and the popularizer of aestheticism. An astonishing number of young Frenchmen took up his new gospel, idolized art, and longed for the artist's life in the France of Louis Philippe. Everywhere, in Bohemian cafés and boarding schools, from the lonely student's room to the idle shop-boy's corner, hot-eyed young men argued days and nights through over "art, the ideal, nature, form, color, and other questions of the same sort . . ." [18]

Many of them—too many—did more than talk and dream about it. In Paris, the center of it all, there was "an immense swarm of secondary authors." [19] Victor Hugo received so many requests for advice and encouragement that he could not answer them all. Editors and publishers were swamped with the manuscripts of ardent neophytes. The turnover in ephemeral "little magazines" of the arts was unparalleled. "I shall open my breast to the great wind of art," one would-be aesthete earnestly informed his diary, "and my quivering heart will ecstatically exult while my ship, upon the wind of beauty, will joyfully sail over the purple sea." [20] He, and countless like him, came up to Paris clutching their manuscripts, happy to accept Bohemian poverty and even the humiliating rounds of the publishers as the true artist's cross. That was the price one paid for greatness in the high aesthetic realm.

The cult of *l'art pour l'art* was clearly—like republicanism, socialism, and the rest—another substitute religion for this generation, starved for something to believe in. "To sanctify and deify art," according to Gautier himself, was the goal of the "Romantic youth" of his time. "It seemed to us," the bushy-haired poet Philothée O'Neddy remembered, "that one day Religion must . . . be replaced by Aesthetics." [21]

Hooligan Maybe—But Not a Greengrocer!

If it was a religion, the creed of the Bohemians was a crusading faith. And the devil, for these disreputable young long hairs, was the middle-aged man with the top hat, the umbrella, and the collar on his shirt.

A cartoon by Gavarni, the newspaper artist whose visual stereotype of the Bohemian lasted throughout the 1830's and 1840's, depicted the confrontation between Bohemian youth and bourgeois middle age with special vividness. The cartoon showed "a dissipated-looking loafer . . . leaning against a lamppost, contemptuously staring at the spruce, trim bourgeois out for his Sunday walk with his wife." The *bousingo* blows a cloud of rank tobacco smoke at the solid citizen's face. "Hooligan!" the latter snorts disgustedly. "Hooligan maybe," snaps the former, "but not a greengrocer!" [22]

Théophile Gautier particularly despised the new industrial system that was the pride of the bourgeoisie. His contempt was as much aesthetic as ethical. His soul was revolted by the ugly, smoky factories, the clanking machines, the ignorant proletariat, the smugly successful entrepreneurs, and the supreme hypocrisy of middle-class morality. Bourgeois talk of order, progress, and prosperity seemed to him and his Left Bank comrades to be a transparent mask for money-grubbing and materialism. Their minds were set on higher things.

The youth movement in literature, announced Philothée O'Neddy, having accomplished so many "beautiful reforms" in art, was now launching "a metaphysical crusade against *society*." Insurgent youth, he wrote, now "dedicates itself exclusively to the ruin of what it calls the *social lie* . . ." And rebellious younger generations from his day to our own would echo his contempt for all the taboos and sanctions of adult society: "I disdain the laws of an impure world." [23]

This Bohemian rejection of the bourgeois society of nineteenth-century France took many forms.

A literary generation that filled its fiction with outlaws and bandits, Gothic horrors and "graveyard humor" also took naturally to a form of spiritual protest almost as old as the Christian Church itself: the defiant worship of Satan, the anti-God. Satan, who had rebelled against God the Father himself, symbolized for them the ultimate revolt against Authority. As the King of Hell, the Devil was also the archetypal pariah, the patron saint of the rejected and condemned. The *jeunes-France* cheerfully accepted the suzerainty of his Satanic Majesty, calling themselves "the accursed of the earth," or simply "the damned." They wallowed publicly in their Satanism and hinted darkly at forbidden rites performed at midnight over blue-flaming bowls of punch.

The Bohemians had, of course, no use at all for middle-class morality. "What is virtue?" asked Petrus Borel, the self-styled "Wolfman." "Nothing, less than nothing—a mere word." [24] Only stupid provincials believed in it anymore. As far as ethics was concerned, the *bousingos* themselves were avowed hedonists. "Enjoyment seems to me the goal of life," another leading light of this generation cheerfully opined.[25] He and his cohorts flaunted their single-minded dedication to the titillation of the nerve ends before the world.

And so it went, through all the bourgeois qualities they had been raised to revere.

The good citizen, for instance, was a patriot, devoted to *la patrie,* the tricolor flag, and the Charter of French Liberties. Théophile Gautier declared that he would gladly exchange all his sacred rights as a freeborn Frenchman for one look at a real Raphael—or a beautiful girl naked. The typical French shopkeeper, bureaucrat, or banker of Balzac's day admired financial success and professional advancement just this side idolatry. The Bohemians called such solid citizens materialists and money-grubbers: they seldom made good at anything themselves. The bourgeois Frenchman loved *order* above all things—goods neatly arranged on the shelves, account books that balanced, gaslight on the pavement, and the meal on the table when he got home at night. The *bousingo* lived a flagrantly *dis*orderly life, owned little or nothing, and sometimes had no idea at all where his next meal was coming from.

In art, in ideals, in style of life, the first Bohemians were at war with the middle-class world of their elders. Theirs was as clearly and self-consciously a counterculture, an alternative way of life to that of the majority, as any that has arisen since. They called it "the Romantic life," a life style "as turbulent, as adventurous, as free as the Arab tribes in their solitudes." [26] It has since come to be known as *la vie de bohème,* the Bohemian life.

4. *THE TWILIGHT OF BOHEMIA*

A Generation Cast Adrift

In the short run, at least, the first Bohemia was a failure. And by 1835, the most ardent disciples of the *vie de bohème* were well aware of the fact.

No one had bought their books or hung their paintings. The public had laughed at their aesthetic exultations and their artistic apocalypses. Even their colorful, hedonistic style of life had brought them more contempt than converts. In time, this universal opprobrium had its inevitable effect upon the spirits of even the most boisterous among them. "A beard! that seems simple enough today," wrote Gautier years later, when beards were fashionable, "but then there were only two in France. . . . It took courage to wear one, a sang-froid and a contempt of the crowd that were truly heroic!" [27] As the thirties wore on, courage began to fail.

It was easy enough to flaunt odd costumes and defy the bourgeoisie at the premieres of Romantic plays, when all the tribes were gathered and buoyant hopes ran high. It was harder to keep the faith alone, in a shabby, freezing cubbyhole under the eaves of some crumbling tenement. Ill-clad, ill-fed, their most carefully crafted work sneered at by the critics—no wonder they began to see themselves as truly damned, lost souls, doomed to artistic failure and a paupers' grave. Under such circumstances, it was possible even to doubt one's genius, to contemplate surrender and retreat to some despicably bourgeois line of work that at least paid a living wage. Most of them did in fact drift away from Bohemia into steady work—commercial art, writing for the newspapers, even into the bureaucracy or the professions.

But such surrender was a gigantic retreat from Moscow for these artistic Bonapartes. Their whole being was bound up in their aesthetic faith. They had found significance and mean ng for their lives in the quest for beauty pure. They had defined theır very selves by defining and diabolizing the bourgeois enemy. To give up was in many cases to empty their lives of significance, to raise terrifying existential questions about their very reason for being.

They saw themselves increasingly as a lost generation now, youth without a future, self-surrendered to damnation:

> Thus careless of antique moralities,
> Lost children of too many exposés,
> We to the rumble of a passing age
> Dance gaily on the edge of the abyss.[28]

The Nietzschean sneer at "antique moralities" undoubtedly stung the bourgeoisie. But it revealed a real sickness in the youth as well. A perceptive contemporary critic put his finger on the psychic peril that underlay the purely economic risks this generation ran. Their aesthetic religion, he pointed out, was simply too weak a reed to support them in the travails to which they were exposed. Cast adrift in the universe with no surer guides than nerve ends and poetry, how could they help but suffer? Floating free in Bohemia, with "no other plan than to encounter marvelous exaltations in order to make odes about them . . . we shall see what strange dreams assail them and torment them." [29]

In the later thirties, the bad dreams were all about them, hissing and beating their bat wings like creatures out of Goya etchings. Something had gone rotten with their world. Young Alfred de Musset pictured this growing despair to the life in his famous *Confessions of a Child of the Age*.[30]

Ours, wrote this disillusioned young man in his middle twenties, is a generation cast adrift, a generation floating between two worlds. The Old World, with its reverence for royalty, religion, and nobility, is gone forever. The Enlightenment, the Revolution, and Napoleon Bonaparte have shattered all faith in thrones and altars. The New World is dimly visible ahead—the world of utopian republics the social prophets speak of so confidently. But that brave new world is a mere glimmer on the far horizon, decades, perhaps centuries away. Neither Musset nor any of his readers would ever live to see it.

All of us, he declared, are thus condemned to an in-between age, halfway between past and future. We cannot believe in the moribund ideals of the dead past. But neither can we truly accept the values of an age that has not yet come into existence. Thus deprived by history itself of any firm convictions, any unassailable ideals, we drift rudderless in a vast Atlantic of despair.

This was the famous *mal du siècle* of the Romantics—the sickness of the age. It was not an ailment peculiar to that age and generation alone. No few alienated generations since, similarly torn from their moorings by the unrelenting surge of social change, have found their own new countercreeds to be fragile life preservers in the typhoons that howl around them. "The dream is over," wrote a melancholy survivor of the Age of Aquarius, the hippie side of the American 1960's. He cited Phil Ochs on the debacle of Manson and Altamont:

> But the decadence of history is looking for a pawn
> To a nightmare of knowledge he opens up the gate
> A blinding revelation is served upon his plate
> *That beneath the greatest love is a hurricane of hate* [31]

Another generation has danced gaily for a time on the edge of the abyss, only to learn at last that in this harsh world, Love—like Beauty for the first Bohemians—is not enough.

From Grub Street to Greenwich Village

In the short run, certainly, the *bousingos* of the Latin Quarter failed of their objectives. Their high hopes for a new Renaissance, a "greening" of French culture and a springtime flowering of the arts, came to nothing. Nor was it possible for them to maintain for long that "Romantic life," as adventurous and free as the Arab tribes in their solitudes, that was the most striking manifestation of the Bohemian revolt. Poverty and public rejection drove the majority to abandon their artistic vocations altogether and seek a living in that very bourgeois society they had once so insolently turned their backs upon.

The first Bohemians were beaten by the system. But the Bohemian way of life lived on.

From the days of François Villon to those of Daniel Defoe, there has always been a Grub Street: a huddle of impecunious writers and artists struggling to survive on the fringes of society.

But Bohemia is something fundamentally new in the world. Villon lived in colorful destitution because he had to; "Wolfman" Borel and his friends withdrew to the artistic ghettos as a matter of choice. The Grub Street hacks of Defoe's day had no objection at all to money and the creature comforts, when they could get their hands on them; Théophile Gautier despised the middle classes for caring about such things. The children of the new Bohemia were thus "the first men of letters to isolate themselves from the general public as if from contamination"—to withdraw deliberately from the system rather than sell their souls to Philistine conformity.[32]

Generational withdrawal of this sort is hard to find before the second-generation French Romantics of 1830. It has spread across the world since then.

In the 1840's, Bohemia renewed itself. Gautier was a middle-aged guru by then, the admired prophet of aestheticism to youths of such diverse genius as Charles Baudelaire and Gustave Flaubert—whose *Sentimental Education* provides perhaps the most brilliant generational autobiography in all fiction. The Bohemia of the forties lacked the bite and fury of the *bousingo* thirties—was, in fact, almost a Disneyland parody of that scathing rejection of middle-class values. But the latter decade did produce the vastly influential work of Henry Murger, whose tales of the *vie de bohème,* on which Puccini's opera was subsequently based, made Bohemia a household word—and a living alternative for increasing numbers of alienated youth.[33]

From the Left Bank to Bloomsbury, from Greenwich Village to the Haight, from Amsterdam to Tangier, the Bohemian subculture has spread. The articulated ideology may change—from "art for art's sake" to "do your own thing," from the cult of Beauty to the cult of Love—but the life style, and the protest it embodies, remains essentially the same. It has been providing what Erik Erikson calls a "psychosocial moratorium" for young people trying to find themselves in our fantastically complex modern society, for close to a century and a half now.[34] It is a striking contribution to the cultural life of our time, and a fitting memorial to one of the most astonishingly unconventional younger generations in modern history.

5

"No Wishes, No Prayers. We Demand!" *
False Springtime of the Youth Revolt
Austria, 1848

They called it the Springtime of the Peoples, that revolutionary year in the middle of the nineteenth century when anything seemed possible, and utopia was just around the corner. In Paris, in Berlin, in Vienna, in Milan and Rome, in Budapest and Prague, everywhere the peoples were rising. New flags were flying that spring, as the barricades went up across the length and breadth of Europe. The reactionary old order, imposed on the Continent after Waterloo, cracked and crumbled away. New ideologies—liberalism, socialism, half a dozen nationalisms—surged forward into the breach.

New ideologies—and hordes of new believers. For the revolutionary year 1848 was in many respects a generational revolt. It marked, in fact, a great leap forward in the swelling power of the Youth Revolution. It gave the new generations of ideologically driven youth their first taste of victory.

The young felt their own strength as they rampaged through the capital cities of Europe that unbelievable spring. Before a year was out, however, the revolutionary youth had learned another lesson too—the bitter truth that they were still too weak a force to change the course of history.

For the Revolutions of 1848 failed in almost every case. Military force and reactionary political intrigue played a part in shattering the victory of the young ideological revolutionists. So did the violence of their proletarian allies and the timidity of their bourgeois leaders. But the failings of the youthful revolutionaries themselves

* A student in front of the *Landhaus*, in Priscilla Robertson, *Revolutions of 1848: A Social History* (New York, 1952), p. 211.

were equally crucial factors in making 1848 the false springtime of the Youth Revolution.

Nowhere was this pattern of youthful triumph and debacle clearer than in old Vienna.

The far-flung Habsburg realms which Metternich still ruled had their share of problems that March of 1848. There was the polyglot nature of the empire—the multinational mix of Germans and Hungarians and Czechs, Italians and Poles and many other peoples who had come, over the centuries, to accept the suzerainty of the house of Habsburg. As nationalism spread among the emperor's subjects, they were bound to grow intolerant of each other and restless under the domination of Vienna.

There were social and economic problems too. The vast peasant majority grumbled under the feudal dues and medieval conditions of servitude—particularly the hated *robot,* or labor service—that still governed their lives. There was little industry in Austria as yet, but there was already a growing proletariat of landless, often jobless workers congregating in the few cities of the empire. When depression settled like a blight over Vienna (or Prague, or Budapest), these could become dangerous classes too.

Politically, the Habsburg realms in the age of Metternich were as autocratic as any in Europe outside of tsarist Russia. Two emperors reigned during the three decades between 1815 and 1848: Francis II (1804–1835) and Ferdinand I (1835–1848). Old Francis was a rigid reactionary who supported the policies of his famous foreign minister without reserve. His deathbed injunction to his son and heir in that age of dizzying social, political, and cultural change was simple: "Govern—and change nothing." [1] Ferdinand, the unfortunate inheritor of this rigid policy, turned out to be a congenital idiot who liked playing in the park with the children and willingly signed anything that was put in front of him. He cheerfully turned the reins of government over to a conglomeration of bureaucrats, courtiers, royal relatives, and the suave and ageless master of diplomacy, Prince Metternich.

For thirty years after the Karlsbad Decrees, then, the Metternich system held absolute sway over the German states, the Italian states, and the Habsburg Empire in between. Prince Metternich's offices in the *Ballhaus* in Vienna were the heart of it. From there the lines of influence and control reached out to all parts of Central Europe. As long as Metternich sat in the *Ballhaus,* the censors and the border guards would ply their trades, the police would spy and provoke and compile their endless dossiers, and the political prisoners would sit helpless in the dungeons of the notorious Spielberg prison.

And yet Vienna, in those old "pre-March" days, was the gayest of European capitals. The good burghers swarmed to the theater and the opera, or waltzed away the night to the music of Strauss. By day they thronged the coffee houses, or strolled on the ancient city walls or in the vast suburban gardens of the Schönbrunn Palace. The luxury shops were second to none in Europe, and at Christmastime—it was said—even the poorest managed a Christmas tree, gay with sugarplums and toys and streamers of colored paper.

The Viennese were considered the most easygoing, charming, even frivolous people a traveler could want to meet. "Who likes not wine, women, and song," they nodded and smiled to the old beer hall tune, "remains a fool his whole life long." [2] As long as there was *The Magic Flute* at the *Theater an der Wien,* or a new play by Nestroy or Grillparzer, or Jenny Lind singing tonight—who cared about the policies of the *Ballhaus,* or the condition of the proletariat?

If a visitor from some comparatively liberal West European country absolutely insisted on discussing politics, however, he was likely to get a startling response. The Habsburg Empire was an absolutist state of the old school—and proud of it. "The *Liberal,*" one curious English traveler was crisply informed, "desires unrestrained power to please himself in religion, morals, politics, and literature, without reference to the wisdom or the will, either of God or man." He blithely claims to need "no protection against all that [political] faction, blasphemy, and obscenity can do against you, your wives and children." In Austria, on the other hand, things were different:

> The *Absolutist* . . . expects and demands from those at the head of the social compact of which he makes a part, that they should sustain that social compact by the power it has itself given—stand firm to their posts—keep constant watch over the safety and happiness of the people—protect them from violence and tumult of every kind . . .

Loyal subjects of all classes, the conservative Viennese assured the British traveler, felt the same reverent love for their rulers as "happy children feel for their parents." [3]

1. *THE STUDENTS ARE IN THE STREETS*

A Riot of Street-Boys

"Dismiss the minister everyone hates!" the wild-eyed young man teetering precariously on the edge of the fountain screamed at the mob.

"What's his name? Tell us his name!" the crowd roared back.

"METTERNICH!" [4]

The mob surged and heaved like an ocean, roaring its approval.

The courtyard in front of the *Landhaus* where the Estates of Lower Austria were meeting was jammed with people. The top hats and frock coats of the burghers from the inner city mingled—for once—with the smocks and caps of the proletarians from the working-class suburbs. But drawn up front and center were the students from the University of Vienna. They had marched to the *Landhaus* in serried ranks, determined to seize the time. And they were seizing it, with a vengeance and a passion too long dammed up, and now unleashed at last. It was the morning of the thirteenth of March, 1848.

A young doctor named Fischhof, only a couple of years out of medical school, outlined the demands of the youth. Perched on the shoulders of two other young men, he called for academic freedom, for freedom of the press and speech and of religion. "Long live Austria and its glorious future!" he shouted. "Long live freedom!"

"Freedom! Freedom!" the people shouted back.[5]

"Listen, comrades!" another young man cried over the uproar, "it won't help us or our fellow citizens to stay here in this courtyard making speeches. We've heard enough orations—let's start a dialogue with the Estates in there!" [6]

The Estates of Lower Austria, a body with neither prestige nor power over the rest of the empire, must be compelled to tackle all the accumulated problems of thirty years of government rigidity and inaction. Representatives of the assembled people must be sent in to "supervise" the activities of the nervous delegates. That was how the French revolutionaries did it, after all, when they brought their governments to heel.

While the mob was busy choosing a dozen representatives, another young man, a student from the Tyrol, shoved his way to the improvised rostrum at the fountain. He was waving a piece of paper.

"Kossuth's speech!" he shouted over the tumult. "Kossuth's speech!"

Here was one oration they would all listen to. Everyone had heard of the inflammatory speech the famous Hungarian radical, Louis Kossuth, had made to the Diet of the Hungarian provinces the week before. It had been censored out of the Viennese papers, of course. Here now was a bootleg translation, to be read aloud for the edification of the mob.

"From the charnel house of the Vienna System"—the Viennese students cheered lustily at this insult to their country—"a pestilential air blows toward us. . . . The source of all the evil lies in the preposterous policy of the Austrian ministers . . ." More of the same, with frequent howls of enthusiastic approval for every gibe at the old men in the imperial palace and the ministry of foreign affairs. And then: "For the common good of us all," the voice of the Tyrolese youth shrieked Kossuth's passionate ultimatum, "it is necessary for us to obtain a Constitution!"

"The Constitution! The Constitution!" [7]

Not even the students had dared to contemplate such a thing.

The echoing chant bounced off the chaste neoclassical façade of the *Landhaus*. Worried faces were already peering down from the windows when someone handed out a paper. A note from the Estates, offering to carry a petition to the emperor, a humble wish that his majesty might consider the question of reform. After Kossuth's fiery oratory, this was lukewarm pap indeed.

"That's nothing. Tear it up!"

"No wishes, no prayers. We *demand!*" [8]

The youth was in the streets, the non-negotiable demands were in the air. Many another shaken city, that tumultuous year and in years to come, would hear that strident imperative: *No wishes, no prayers—We Demand!*

Things escalated rapidly after that.

There were more speeches, more shouting. Suddenly there were voices from the upper windows of the *Landhaus*—the dozen delegates of the people, calling that they were trapped, that they had been lured into a snare. A delusion undoubtedly: but in this inflammable situation, it was enough.

The crowd, the students at their head, charged into the hall, smashing windows, breaking furniture. Within an hour, the liberal chairman of the assembly was reluctantly leading a delegation of students and representatives of Lower Austria to wait upon the emperor. As the parade pushed through the growing crowds toward the ancient imperial palace in the *Hofburg,* the shout went up again, and still more violently: "Down with Metternich!" [9]

The delegation was received, their vigorous petition accepted. The emperor, they were informed, would give the matter every consideration. It was an answer they had heard before. In the streets and squares before the palace and the hall where the Estates were still nominally in session, troops were hastily deployed.

People jeered and shouted at the soldiers, refusing to believe the guns were loaded. A royal archduke rode among them, calling for calm: he was pelted with stones. The mob began to throw things at the soldiers.

A volley was fired in the air. A second was fired into the faces of the mob.

Five were killed and many more wounded in that first fusillade in front of the *Landhaus.* The first to fall was an eighteen-year-old student, a mathematics major with a brilliant future, at least according to his horrified friends. "Whoever gave the order [to fire]," a liberal observer commented shrewdly, "brought the monarchy to the edge of the abyss by giving to a riot of street-boys the character of a revolution." [10]

A Regiment of Freedom Fighters

The first shots were fired about two in the afternoon. For the next dozen hours, Vienna was engulfed in violence.

Soldiers fired on rioters and demonstrators in other streets. Working men from the industrial suburbs forced the city gates—hastily closed that morning—and thronged through the narrow lanes of the old city, clashing repeatedly with troops. As evening fell, government toll booths, where customs duties were collected on food coming into Vienna, were put to the torch by underfed proletarians. Several factories were attacked, the shiny new steam-powered machinery destroyed, the buildings set on fire. There had been a bad depression in the late forties, and the working classes were bitter.

In the Aula, the great hall of the University of Vienna, the two thousand students of the university rallied. They demanded arms to help maintain order, and to guarantee just redress of grievances. They swore that if they didn't get weapons by nine that night, they would march on the imperial arsenal and attack it with their bare hands.

In the tangled complex of ancient government buildings known as the *Hofburg,* total confusion reigned. The feeble-minded Emperor Ferdinand himself was deeply disturbed by the thought that his army had been forced to fire upon his people. The reactionary but superannuated minister of police was, according to an eyewitness, "completely paralyzed." [11] Delegations from the city's civilian militia, the National Guard, waited on the emperor to warn him that if concessions to the liberal spirit were not quickly forthcoming, they would themselves have to go over to the side of the insurgents. The sight of the unarmed students confronting three ranks of grenadiers with muskets raised had in fact won the admiring support of many middle-aged, middle-class, but fundamentally liberal-minded citizens of Vienna. The workers, meanwhile, were beginning to build barricades in the streets—the first barricades in the history of the ancient Habsburg capital.

Two demands above all others united the students at the Aula, the workers in the streets, and the agitated delegations that waited on the emperor: arms for the people, and the head of Metternich.

In his office in the foreign ministry, Prince Metternich, an urbane old man in his seventies, went coolly about his duties. Somebody peered out the window and reported nervously that many well-dressed citizens seemed to be in the seething crowds below. "If my son were among those people," the aging aristocrat responded dryly, "I would still call them rabble." [12] But if his continuance in office was no longer of value to his country—he awaited the imperial decision.

It came at eight-thirty that night. Metternich signed his resignation with a steady hand. He slipped quietly out of the strife-torn city the next day in an ordinary public cab. A gentleman who entertained the Austrian foreign minister on his journey into exile remembered how the old man discoursed on fine wines, and how exquisitely he played the violin. He would play the "Marseillaise" over and over in the moonlight, humming a creaky accompaniment to his own sure hand upon the bow.

By nine o'clock on the night of Metternich's resignation, they were passing out guns at the Aula. It took all night, by the light of flickering torches, to turn the student body of the University of Vienna into a regiment of freedom fighters.

2. *STUDENT POWER: THE ACADEMIC LEGION*

From Biedermeier *to* Burschenschaft—*The Shaping of a Generation*

Something had clearly happened to this university generation in the most frivolous and apolitical capital in Europe. Once again, we must glance briefly backward into the past for an understanding of the forces that turned these children of the years around 1830 into the revolutionaries of 1848.

This generation of young Austrians, like their neighbors elsewhere in the German states, had had one great advantage from the beginning. They had been born in the middle of the celebrated *Biedermeier* period, the "era of good feeling" that followed the Napoleonic wars. It was a time of good-natured Philistinism, of eat-drink-and-be-merry frivolity, with plenty of theaters and dance halls laid on, especially in Vienna. At home, the youth that took to the streets in the forties had been coddled and petted throughout the thirties in a great wave of family "togetherness." [13] Once again a generation was raised to expect wonders from the world, only to find realities instead.

At the same time, however, the Austrian student generation of 1848 may actually have been closer to the economic realities of life in the "hungry forties"—the great Europe-wide famine that drove Irishmen to America and Berliners to the barricades—than one might expect. A surprising percentage of the University of Vienna student body just before mid-century was apparently far from aristocratic in origin. A fifth were sons of small and middling businessmen; another fifth were the offspring of artisans. Some thirty-nine percent of the students were too poor to pay tuition.[14] Such an expansion of educational opportunities to the children of the underprivileged classes of society—to the *raznochintsy* in Russia in the 1860's, for instance, or to ghetto-bred blacks in the American 1960's—has often had explosive results.

Beneath the gaiety of old Vienna, then, there was real suffering, and more knowledge of it than one might expect among the young gentlemen of the university. But there were even more subversive influences at work. Beneath the censorship and thought control of the Metternich system, a number of liberal and even radical intellectual influences operated to shape the growing minds of this generation.

The Viennese were a literate, cultivated people, and no amount of censorship and border checks could keep them in ignorance of the ferment of new ideas in the world at large. They were, in the first place, quite conscious of the system of thought control itself. From the 1830's on, they had, if anything, an exaggerated idea of "the sinister Metternich 'System,' with its spies, its police repression, its high tariff walls, its cultural 'iron fences,' and its snobbish officialdom." [15] Nor was it so difficult to get hold of subversive literature. Political police were still quite inefficient in the nineteenth century. The forbidden books of Voltaire and Rousseau were readily available under the counter, and political pamphlets were easily smuggled across the frontiers from the German states.

Beneath all the official subservience and apparently mindless *Gemütlichkeit* of pre-March Vienna, then, there was a certain amount of liberal sentiment, at least among progressive businessmen and enlightened aristocrats. It was the most moderate drawing-room liberalism, of course: an interest in civil liberties and abstract constitutionalism; conversation over cigars and wine at the Reading Club or the Chamber of Commerce. But, as recent sociological research has shown, such moderate-minded liberal fathers not infrequently produce a generation of radical sons.[16]

The University of Vienna itself provided a further radicalizing experience for the youth who matriculated there in the middle 1840's.

There were the usual youngish liberal professors, men like Professor Hye of the Law Faculty, or Fürster, the burly Catholic priest, a militant champion of clerical marriage. These teachers dared to demand the right to speak their minds across the lectern, and they quickly became heroes to the more liberally inclined students. The Polytechnic and the famous Medical School in particular won a startling amount of academic freedom in the early forties, mostly because the government could see no danger in free speech on such purely technical subjects. Students from Switzerland and the German states and elsewhere thronged to these institutions, bringing a subversive breath of free air with them.

In the middle and later forties, the *Burschenschaft* movement at last reached Vienna. Secret societies with names like *Liberalia* and *Teutonia* were organized among the students—nine of them in all during the three or four years before 1848. These Student Unions had their hedonistic side, of course, hikes and picnics and other essential trivia to keep young bodies from growing restless. But serious concerns preoccupied them too. Some of them at least took their subversive literature seriously. They studied social issues and discussed them eagerly. They corresponded secretly with their opposite numbers at Jena and Tübingen and elsewhere in the Germanies.

> In spring or summer [a one-time Austrian *Burschenschafter* recalled], the societies would take long walks to the old Greifenstein Castle, to the Sophienalp or to Heinbach, would hold parliamentary sessions, make speeches and work up great enthusiasm over what they would do after the absolute rule of the present [was over], in the freedom of the future.[17]

The Student Unionists were deeply involved, in short, with the problems that beset their country. And there were plenty of problems to be concerned about in those last years before the deluge.

After three decades, the system that had held the line since Waterloo seemed at last to be cracking. Nationalistic passions were spreading among the minority peoples of the empire. Discontent was increasingly apparent among the new, industrial working classes, and there were rumblings from the countryside. There were peasant uprisings in the Polish provinces. Factory workers rioted in Prague. The famine of the hungry forties was no respecter of Metternich's border guards.

Depression settled over the rapidly industrializing suburbs that loomed beyond the medieval walls of Vienna itself. The workers in the silk and cotton mills, in the machine shops and railroad yards found it hard enough to keep body and soul together in the best of times. In the late 1840's, there was widespread unemployment. Soup kitchens were set up, and beggars appeared in unprecedented numbers. The crime rate soared: the streets of the capital were no longer safe at night.

The socially concerned *Burschenschafter* had plenty to talk about.

Then suddenly, in the last days of February, 1848, came the news that was to blow the lid off old Vienna: the electrifying intelligence that Paris had risen once again, that Louis Philippe was driven from his throne, and the tricolor of the Republic flew over Notre Dame once more.

The World Turned Upside Down

The story of the Academic Legion, the celebrated student militia that seized power in Vienna in 1848, evidently goes back to well before that fatal thirteenth of March when the students set out to march upon the *Landhaus.* In a sense, the story must begin with the moment this student generation first became conscious of the ambiguous and deeply flawed world in which it was growing up. Certainly, it must go back to the organization of the new Student Unions in 1845 and '46 and '47; for it was the established heads of these associations who took the lead in setting up the Legion. Most obviously, however, it was the news from Paris that galvanized the Viennese students—as it did young people all across Europe—and drove them shouting into the streets at last.

Ever since 1789, France had been the revolutionary weather vane of Europe. Liberals, radicals, revolutionaries everywhere looked to Paris for inspiration and example. "When France sneezes," grumped Metternich, "Europe catches cold." [18] When the tricolor went up in Paris in 1848, the barricades went up in cities all across the Continent.

From the Baltic to the Mediterranean, the Metternich system collapsed. The King of Prussia, like the Emperor of Austria, was humbled by an uprising in his own capital. The Austrians were driven out of Milan and Venice, and radicals seized power in the Czech and Hungarian provinces of the empire. In a number of German and Italian states, petty despots, who had looked to Vienna or Berlin for support, were compelled to grant constitutions to their peoples. Even the Pope, after desperate efforts at compromise, was forced to flee from Rome. For a time, at least, it looked like total victory for the forces of revolution. The young Russian anarchist, Bakunin, remembered it all vividly:

> It seemed as if the entire world was turned upside down. The improbable became commonplace, the impossible possible. . . . In a word, people found themselves in such a state of mind that if someone had said, 'God has been driven from heaven and a republic has been proclaimed there,' everyone would have believed it and no one would have been surprised.[19]

In Vienna, the world began to tilt on its axis when a handful of student leaders, drinking and talking excitedly in the bar of a suburban inn, came up with the idea of a university petition to the emperor. The Estates of Lower Austria were meeting in a week, and some of the bourgeois liberals there assembled were expected to submit some sort of address to the throne. Why not a student petition too? The Emperor Ferdinand—"poor Ferdy," they called him—was an idiot, but he was well-meaning enough. He might even read their missive. Why not do it? In these exciting times, one had to do *something.*

For several feverish nights, leading Student Unionists and other university liberals met in secret, guards posted to warn them of the political police. They constructed a reasoned plea for civil liberties, for academic freedom, for a national assembly representative of all classes of society. The word *constitution,* with its nasty implications of limits on the absolute power of the house of Habsburg, never once appeared.

It began as the affair of a few emancipated students and a liberal teacher or two. By Sunday, March 12, it had mushroomed into a mass meeting in the Aula, the assembly hall of the university.

The husky, energetic, and vigorously liberal professor of theology, Father Fürster, kindled a militant mood at once with a ringing sermon urging the youth to let their conscience be their guide. "In your country's cause," he cried, "no sacrifice can be too great!"

The draft petition was read in an atmosphere of rising enthusiasm. There was no discussion: "Pens—a table—sign, sign!" the students shouted, pushing forward, eager to be the first to get their names on the historic document.[20]

At that point, Professor Hye and some other less miiltant liberals on the faculty intervened. The police had warned them to control their students, and they were genuinely frightened for their charges now. They reminded the fired-up youth of the Polish students who had been dragged off to prison for insurrectionary acts in earlier years; of Czech and Italian students drafted into the imperial armies and assigned the most ignominious labor in the baggage trains. They agreed to take the petition to the palace themselves, if only the students would stay calm and refrain from tempting fate.

That Sunday night, two professors carried the university petition to the *Hofburg*. The document was received. The professors were informed that the emperor would take the matter under advisement.

This word, returned to the students at another mass meeting the following morning, a few hours before the Estates were to begin their deliberations across town, was the final straw. Many held back that first day, "fearing that their names would be inscribed in the government's 'black book.' " Not surprisingly, it was "mainly . . . the more reckless portions" of the student body who formed up and marched in a long procession to the *Landhaus*.[21] But that night, with their comrades dead in the streets and the red glow of flames clearly visible beyond the city walls, few refused the weapons, long barrels glistening redly in the torchlight, as their professors passed them out. And it was the guns, the arming of the student body, that turned the academic community into the Academic Legion of Vienna.

Watchdogs of the Revolution

A week after the explosion of March 13, the armed students formally organized their Legion. The Academic Legion was intended to help keep the peace and to guarantee the newly won rights of the people. It soon became a political power in the land—perhaps the most powerful of all the committees, clubs, unions, and various armed bodies that jockeyed for authority in revolutionary Vienna.

Any student was eligible to join, as were professors, graduates of the university, and a ragtag of others who could claim some sort of academic background. During the brief six months of its ascendancy, the Legion grew to number some five thousand young heroes of the revolution.

They wore dashing blue-and-gray uniforms and broadbrimmed, black "Calabrian" hats garnished with ostrich feathers. They tied black, red, and gold sashes around their waists, the colors of the *Burschenschaft,* and of the new "United States of Germany" the liberal statesmen were laboring to forge at the all-German Frankfurt Assembly. Long steel swords hung low enough at their sides to clang romantically on the cobblestones as they strolled the streets of the city. They also sported beards and mustaches and let their hair grow long.

They became the watchdogs of the revolution and the most militant advocates of every radical measure over the months that followed.

The prime source of the very real power wielded by the Vienna students of 1848 seems to have been the special relationship they enjoyed with the artisans and workmen from the grimy industrial suburbs. The students' book learning and their attendance at the *Hochschule,* the most prestigious of Austria's educational institutions, gave them an automatic ascendancy over the working men in those class-conscious days. Their youthful militance made them natural leaders for the discontented proletariat. Most important, the young men from the university took the workers' cause to heart: they became the tribunes of the people and earned the support of the masses by real services rendered.

Thus, for instance, medical students provided free medical care for the poor, and law students free legal aid. Students of all the schools took up collections for the destitute. The Academic Legion and the Aula ferreted out corrupt or highhanded officials and joyfully hacked their way through bureaucratic red tape wherever the interests of the poor were involved. They "arbitrated" between factory owners and workers, usually to the advantage of the latter. They demanded—and got—the right to vote for the proletariat, and public works programs to provide jobs for the unemployed. They became the voice of the voiceless masses in the government, and the lower orders responded with vigorous support that, for those few months at least, made the Aula almost impregnable.

Thus fortified, the Academic Legion patrolled the streets, adjudicated disputes, issued manifestos, and made increasingly radical demands upon the feeble shadow of a government that survived the fall of Prince Metternich.

In the months that followed March, the students demanded the resignation of other ministers besides Metternich. Sometimes they even invaded the homes of these distinguished gentlemen at the head of unruly mobs to enforce compliance. They almost always got their way.

They demanded a totally free press. Soon every sort of radical tract was being hawked on the streets of Vienna. The number of newspapers published in the capital spiraled upward from less than half a dozen to nearly a hundred separate publications before that wild year was over.

They demanded a constitutional convention elected by universal manhood suffrage, and the nervous cabal of courtiers around Emperor Ferdinand agreed. They demanded that Austria join the new united Germany that the Frankfurt liberals were building, and poor Ferdinand himself responded by stepping out on a palace balcony smiling vaguely and waving the new black, red, and gold banner. Thereafter, anyone who dared display the old black-and-yellow Habsburg colors was likely to have his windows smashed and his home invaded by the militantly nationalist youth.

The Flags Fly Free

Backed by the mob outside the walls, the students stood firm against every effort by the government to reassert its own supremacy. In May, they were peremptorily ordered to disband their Legion and even close the university. The uniformed youth summoned the workers to their aid, flung up barricades—some rising to the second stories of the houses on either side of the narrow medieval streets—and compelled the imperial government to rescind the order. It was a sight even the most unsympathetic witness never forgot, those tense May nights in the streets:

> During the whole night, the students, the National Guard, and workmen remained upon the barricades. Fires were made in the middle of the streets; students with their Calabrian hats and feathers, National Guards with their helmeted caps, *ouvriers* without coats, and peasant women without bonnets, seated on

> paving stones around the bright blaze, indulged in coarse jokes and laughter, or in songs.
>
> It was a strange and painful sight to see these camps in the heart of a city; yet the motley groups by the dusky light of the watch-fires, with the houses high and dark for a background, were picturesque in the extreme.[22]

But the imperial troops never materialized. The government gave way once more, and the power of the students rolled on unbroken.

The Aula itself must have resembled nothing so much as an "occupied" American university of the later 1960's. The students moved bodily into the great assembly hall. They ate there, slept there, partied there. They strewed the hall, and the lecture rooms as well, with straw for sleeping. They vandalized the stately portraits that ran around the walls, drawing mustaches on the stiffly formal faces of the famous dead, or cutting out the faces entirely and replacing them with the grinning faces of monkeys. They lived on free food donated by the citizens. They introduced wine, women, and choice cigars to the sacred precincts. They littered the place with their gear and their guns and their own bodies, collapsing exhausted after a long night's patrol to sleep in a tangle of blankets on the floor.

Wherever they went, the university youth were feted and admired. Women brought them baskets of bread and wine on the barricades. The dashingly uniformed Legionnaires were the most sought-after partners at every dance. They took a leading part in all the endless parades and celebrations of that long spring and summer. They exchanged flags and encomia with young revolutionaries in Paris and Prague and half a dozen other cities. They were respectfully listened to in peasant villages and genteel drawing rooms—especially when there were young ladies present. A widely circulated song of that year hailed them as the saviors of their people:

> Lo, who be these so proud in bearing?
> The bayonets flash, the flags fly free;
> They come with silver trumpets blaring,
> The University! [23]

As summer came on and they began to drift away to other German cities, and even to other countries, to see how the revolution fared elsewhere, they found themselves hailed everywhere as the heroes of the hour. This was the youth that had overthrown Metternich himself. This was the generation that had transformed Vienna at one blow from the chief center of European reaction to "the greatest city of liberty on the continent." [24]

It was a beautiful, blue spring in Vienna, the loveliest in years. Life was one long celebration—between crises, that is—for the student masters of the city. For if any single group dominated the cacophony of voices that filled revolutionary Vienna, it was surely the aggressive young ideologues of the university.

3. *THE LAST BARRICADE*

The Vices of Their Qualities

Disaster, tragically but typically, loomed just around the corner. While the young revolutionaries strutted the streets of barricaded Vienna, their enemies were gathering—on both sides of the barricades.

The "Camarilla," the loose grouping of courtiers and royal relatives who surrounded Emperor Ferdinand, chafed bitterly at their humiliation. Archduchess Sophia, Ferdinand's sister-in-law and the mother of the next emperor, was particularly outraged at the situation. "I could have borne the loss of one of my children more easily," she swore, "than I can the ignominy of submitting to a pack of students." [25]

In May, the royal family and the court slipped out of Vienna and settled for the summer at Innsbruck, surrounded by loyal peasants who had no knowledge of any *-ism* whatsoever. In June, the royalist general, Prince Windischgrätz, crushed the Czech freedom fighters—mostly student barricade-builders—in Prague. By August, Count Radetzky's troops had reoccupied Milan. As the summer drew to a close, the rebels still held sway only in Hungary, under Kossuth's fiery leadership, and in Vienna itself.

Even inside the imperial city, student power had its enemies. As so often happens, rebellious youth rapidly alienated their reform-minded elders. By autumn, almost all the university faculty had turned against the radical students. On one celebrated occasion, middle-class National Guard units joined the Imperial Army in an abortive face-down with the Academic Legion. The peace-loving, tidy-minded burghers of Vienna were increasingly desperate for an end to anarchy and disorder, for the return of the emperor, and the final repression of "the ignorant masses and fanatical youth," as they described the worker-student alliance that ran the city.[26]

The workers themselves, finally, grew more and more unruly as the year went on. In August, the students proved unable to prevent a massive cutback in the expensive public-works projects on which the unemployed had come to depend. The Academic Legion failed to support the working men in a bloody clash with middle-class National Guard units that same month. The explosive violence of the proletariat and the artisans would prove to be a prime catalyst in the brewing of the final catastrophe.

In the last analysis, however, the student militants of 1848 proved to be their own worst enemies.

They themselves, like their worker allies, were fatally prone to violence whenever their ends could not be gained by any other means. They forced unpopular ministers to resign by mobilizing the mob. They submitted "Storm Petitions"—non-negotiable demands backed by loaded muskets—to the shell of a government that remained. They armed themselves and barricaded the city against the Imperial Army. All of which was natural enough, given their ideological enthusiasms, their youthful impatience, and the revolutionary tensions of the times. It was also, however, clearly counterproductive in the long run. As is usually the case when youth rises in arms against the modern state, the bigger battalions were on the other side.

To their willingness to resort to violence may be added a rather naive extremism as a major weakness of the Youth Revolution as it took shape in 1848 Vienna. This younger generation wanted everything *now*—freedom now, German unification now, utopia perhaps the day after. They insisting on pressing the revolution too far, too fast. Compromise was a dirty word in their vocabularies; half a loaf was a liberal cop-out. "The university students," as one historian has pointed out, "were the field officers of the revolution; they had not the maturity to provide responsible leadership." [27]

Another fatal weakness of this, as of subsequent younger generations in revolt, was their hopeless infatuation with radical rhetoric. Radical agitators swarmed to Vienna from all over the German states, indeed from all over Europe, in the months after the March Revolution. Men like the notorious liberal nationalist, Dr. Anton Schütte, had only to tell the youth that they were universally applauded for having made theirs the freest city in Europe to stir them to even more passionate ardor for their cause. He had only to suggest some new and even more radical tactic—a "Storm Petition," for instance—to win their enthusiastic acquiescence. If older men are generally moved primarily by self-interest, younger ones are all too frequently impelled to violent action by the powerful appeal of words.

Behind the radical rhetoric, of course, lay radical ideas. In their excessive preoccupation with theoretical constructs lay a final major flaw in the Youth Revolution as it existed in 1848, less than half a century into its colorful history.

The heads of the young gentlemen of the Aula were full of revolutionary ideas, most of them foreign in origin and all too many of them essentially irrelevant to the real problems that confronted their country. Austria's most powerful discontented class, for instance, was her vast peasantry: industrialization was only beginning to spread, and the proletariat was a tiny minority. But the much admired young revolutionaries of France—a far more industrialized nation—had been making common cause with the workers for some twenty years, and so the Austrians must do the same. The oppressive feudal dues of the peasantry were in fact abolished, at the instigation of a young law student named Hans Kudlich. This crucial act of liberation, however, came largely as an afterthought, and little energy was ever devoted to winning over the peasants—the majority of the emperor's subjects—to the revolutionary cause.

Take one other instance. The presence of large national minorities was undoubtedly the greatest single problem that afflicted the Habsburg Empire. But the North German *Burschenschaft* was dedicated to the notion of a United States of Germany, and so, inevitably, were their Austrian imitators—even though this attitude quickly fragmented the forces of revolution in the multinational Habsburg realms. The Hungarians alone, of all the minority nationalities, were admired and courted by the Viennese student rebels, and Kossuth's rather minimal support was not enough to save Vienna from disaster when the final confrontation came.

Where ideology comes to grips with actual circumstances, it can be a great source of strength to the modern Youth Revolution. In 1848, however, the Academic Legion was simply too full of fashionable French and North German ideas to come to terms with Austrian realities.

The youth of 1848 had courage, commitment, and the willingness to take vigorous action against evils their elders had apathetically tolerated for generations. But they had the vices of their qualities as well: a proneness to violence and extremism, a weakness for rhetoric, and a tendency to see the world in ideological terms that simply did not correspond to their own real circumstances. In the violent March days and on the barricades of May, their virtues had carried them to astonishing victories. In October, as their short, six months' tenure in power drew to a close, their weaknesses were clearly to the fore.

A Juggernaut Unleashed

The bête noire of the students that fall was Count Latour, the minister of war. It was Latour who secretly kept the imperial armies supplied and in the field as they methodically reduced all other centers of revolution in the Habsburg realms. He accused the students themselves of plotting yet another rebellion and repeatedly urged the Camarilla to move against the Academic Legion. The students responded in kind, urgently warning the working men that Count Latour was now the greatest enemy of the revolution left at court, a dangerous man about whom something must be done.

On October 5 and 6, the bloody climax to this angry feud stunned the city—and set the stage for the final cataclysm.

On October 5, War Minister Latour ordered troops from the Vienna garrison to entrain for Hungary to reinforce Baron Jellachich's efforts to crush the insurrectionary forces of Kossuth. The students, the workers, and some sympathetic units of the National Guard (primarily those recruited from the industrial suburbs) responded with desperate efforts to prevent the troops from leaving. They mingled with the grenadier regiments, plied them with wine, urged them to refuse to march against their revolutionary brothers in Budapest. They tore up railway tracks and sabotaged a key railroad bridge leading out of the city. They blocked the station with their own bodies. And they won, this last time: the troops did not leave the capital.

But this time the juggernaut the student radicals had unleashed could not be controlled. On October 6, firing broke out between suburban and inner-city Guard regiments, and working-class mobs attacked regular army troops with six-foot iron bars. That evening, a maddened mob stormed into the war ministry. They clubbed and stabbed Count Latour to death, stripped and brutalized his body, and ended by stringing up the bloody corpse to a lamp post in the street.

If there was any hope for the revolution in Vienna, the savage murder of the war minister finished it. Within a few days, many thousands of well-to-do families had fled the city in terror, along with most of the liberal, middle-class Guard officers. Before the end of the month, the armies of Windischgrätz and Jellachich were encamped within artillery range of the Habsburg capital itself.

In the last week of October, the siege of Vienna began.

What a Quantity of Beards and Long Locks Have Fallen . . .

The Academic Legion gave a surprisingly good account of itself in those last harrowing days. Their numbers had shrunk to perhaps a thousand by autumn, as members drifted off to fight in Italy or Hungary, or went home because they were too poor to survive without subsidies in Vienna. But chemistry students could still make gunpowder and future engineers could manage the artillery. Students distributed supplies, ran key observation posts, treated the wounded, and often commanded units of working men on the barricades.

The long-haired Legionnaires seem to have maintained much of the gaiety of March and May even in those dark October days. But their jokes and songs were soon lost in the crash of cannon fire and the screams of the injured. Their dapper uniforms and cocky plumes were indistinguishable in clouds of powder smoke so thick the desperate defenders could hardly see each other's faces in the gloom.

The city fell on the last day of October.

On the first of November, an eyewitness marveled: "What a

quantity of beards and long locks have fallen since yesterday!" [28] Everyone seemed to have cut his hair, and there was not a Calabrian hat or a red, black, and gold sash to be seen on the streets of the occupied capital.

Students were routed out of the most incongruous hiding places —including even the boudoirs of the admiring young ladies with whom the dashing Academic Legionnaires had danced so gaily in the spring. Some were imprisoned, some were banished. Some slipped out of the country and went into self-imposed exile. A few fled even as far as America to build new lives in a country where a man was free to speak his mind.

But some of this revolutionary generation of young Austrians neither hid nor fled. After the fall of the city, the bodies of those who had died defending it were laid out in long rows on the dirty floor of the public mortuary to be identified by relatives and friends. "Most of them," remembered one who went to view the dead, "were young men . . ." [29]

An experiment in student power. An experiment that failed.

And yet the Viennese student rebels of 1848 did accomplish something: they started their country on the road to constitutional government. For the demand for an Austrian constitution, first raised in the crowded courtyard of the *Landhaus* that wild March morning in 1848, was never after stilled. Even the autocratic Emperor Francis-Joseph, who succeeded "poor Ferdy" that same year, saw the need to play, at least, at constitution-making. Thus there was the Kremšier Constitution of 1849; the "Diploma" of 1860 and the "Patent" of 1861; the establishment of the Dual Monarchy in 1866–67; and the gradual extension of the suffrage that continued beyond the turn of the century. Twenty years after that first shrill student demand for "Freedom! Freedom!" Austrians were granted a modern bill of rights. Sixty years after the March Revolution, almost all Austrians had the right to vote. When Francis-Joseph finally passed away in 1916, the Austrian Republic was only four years away.

As the German Student Unions of 1815 set the Germanies on the road to national unification, so the Viennese Academic Legion made a beginning, at least, in the liberalizing of their country. For all their weaknesses and follies, rebellious younger generations do seem to have a knack for making significant beginnings.

6

"The Nihilists Are Setting St. Petersburg on Fire!" * *From Nonviolence to Terrorism Russia, 1881*

Among the qualities of the Youth Revolution, none has been more widely discussed than the *extremism* of the younger generation in revolt. Whether they rebel against or withdraw from society at large, whether they win or lose, rebellious young ideologues are always accused of "going too far." They inevitably demand too much, too fast—or so their elders repeatedly insist.

On a less purely pragmatic level, the extremes of commitment and dedication of which youth has proved capable have often stirred sympathetic elders to extravagant admiration. The nonviolent civil rights crusaders of the early 1960's seemed well-nigh saintly to some Americans. But youth in revolt, especially when its nonnegotiable demands are frustrated, is also capable of extremes of irrational violence, like that of the ghetto-burners and Black Panthers of the later 1960's. Such exalted idealism and shocking violence have been key qualities of the Youth Revolution from the beginning.

Nowhere was this more true than in nineteenth-century Russia, the land of Turgenev's archetypal *Fathers and Sons.* Tsarist Russia, a nation sunk in political repression and hopeless backwardness, produced some of the most extravagant dreams and brutal tactics in the history of the accelerating revolt of the younger generation.

By the middle of the nineteenth century, Romanov Russia was already the largest nation on earth, and by far the most populous in Europe. Unfortunately, it was also the most culturally isolated, the most economically underdeveloped, and the most politically auto-

* Ivan Turgenev, *Literary Reminiscences and Autobiographical Fragments,* translated by David Magarshack (New York, 1958), p. 174.

cratic of all the great powers. The differing attitudes of succeeding generations of Russians toward their country and its peculiar institutions were the cause of one of the most famous generational conflicts of modern times.

The keystone of the autocracy that ruled this strange medieval anomaly looming along the eastern frontiers of modern Europe was the Romanov emperor himself, the Tsar of all the Russias. In Western Europe, parliaments and written constitutions were becoming commonplace in the second half of the nineteenth century. Even Bismarck had to haggle on occasion with the people's elected representatives. Only in St. Petersburg was the sovereign's will still the first and final principle of government.

There was no Russian constitution, no parliament, no local or provincial assemblies capable of limiting the tsar's power. Freedom of speech, assembly, and the press, equality before the law, equal opportunity for advancement—all these half-mythical Western civil liberties were not even that in Russia. The emperor in St. Petersburg, the "little father" of the Russian people, still ruled as his ancestors had—by God's will. The liberal who dared suggest that the emperor share his absolute authority with his subjects was thus not only a political offender of the first order: he was guilty of blaspheming against the Lord's anointed.

As in Habsburg Austria, the Romanov tsars depended not only on the church, but on the bureaucracy, the secret police, and, in the last resort, on the army to maintain their hold over the vast realms they ruled. The Russian bureaucracy was the largest, and one of the most inefficient, in Europe. The Russian army was the biggest in the world, and its Cossack cavalry had long been notorious as suppressers of civil disorders. The political police force—the Third Section of His Majesty's own Chancery, popularly known as the "Third Section"—was ubiquitous in Russia long before the Communists came to power.

The most conservative West European travelers winced at the absolute authority wielded by the Russian emperor over his acquiescent subjects. The Marquis de Custine wrote that due obedience to constituted authority was one thing, but that until he visited Russia he "did not know what it is to come across an absolute government and a nation of slaves." The self-exiled Russian liberal, Alexander Herzen, judged his country's political system even more harshly: "Free speech with us," he wrote, "has always been considered insolence; independence, subversion; man was engulfed in the state, dissolved in the community." The despotic authoritarianism of the tsars, he declared, "reached at times a degree of unbridled violence that has no equal in history." [1]

Nine-tenths of the seventy million people who lived in this huge, half-European, rigidly autocratic state were peasants. They were the creatures of the Russian land, the "black earth" that no nationalistic ideologue had to teach them how to love. They structured their simple lives according to its primeval rhythms of season and climate, sunshine and rain. They were the "dark folk," still wearing long beards and flowing caftans in the Old Russian style. They were deeply distrustful still of the shaven chins and frock coats of the Westernized elite who had dominated their country since Peter the Great's time. City-dwelling intellectuals were beginning to think of this vast unlettered peasantry as the salt of the Russian earth. The fact was that the typical *muzhik* was, as he had been for centuries, ignorant, dirt poor, and legally unfree.

Serfdom had reached its apogee in Russia, not in the middle ages, but in the enlightened eighteenth century. By 1800, more than half the peasants in Russia were serfs on the great estates of the Russian nobility and country gentry. Most of the remainder were "crown peasants," personally free in theory, but bound in pragmatic fact to labor all their lives on the immense acreages owned by the state. Theoretically, serfdom was a step ahead of the chattel slavery which still persisted in the United States in the first half of the nineteenth century. In practice, the Russian serf was often little better off than his black counterpart in America.

In every way, Russian society was retrograde and primitive. The Industrial Revolution had hardly touched the country. The middle classes, the aggressive champions of liberal institutions and economic progress elsewhere in Europe, were feeble and unprogressive in Russia. The only force for change that stood between the "little father" and the masses of the peasantry was the small Westernized intelligentsia of enlightened officials and liberal landowners. But the liberal and the enlightened were a tiny majority, even among the Europeanized elite. They were generally regarded as mere grist for the Third Section's mill.

Most Russians of all classes simply accepted their country's shortcomings as "givens," like the weather. Autocratic government, economic backwardness, the servile status of the peasant majority were simply "facts of life."

And then, as the second half of the nineteenth century got under way, strange things began to happen in the Russia of the tsars.

1. *A GENERATION OF NIHILISTS*

Liberal Fathers—Radical Sons

The Russian younger generation of the 1870's—the revolutionary generation whose surviving remnants struck their final blow at tsarism in 1881—was the product of a considerably more complicated generational background than that of the Austrian youth of 1848. Like the Viennese Academic Legion, the Russian *narodniki* were, generationally speaking, the radical sons of liberal fathers. But they were also the "little brothers" of one of the most violently alienated of all rebellious younger generations—the famous Russian nihilists of the 1860's. Both the liberal "men of the forties" and the radical "men of the sixties" contributed largely to the militant idealism and the crescendo of violence that made the Russian youth of the 1870's notorious across the length and breadth of Europe.

The sixties: for the young Russian who came of age around 1870, the decade just preceding his was an age of giants. It was the age of the nihilists—the "new people"—the generation that dared to say No.

> "A nihilist," said Nikolai. "That comes from the Latin word *nihil,* nothing, so far as I can tell; it must mean a person who—who acknowledges nothing."
>
> "Say rather: who respects nothing," [Uncle] Pavel put in, and began buttering his bread again.
>
> "Who examines everything from a critical point of view," Arkady [Nikolai Kirsanov's college-boy son] observed.
>
> "And isn't that exactly the same thing?" asked Pavel.
>
> "No, it isn't the same thing. A nihilist is a person who does not bow to any authorities; who doesn't accept any principle on faith, no matter how hallowed and venerated . . ." [2]

The emancipated youth of Turgenev's generational classic, *Fathers and Sons* (1862), make a number of similar attempts to communicate their "views" to their irritatingly obtuse elders. Bazarov, the archetypal nihilist of the book, speaks out most clearly for this disenchanted younger generation. A nihilist, he snaps, is one who genuinely believes that there is not "one institution in our contemporary existence, in private or public life, which doesn't deserve complete and merciless annihilation." [3]

This sweeping condemnation of all existing values and institutions was to win for the Russian youth of the sixties a reputation as the first totally nihilistic generation of modern times. To many, it seemed as if this iconoclastic new youth had sprung out of nowhere, fully armed at birth with the jeering, sneering negativism that became their trademark. Actually, the nihilists of the 1860's were the end product of an insurrectionary opposition movement in Russia that had begun to develop as early as 1815—and that did not end when the nihilists, and the *narodniki* who followed them, passed out of history.

The famous Decembrists of 1815–25 were a generation of aristocratic young army officers who had picked up subversive democratic notions while serving in the army of occupation in Paris after the Napoleonic wars. They were the founders of the Russian revolutionary tradition. But their abortive insurrection in December of 1825 sent most of them to Siberia. It sent a handful of their leaders to the gallows. The Decembrists thus contributed little but a pantheon of martyrs to the revolutionary tradition they began.

Through the 1830's and '40's and on into the '50's—throughout the grimly authoritarian reign of Nicholas I—the only opposition the tiny Russian liberal community could muster was that of the hopelessly ineffectual "superfluous men." For to be liberally inclined in the Russia of Tsar Nicholas, when enthroned autocracy and subservient peasant masses meshed perfectly into Custine's "nation of slaves," was to be utterly unnecessary and unwanted by anybody —to be, in a word, *superfluous*. These generations—the generations of Turgenev's Nikolai and Pavel Kirsanov—did add utopian socialism to the fund of democratic ideas inherited from the Decembrists. Beyond that, they did little but wring their hands in secret, and bury themselves in Hegelian metaphysics and the poetry of Pushkin.

These "conscience-stricken gentry" comprised one of the most memorable "silent generations" of modern times.

Herzen and Bakunin the anarchist, both of whom fled to the West to speak their minds from exile, were among them. So was Turgenev himself, who judiciously expressed his views in fiction. These were the "fathers" of the generation of the 1860's—and of their admiring "little brothers" of the astonishing 1870's.

The tie between these metaphorical fathers and sons was probably not often a literal blood relationship. For one of the distinguishing characteristics of the nihilist generation was the fact that, unlike its aristocratic predecessors, it included a large admixture of the lower orders.

The children of the lower classes were admitted to the universities in considerable numbers for the first time in the reign of the reforming tsar Alexander II (1856–1881). These new students were neither peasants nor proletarians: they were the lowest levels of the literate population, the so-called *raznochintsy*—sons of petty officials, lower-ranking army officers, village priests and country doctors. Nor were the *raznochintsy* a majority in the Russian universities of the 1860's: the sons of the gentry and the titled nobility still predominated in the typical demonstration.[4] But their influence was great within their generation. They lent a new tone of crude belligerence to the generational upheaval of the sixties.

But the new youth was more than a class phenomenon. The nihilist generation was, in large measure, the consequence of the sort of twist of history that not infrequently produces a generational rebellion: a great reform movement that fails to live up to its own exalted goals.

Alexander II, the "tsar emancipator," actually did more to transform Old Russia than any ruler between Peter the Great and Joseph Stalin. The great achievement of this unaggressive little man with the mild eyes and the mutton-chop whiskers was the emancipation of the serfs in 1861. His reforms during the decade of the sixties encompassed every area of Russian life, from the judiciary to the military, from local self-government to the expansion of educational opportunities. But they did not go far enough to satisfy the liberal youth whose hopes he had raised beyond all possibility of fulfillment.

Nor did those reforms, it is only fair to add, go far enough in many cases to solve the problems to which they were addressed. The serfs, for instance, were freed. But they were given too little of the land they had formerly cultivated. They were saddled with heavy debts to the government ("redemption payments") for what land they did get. And they were sometimes turned out without an acre to beg their bread, or to swell the dislocated new proletariat of the cities. Tsar Alexander solved the "serf question" only to replace it with a "peasant problem" that still plagues Soviet Russia today.

Their great expectations thus betrayed by the reformers themselves, the educated, liberal-minded youth of 1861 angrily turned their backs on the society that had first raised, then dashed their hopes. They quickly drifted into one of the most celebrated counter cultures of modern times.

Long Hair and Blue Spectacles

The nihilists "suddenly sprang up in families," wrote the aging and increasingly jaundiced novelist Goncharov, "on the streets—everywhere, flooding the cities . . ." Like most of his generation, Goncharov had little use for these, "the latest type of urchins, ignoramuses, with their pretensions of leading society forward . . ." Dostoyevsky, who savaged the new youth in both *The Possessed* and *Crime and Punishment,* spoke for many a soured man of the forties when he declared angrily that "Nihilists . . . should get the knout once and for all." [5]

They were a typical enough bohemian subculture: hairy, dirty, foulmouthed, oddly costumed, and violently anti-social. Nihilist men let their hair grow long, and some wore full beards as well. The typical *nigilistka,* the female of the species, showed her contrariness by cutting *her* hair short, as determinedly bobbed as any emancipated woman of the 1920's. The clothing of both sexes was usually dirty and in disrepair. Some wore plaids over their shoulders and affected heavy boots and large blue spectacles. Some sported baggy peasant costumes. In far-off provincial Kazan, they were said to dress in the skins of wild animals and go around with sticks.

They were clearly a counter culture as well, espousing strange new values and *Weltanschauungen* utterly at variance with those of their society. The nihilists of St. Petersburg or Moscow, for example, often lived together in communes and were widely rumored to practice "free love." Beyond question, they were freethinkers—in the nineteenth-century sense—to a degree unheard of before in Old Russia.

There was nothing Romantic about these Russian descendants of the Paris Bohemians of the 1830's. The nihilists were atheists and philosophical materialists, worshipers at the shrine of modern science, and idolators of Charles Darwin. They regarded themselves as hard-boiled realists, a generation that, unlike the Romantically inclined men of the forties, did not deceive themselves with vaporings about Art and Beauty. What use was Pushkin's poetry, these real-life Bazarovs demanded, when there were peasant babies going hungry in Russia?

The cult of materialism which swept all Europe in the second half of the nineteenth century made this a fact-oriented generation, dedicated to "telling it like it was." What was needed, they angrily insisted, was empirical study, concrete data, and then positive application of the most advanced scientific ideas to the problems of the day. The Romantic escapism of the older liberals was as bad as the religious obscurantism of the reactionary establishment.

What Is To Be Done? demanded the thick-spectacled radical journalist Chernyshevsky, in his widely read nihilist novel of the same name—a book written in prison, before his exile to Siberia. What was to be done—that was the key question for this generation. Facts first, then action—that was their program. Not for them thirty years of wringing their hands and wishing things were different.

The Woman Question

In actuality, they took action in only two areas: the liberation of women and the reform of the universities. Only very late in their career did the nihilist counter culture turn militantly against society at large, to slip at last into political agitation and the dream of revolution.

Which is not to say that they did not object, publicly and noisily, to a number of government policies. It was only that, as they soon discovered, they could do very little about most of them.

They were bitter about the "false emancipation" of the serfs, for example, and about the "Bezdna massacre," in which scores of peasants who rebelled rather than accept liberty without land were shot down by the troops. They were outraged when the government resorted to military force to suppress violent radical agitation in the Polish provinces—a periodic necessity ever since the partitions of Poland in the eighteenth century, but none the less immoral to the nihilist generation. In both cases, however, their protests took the comparatively innocuous form of ostentatiously celebrated masses for the souls of those Poles and peasants who had died in rebellion against the Lord's anointed.

In the matter of female emancipation, on the other hand, the nihilists generated new cultural forms that genuinely horrified their elders.

The "woman question" became a burning issue among Russian youth during the 1860's. The nihilists championed the rights of women to education and careers of their own, to freedom of movement and life style, even to sexual emancipation. Paternal authority over the unmarried daughter, they declared, was moral tyranny. Marriage was just another of the antiquated institutions that deserved "complete and merciless annihilation." The preachings of John Stuart Mill on women's liberation, and George Sand's practice of it, won their unqualified approbation. Chernyshevsky even proposed a reverse double standard, by which men must remain faithful, but women would be free—by way of compensation for centuries of sexual oppression—to take as many lovers as they wished.

The girls took them up on it—on some of it, at least—and the *nigilistka* was born. Soon bright-eyed young women with bobbed hair and determinedly plain dresses were sitting in university classes—to the intense irritation of the more conservative professors. They participated frankly and freely, though usually not sexually, in the life of the communes. Despite all the lurid prose that was written about them, it was apparently the "new ideas" that interested the *nigilistka,* not sex. The cult of sexual freedom would have to wait for another time and generation.

Nihilist women insisted above all on their freedom from male domination. Girls in their 'teens ran away from unfeeling fathers to join the nihilists. Young married women abandoned husbands who lacked sympathy for the cause. The female nihilists cheerfully "married" friends or even strangers with whom they had no intention of living in order to gain their legal freedom. They had no respect at all for the traditional feminine roles of wife and mother. "A wife who did no useful work, but merely saw to household affairs," they firmly believed, "was no better than a kept woman . . ."[6]

The University Revolt

The nihilists, most of whom were (or had been) students themselves, made even more serious efforts to transform the Russian educational system. They founded the short-lived Russian "Sunday schools" for illiterate working men who had no other time free for self-improvement. They championed women's rights to education. Above all, they attacked the antiquated, authoritarian university system of their day.

They rejected the rigid discipline of the typical Russian university—the rigorous attendance regulations, the rules on haircuts and smoking, the uniforms, the militaristic saluting of teachers and administrators on the street. Now they let their hair grow, smoked in the halls, wandered into classes when they felt like it. They organized themselves as a student body and began to hold meetings—a sinister activity indeed in Romanov Russia. They set up student-run reading rooms and lending libraries and subscribed to such radical underground papers as Herzen's *émigré* journal, *The Bell.*

The "new people," as they called themselves, went even further. They began to boycott the classes of teachers they regarded as incompetent. Sometimes they staged riotous demonstrations outside classrooms, drowning out the lectures going on inside. Here and there, they developed enough "student power" to compel the firing of an unpopular instructor. And when even the tsar emancipator's liberal officials began to clamp down, the new people responded by taking to the streets.

The first such protest march in Russian history—an impromptu demonstration against a new and more rigorous set of university regulations—took place in St. Petersburg in the fall of 1861:

> A sight like it had never been seen [a participant recalled in later years]. It was a wonderful September day. . . . In the streets the girls who were just beginning to go to university joined in, together with a number of young men of differing

> origins and professions. . . . When we appeared on the Nevsky Prospekt, the French barbers came out of their shops and their faces lit up and they waved their arms cheerfully, shouting *"Révolution! Révolution!"* [7]

It was nothing so serious as that, of course. "This is not an insurrection," they earnestly assured the mounted police who hastily ringed them in.[8] But when the troops were called out, when their leaders were arrested in the night by the gendarmerie, things quickly escalated to violence.

By and large, these seem to have been "police riots." In Moscow, for instance, the police clearly egged on an already hostile crowd into attacking a student protest march. The forces of law and order then intervened "to keep the peace," clubbing the students and arresting them by the hundreds. Mounted policemen ranged far from the scene of the demonstration, galloping up and down neighboring boulevards, sweeping up the university youth wherever they found them. "They grabbed the students from the sidewalks," an eyewitness remembered, "dragged them from the droshkies [horsedrawn cabs], and hauled them by their [long] hair into the police stations. The police horses trampled some of them with their hoofs; some were seriously wounded . . ." [9] In all, 340 students were taken into custody on that one occasion, many of them injured.

"Processions, protests, troops called out to disperse students," wrote a correspondent for the London *Times* "—all this is certainly very new for Russia." [10] It always comes as a shock to a comparatively stable society when the young barbarians take to the streets for the first time.

The Rise of the Politicals

Nihilism began as a counter culture, a turning away from society in search of self-development and close association with other "thinking realists"—another of its adherents' favorite sobriquets. In the face of increasingly vigorous repression, however, the new youth soon found itself drifting into political militance. What we may think of as the second nihilist generation—the generation of the later 1860's and the early 1870's—produced the most notorious would-be revolutionist before the *narodniki* themselves—the "unmentionable" Nechayev.

Even in the early sixties, however, there were a few "politicals" among the blue-spectacled, heavy-booted, long-haired denizens of the nihilist counter culture. There was a handful of incendiary pamphlets like *Young Russia* (1862), which demanded the raising of the red flag and a march on the Winter Palace, massacring "the imperial party" on the way. There were one or two attempts at organizing secret societies—feeble efforts, but enough to convince even liberals of the older generation that "among the students and the men of letters there is unquestionably an organized conspiracy," probably directed by outside agitators.[11]

Then there were the terrible fires which swept several Russian cities, including sections of St. Petersburg itself, in the spring of 1862. Arson was of course suspected, and the negative thinkers who talked so belligerently about "clearing the ground" for the utopia of the future were inevitably the prime suspects. Turgenev's *Fathers and Sons* appeared in print that spring, and "the first exclamation that escaped the lips of the first acquaintance I met on the Nevsky Prospekt"—as the author subsequently recalled—"was 'Look what your nihilists are doing! They are setting Petersburg on fire!' "[12]

In 1866, there was even an attempt to assassinate the tsar. A disturbed youth named Karakozov took a shot at Tsar Alexander as he emerged from a public park in St. Petersburg. The bullet missed, and the assassin was quickly seized by the horrified crowd. Not surprisingly, the crime of Karakozov triggered a new wave of repression. "The younger generation," a government investigating committee quickly concluded, was "steeped in atheism, materialism, and socialism, inculcated not only by the teachers, but also by the radical 'progressive' press."[13] Karakozov was, of course, executed. Chernyshevsky, the journalistic idol of the nihilist youth, had already been bundled off to Siberia, but a number of his surviving colleagues followed him now. And the student population of that inhospitable province began to grow apace.

But militance reached its apogee in the pre-*narodnik* generations with the sensational case of Sergei Nechayev.

The Nechayev trial of 1872 shocked Russia. The long-haired

young proletarian revolutionist had apparently tried to organize a nation-wide Russian underground. He claimed the authorship of a bizarre *Catechism* for the full-time professional revolutionary. He had certainly been responsible for one killing, the bizarre murder of one of his own student followers, whom he claimed to suspect of being a police spy. He was, to his horrified elders at least, the epitome of Bazarovian nihilism. His *Catechism* laid down a clear distinction between his world and that of his fellow Russians: "The laws, the conventions, the moral code of civilized society have no meaning for [the revolutionary]. . . . To him, whatever promotes the triumph of the revolution is moral, whatever hinders it is immoral . . ." And then the sweeping negation the youth of the sixties had made their battle cry: "Our business is passionate, complete, ruthless destruction." [14]

They locked Nechayev up in an isolated cell in the Peter and Paul Fortress, the maximum security prison of St. Petersburg. He died there ten years later, defiant to the last. Sergei Nechayev was almost certainly a pathological case, and a caricature of his generation. At the same time, however, he stood as a towering symbol of the main contribution of the men of the sixties to the Russian revolutionary tradition: the final break with the past, the total defiance of the Old Russian way of life.

These were the big brothers of the "populist," or *narodnik* generation of the middle and later 1870's. They were a challenge, a model, an inspiration to their successors. But they also posed a problem for these ardent, ideologically driven men and women a decade younger than they.

What was there left for the youth of the seventies to do? Growing up in the shadow of such giants, what could even the most ardently anti-Russian young rebel add to the urgent appeal of a Chernyshevsky, to the monumental defiance of a Nechayev? What was left for the *narodnik* generations—except perhaps, just perhaps, to succeed where the nihilists had failed?

2. THE CHILDREN'S CRUSADE

If They Whip the Muzhik, *Let Them Whip Me Too!*

The youth scene certainly looked remarkably unpropitious in the early seventies, at least by comparison with the turbulent decade just preceding. The leaders of the nihilist revolt were gone, fled to the West, exiled to Siberia, dead in their twenties. Their followers had cut their hair and changed their clothes and faded back into the general population.

For many liberal-minded Russians, it was a sterile and weary period, disillusioned and frivolous. There were no radicals left, it seemed. Yesterday's extremists now sought only to bury the past and to avoid all compromising involvements for the future. "The more radical they had been ten years before," one young seeker recalled, "the greater were their fears." Among the intellectual leaders of the capital, "the moment the conversation began to lose its frivolous character," the moment some brash young man wanted to discuss the state of the nation, "some sort of interruption was sure to occur. 'What do you think, gentlemen, of the latest performance of *La Belle Hélène?*' or 'What is your opinion of that cured fish?' was loudly asked by one of the older guests . . ."[15]

But a new term was already spreading among the educated youth of Russia. In the history books, it is called Russian populism, the cult of the peasant. To the literate, concerned young people who made the "To the People" movement of the middle seventies, it was the great crusade of their lives.

"The old 'nihilism' . . . described by Turgenev," wrote one shrewd commentator on the Russian scene, "was over about 1870."[16] A new and more socially oriented, more unabashedly altruistic ideology soon became the talk of the tea shops and the smoky student rooms. In place of the egocentric nihilist there arose a new type of rebellious youth, the *narodnik*—the populist, the peasant socialist, the worshiper of the *narod,* the Russian *Volk.* The new rebel no longer demanded merely his own personal emancipation, his own self-development above all. Instead, he identified with the sweating peasant masses, made their cause and their unjust suffering his own. "If they whip the *muzhik,*" wrote

Nikolai Mikhailovsky, one of the journalistic prophets of this first populist generation, "let them whip me too." [17]

Many streams of thought, some West European, some native Russian, flowed together to form the faith of the *narodnik*. The romantic belief in the spiritual superiority of simple folk—children, noble savages, and above all peasants—played its part. Germanic mystical-nationalist enthusiasm for the ancient *Volk* infected many Slavic countries, including Russia. Anglo-French democratic and socialist notions, with their emphasis on Everyman's right to control the state and the economy, made their contribution. Indeed, in the century of the "religion of humanity," the century that saw the symbolic excesses of Jacksonian democracy and the Marxist exaltation of the proletariat, it would have been surprising if the Russians had not gotten around to worshiping the *muzhik*.

But there were some strictly Slavic components to Russian populism as well. There were the special virtues which the peasant epitomized in the eyes of the intelligentsia of Petersburg and Moscow. All the piety and patience, the fundamental honesty and simple sense of justice, the hospitality, the kindliness, the unswerving loyalty of this great brooding Slavic nation were—as the populist youth believed—embodied in the Russian peasantry. To those of a revolutionary bent, furthermore, the "dark folk" were more than the national character incarnate; to the revolutionary, the peasants represented a potentially irresistible force for the reshaping of Russia. In the sheer might of their overwhelming numbers, they comprised an unstoppable army that had only to be set in motion to bring certain victory. Generations of young rebels would labor to find the lever that would set that peasant army moving.

More than Russia's destiny might well be at stake. All the world, after all, was to benefit from the broadly democratic, utopian, socialist community of the future. It had been universally assumed that Western Europe would lead the way; but ever since the triumph of reaction in 1848–49, Russians had questioned this assumption. In Russia, they pointed out, there already existed an indigenous peasant socialism, the village commune called the *mir,* which should make the transition to utopia far easier than in other lands, where the humblest cottager was a capitalist. Within the *mir,* all land was owned in common; it was even periodically redistributed, as changes in soil quality, the sizes of families, and other factors dictated. The *mir* as a whole decided when to plant, when to harvest, and other matters of concern to all. "The *mir* is like a wave," a peasant proverb ran, "one man's thought is everybody's thought." [18] Here, surely, was a solid foundation on which to build a socialist Russia—the first step to a socialist world.

Beneath all this ideologizing, however, lay a much more powerful motive for the impending generational upheaval. For this was a generation gripped by a fantastic, obsessive, inescapable guilt complex.

Young Prince Peter Kropotkin, who began as a populist and ended as Russia's most famous anarchist since Bakunin, discovered his own guilt standing in a rocky clay field in Russian Finland. He was there as a geologist, studying the land; the peasants were there as they had always been, struggling with dumb hopelessness to scratch a living from this same sterile earth. Kropotkin loved science. But:

> what right had I to those highest joys [he could not help asking himself] when all around me was nothing but misery and struggle for a mouldy bit of bread; when whatsoever I should spend to enable me to live in that world of higher emotions must needs be taken from the very mouths of those who grew the wheat and had not bread enough for their children? [19]

"We are debtors of the people," wrote Mikhailov, the Chernyshevsky of the seventies.[20]

How to pay the awful debt, how to exorcise the oppressive sense of guilt, became the great problem for this generation of concerned young Russian intellectuals. They found the solution, as rebellious youth so often does, in the writings of their despised predecessors in this developing revolutionary tradition.

Herzen had given them their answer a decade earlier, when the students of St. Petersburg had been turned out of their university in 1861. "To the people!" that vanished prophet had written then. Take your knowledge to the dark folk: "This is your place, exiles of knowledge, soldiers of the Russian people." Kropotkin and many others found their answer in that simple imperative: "*V narod!* To the people!" Wherever Chernyshevsky's crucial question was raised, *What is to be done?* the answer came back quickly now, with a mighty outpouring of psychological relief: "Go among the people, and the question will solve itself!"[21]

The first populist generation had found their crusade.

V Narod!

They talked of little else, that spring of 1873. They would leave the universities and return to the countryside, go back to the People (the *muzhik* was rapidly becoming such a capitalized abstraction for them now). They would live among the simple peasants, share their hard black bread, labor by their sides, repaying with their own sweat that mountainous, heartfelt debt. They would learn too, learn truths you could not find in books—how the dark folk really lived, for instance, and that deep spiritual wisdom only the *narod* had to teach. Most important, they would carry their own gospel, the creed of socialism, to these victims of the system; would show them how they themselves, rising up in their millions, might transform Old Russia once and for all.

Through long nights they talked about it, strolling on spring evenings by the Neva . . . in the shadow of the ancient Kremlin . . . beneath the Byzantine churches of Kiev. There were wild gestures of renunciation. Some quit school within weeks of graduation; some tore up their diplomas; some came swarming home unbidden from the West, abandoning the sure success a European degree would give them, to fling themselves into the movement.

Desperate measures: but then, these were desperate, glorious times. The death knell of the old order was sounded: in its place would rise "a new world, based upon the fraternity of all men, in which there will no longer be either misery or tears . . ." A whole generation was seized by the spirit of the crusade, driven by its twin passions: the desire to share in "the great work of the redemption of the country, of humanity," and by "an aspiration towards their own moral perfection." Powerful drives indeed for bright young people stifled and suffocated by the system, chafing to carry on in the great tradition of the sixties. They rose in hundreds, in thousands, and "threw themselves into the movement," as a participant recalled, "with a joy, an enthusiasm, a faith, such as one experienced only once in a life . . ."[22]

In 1873, after all the talk and very real enthusiasm, the Moscow *narodniki* went out almost alone, tramping the country roads in peasant garb, to seek out the People. In 1874, a mighty exodus of committed youth flooded across the land, thousands going on crusade. In 1875, a smaller but still determined band of true believers sallied forth in the spring. After that, the children's crusade was over: there was only the piper to be paid. But for those three years, their elders sat up and stared at this most astonishing upsurge of rebellious youth since the blue-spectacled nihilists had first burst upon the scene.

There were women on the great crusade, and some of them seem to have had an even harder time than their male companions. The wanderings of Catherine Breshkovskaya—famous more than four decades later as "the little grandmother of the Russian Revolution" —provide a case in point.

Catherine Breshkovskaya was thirty years old already—"comrades of my . . . age," she remembered, "were very few among the mass of youngsters"—when she set out to travel among the villages in the summer of 1874.[23] The daughter of a family of aristocratic liberals, well and safely married in her twenties, she had put it all behind her four years earlier, to devote herself entirely to the people's cause. She had taught the poor; she had distributed socialist propaganda to the workers. Most recently, she had been living in a radical commune in Kiev.

She has left us a vivid picture of this hotbed of young revolutionaries of the populist generation:

> On the outside, "the commune" differed little from other houses; but inside, it was like a different world. There were many large rooms, and each looked like a workshop. In one were carpenters' tools, with noblemen working as apprentices to the trade; in another students were learning shoemaking; in yet another etchers were preparing metal seals to stamp false passports.[24]

Here and there about the commune, "young men and women could be seen discussing political and economic questions." Some were already clad in the rough, uncomfortable clothing of the *muzhik*. "The whole community," Catherine reminisced long afterward, "was absorbed in the study of the peasants. They would get together in the sitting room and sing folksongs, or tell stories of the peasants illustrating their simplicity and good nature. . . . There was much laughter. The members of the community were merry and full of hope."[25]

On a June day in 1874, Catherine Breshkovskaya set out with two comrades to carry the word to the dark folk. Her companions on this pilgrimage were a priest's son named Stephanovitch and "little Masha," an even more delicately nurtured young lady than Catherine herself. Both were twenty-one years old.

Stephanovitch, a strapping youth, had learned the shoemaker's trade without much difficulty. Catherine and Masha had spent some time among the dye-workers, and proposed to earn a living by dyeing dresses and decorating handkerchiefs. All three were dressed now in rough but serviceable peasant costumes. And all their hearts were "overflowing with good will towards all mankind."[26]

The two women in particular had a hard time of it. Masha, who was somewhat frail, was exhausted by the day-long tramping over the rutty roads with a pack of tools on her back. Catherine almost choked on peasant food: the memory of her first *muzhik*-style barley bun, wrote one who spoke to her years later, "fills Catherine with horror to this day." Both the girls found it almost impossible to sleep on straw pallets in windowless peasant shacks, where "armies of bugs and insects" swarmed around them all night long.[27]

When they set up shop in their first village, the deserted hut they settled in proved to be indescribably filthy. "Get some fresh, warm manure from the fields," a peasant woman cheerfully advised them, "and mix it with lime. That makes a good wash for the floor." Gagging at the very thought, the two genteelly raised young ladies appealed to their more proletarian comrade. But Stephanovitch only grinned. Scrubbing floors, it seemed, was "women's work" among the dark folk: it would be as much as his disguise was worth to help them with it. He watched with obstinately folded arms while Catherine and Masha, "overcome with nausea," labored on their knees, "kneading lime and steaming manure into a paste to varnish a worm-eaten floor . . ."[28]

No sacrifice would have been too great, of course, if the work had gone well. But the little party from the Kiev commune had no luck propagandizing the Ukrainian peasants.

Despite all the hardships and all the reforms that had failed to materialize, there was still a deep reservoir of reverence for their emperor among the common folk of Russia. "The tsar is good to his peasants," a young *muzhik* named Ivan insisted doggedly. "They are his children. Everything that is bad comes from the barons and the lords."[29] All their arguments could not shake his faith.

Fear, too, proved to be a force more powerful than revolutionary logic. A healthy fear of overbearing bureaucrats and sadistic Cossacks was built into the peasantry, reinforced by memories of the repressions that had followed the emancipation a dozen years before. "One soldier stood on one arm, another on the other, and two on my legs," one leader of such a serf insurrection recalled. "I was beaten, beaten until the earth was soaked with blood. . . . I was exiled to Siberia, came back and began all over again; but I can't do it any more."[30] More timid men than this broken hero would never dream of trying it even once.

This was the pattern everywhere. There was a prudent fear of landlords and officials that outweighed all bitterness against them. And there was a stubborn, childlike faith in the dear father tsar that no argument could undermine. Long before the little group of missionaries broke up, long before Catherine Breshkovskaya herself was flung into a ramshackle jail by a local gendarme, she and they knew their mission had not been a success.

Hardly Anyone Over Thirty

Everywhere, the unhappy story was the same. The scattered survivors of the movement admitted it themselves, when they gathered once again, in their old city haunts or in prison cells, for what amounted to a generational post-mortem.

Each year, many had given up before the summer's end and wandered home, broken by the sheer physical hardship of tramping the roads, sleeping outdoors, bending their backs to unaccustomed labor. Some had simply been unable to find jobs; most had proved incompetent workmen in any case. A few, in their determination to shuck off the stigma of the college boy, had dressed so shabbily that no self-respecting peasant would give them house room.

Even when they reached the *muzhik* physically, they had seldom done so intellectually. Some totally illiterate peasants had cheerfully accepted populist pamphlets despite their inability to read: it seemed they made good cigarette papers. Some had simply been too tired of an evening to listen to the radicals. Some had listened, but had utterly failed to comprehend. "Won't that be great when we divide up the land!" one apparent convert to socialism exclaimed: "I'll hire two farmhands and live like a lord!" [31] A few—far fewer than the authorities subsequently claimed—actually turned the agitators over to the police, or beat them up for slandering the tsar.

And, of course, the police were after them like terriers everywhere.

The government of Alexander II had responded like Pavlov's salivating dog to the "To the People" movement of 1873, '74, and '75. The crusade had been totally nonviolent, utterly lacking even in the verbal fury of the nihilist generations. But the populists' ideology had been foreign and radical, their ultimate goal the destruction of Old Russia. They had been much more numerous than their predecessors, going out in thousands, by contrast with the few score members of the embryonic secret societies of the previous decade.[32] It was best—indeed essential—to put an end to this new youth revolt at once, the authorities decided. Massive counterforce—make an example—nip it in the bud. *Young Russia* had been only a pamphlet, only words—and then St. Petersburg had been in flames. Nechayev had succeeded in killing no one but one of his own people, but Karakozov had taken a shot at the tsar. It would be the worst kind of governmental irresponsibility to take chances with this new upsurge of youthful dissent.

It was not hard to track the *narodniki* down. Strangers in the countryside, they betrayed themselves by every word and gesture. They betrayed each other too—by the mail left in their amateurish "drops," by unwittingly leading the law to their comrades, by their complete lack of security preparations. Even the inefficient tsarist police could hardly fail to find them.

They were arrested by hundreds—eight hundred during the "crazy summer" of 1874 alone. They were tried in mass lots: the Trial of the 50 (1877) and the Trial of the 193 (1877–78) were *causes célèbres* of the decade. All told, more than sixteen hundred were taken into custody for a longer or shorter period. Of these, 525 were held for trial; 450 more were put under police surveillance; and eighty were sent directly into exile by administrative order.[33] It was a sweeping repression that made the punishment meted out to the first nihilist generation seem mild by comparison.

They fought back as best they could, with the standard weapons of young radicals in the toils of the law. They turned courtrooms into debating societies, open forums for their attacks on the establishment. The more gifted or determined among them composed and carefully rehearsed set speeches, not defending themselves but assailing the system that dared to put them in the dock. Sometimes their verbal assaults on the autocracy churned a courtroom into bedlam. Often they clearly won the sympathy of their liberal-leaning audience.

Their very appearance in the prisoners' benches was frequently enough to sway the crowd in their behalf. They were all young, after all, with the attractive idealism of youth. The defendants in the Trial of the 50 were "young men in their early twenties." The accused in the Trial of the 193 were at least as young: fully a quarter of them, in fact, were still minors, even after two years in prison awaiting trial. "The observation has been made," reported one foreign visitor, "that, in the numerous political trials . . . hardly anyone has been convicted who was over thirty years old . . . the ages of the majority varying from seventeen to twenty-three." [34]

The presence of young women among the accused further predisposed respectable liberals to pity. At one of the famous mass trials, almost one in every ten defendants was a girl. They were generally "plain, rather unattractive" young women in the nihilist tradition, often "thin, very serious, and careworn." The government claimed that the women were generally "more fanatical than the men"—a not uncommon situation in such generational movements. To sympathizers in the courtroom, however, they looked like "pale nuns." [35]

But all their inspired flights of oratory, and all the sympathy of the liberal intelligentsia, did the *narodniki* no good. They paid excessively for one wild summer of preaching the populist gospel to the people.

By the beginning of 1878, when the last mass trial of the "To the People" crusaders came to a close, one thing at least might be said for the government's hard-line policy: it worked. Or seemed to work, at any rate. There had been no mass exodus to the countryside for two summers past. A *narodnik* underground had formed, but it buzzed and swarmed with the hectic desperation of ants on a burning log, accomplishing nothing while the Third Section ferreted its members out. Sentimental, liberal intellectuals might shower gifts and poems on the young prisoners, but the state would have its eye on them for the rest of their lives. A strong hand was best, at least with Russian radicals.

The Trial of the 193 ended on January 23, 1878. The following morning, a young woman named Vera Zasulich called at the office of Petersburg's police chief, General Trepov, claiming she had a petition to present. She had a pistol; she shot him. The revolutionary terror had begun.

3. *A SAVAGE INSTINCT FOR DESTRUCTION*

Knives and Guns and Dynamite

The nonviolent crusade of the *narodnik* generation had led to nothing but show trials and prison cells. The shift to violence was almost inevitable for the small minority who were not prepared to surrender their cause.

They tried a whole rash of new slogans and new tactics first. "To the People" had failed: they tried "Propaganda by Fact"—a handful of heroes going to live full-time in the villages, serving as teachers or nurses and passing out new truths with every pill. They tried "Let Us Organize," setting up the underground organization called Land and Liberty, with cells in a number of cities, a secret press, and even a counterintelligence unit called the "Disorganizing Section." Only when Land and Liberty finally split in half—a time-honored practice on the revolutionary left—did some of the survivors of this generation finally turn wholeheartedly to political terrorism. Only then did the People's Will Society emerge—the Weathermen of the Russian 1870's.[36]

To all the dedication of the young, to every desperate effort of the movement to find a lever that might shift the nation off its set, reactionary center, the old men in St. Petersburg had had only one response. Between 1877 and 1879, almost 2,400 persons were indicted, either for specific political offenses or for the catchall crime of *lèse-majesté*. Unrecorded numbers were imprisoned for long periods "on suspicion," or banished without trial, by administrative decree. When the universities began to seethe with activism once more, the authorities expelled "hundreds" annually.[37]

To the authorities, this might be stern paternalism, the use of legal force for the protection of society. To the young militants, it was violence pure and simple. The program of the People's Will justified terrorism by declaring that "the existing governmental bourgeois excrescence" was "maintained solely through the exercise of naked force, through its army, its police and its officialdom, just as, in the past, the Mongol tyranny of Genghis Khan was maintained . . ." The famous terrorist Kravchinsky declared that the tsarist regime was "no longer a guardian of the will of the people, or of the majority of the people." It was "organized injustice," government by "brute force." He and many of the survivors of his generation concluded that "against such a government, everything is permitted."[38]

In the late seventies, all the alternatives seemed to involve violent action of one sort or another. Student demonstrations boiled out of the universities once more in the years 1876–78. They seized upon a famous funeral, or perhaps a death sentence, as the occasion for bursts of militance that often ended in bloody clashes with the law. In one wild street battle in Odessa, fatalities were reported.

In the underground, the so-called *buntari* ("fanatics"), sworn to a mass uprising or nothing, found support in Kiev, Kharkov, and elsewhere. The police broke up most of their plots before they could make any serious progress. In the particularly disgruntled Chigirin section, however, one young revolutionary had perhaps a thousand peasants organized and armed, mostly with "homemade pikes," before the law laid him and his comrades by the heels.

Violence began to play a part in the run-of-the-mill propaganda activities of the Land and Liberty Society. The "Disorganizing Section" began to find work to do. Embittered revolutionaries beat up suspected police agents or traitors in their midst. One or two were actually done away with, in the Nechayev tradition. Members of Land and Liberty began to resist arrest, even to engage in gun battles with the police who came for them. In one sensational case, an Odessa propagandist named Kovalsky defended his secret press with knife and gun, while comrades shouted out the windows, urging the gathering crowd to come to their rescue. The tendency to keep weapons about, and the tradition of not "going quietly," spread rapidly in the movement.

From such defensive tactics, it was a short step to aggressive terrorism, to the adoption of political assassination as a new weapon in the arsenal of the revolutionaries.

They argued about it, of course: Russian revolutionaries argued about everything. Some felt that terrorism, by bringing down redoubled police repression, would be too costly in personnel. The more orthodox socialists pointed out that the real target was private property; chipping away at the dictatorial political superstructure would have no effect on the capitalist economic foundations of the system. Some among them still felt a simple moral repugnance to murder, though as "realistic" rebels in the old nihilist tradition, they seldom raised this point.

But the pull of terrorism was far more visceral than intellectual. This aging generation needed to accomplish something concrete, to succeed at last. They had failed humiliatingly once too often. They had wept too many tears of helpless frustration at reports of the mistreatment of their comrades in the prisons of the Third Section. "Action," Kropotkin trumpeted, "is the imperative need of the hour!" [39] For it was violent action, the appeal to knives and guns and dynamite, that won them the attention, the headlines, the mingled fear and admiration that they so intensely needed after their years in limbo.

In the late seventies, then, the fighting groups formed—the Disorganizing Section of Land and Liberty, the Executive Committee of the People's Will. The darkly inspired individuals struck out: Vera Zasulich, for instance, had no orders from any secret society when she entered Trepov's office. The killing began, and with it the last stage in this escalating guerrilla war between insurrectionary youth and autocratic age.

A House of the Living Dead

Through 1878 and 1879, the revolutionary terror grew. The captain of the Kiev gendarmerie was stabbed to death on a street corner. The Governor-General of Kharkov was shot dead in his own carriage. In August, 1878, Sergei Kravchinsky, a twenty-six-year-old veteran of the *narodnik* crusade, of a wide variety of propaganda work, and of two foreign revolutions, walked up to General Mezentsov, the head of the Third Section itself, in a public square in St. Petersburg. Kravchinsky had a knife wrapped in a newspaper. He strolled past his intended victim, wheeled, and stabbed him in the back, twisting the blade with vigor before he pulled it out. Then he leaped into a carriage pulled by a horse well known for speed, and got clean away.

Shocking, but worse was yet to come. In April, 1879, a young man named Soloviev fired five shots at Tsar Alexander himself as he walked in the grounds of his own Winter Palace. The sixty-year-old emperor ran, dodging and weaving through the flower beds. Soloviev was caught and hanged, another Karakozov to add to the roll of martyrs.

The martyr roll was growing fast. The advent of premeditated terrorism was a deeply disturbing development; the government responded by sharply intensifying the repression. All political crimes were turned over to the military courts, which had the power to inflict the death penalty. Military governors were put in charge of Odessa, Kharkov, and other particularly infected areas. The use of "administrative decree" to punish revolutionaries without any court hearing at all became increasingly common. Eastern Siberia, an area seldom used for penal colonies in the past, was opened up to larger and larger numbers of politicals. And as a last resort, the government began to execute the terrorists. "Nihilists," as the popular press still called the revolutionaries, were hanged or shot for arming and organizing the peasantry, for armed resistance to arrest, for having dynamite in their possession, and in one case simply for propaganda work and financial backing of conspiratorial groups.

Hundreds of young people now found themselves sitting in five-foot cells staring at the walls. They had little to eat and no one to talk to, were charged with nothing, were interrogated only at intervals of months. There was little brutality: little was necessary. They were simply left in their solitary cells till their bodies bloated and disease found root, till their minds rotted to the edge of insanity, or until the creaky police bureaucracy got around to charging, convicting, and sentencing them to further punishment.

Hundreds more found themselves tramping the long road into

the Siberian wilderness. It was a thousand miles from the forwarding prison at Tomsk to the isolated penal colonies in Eastern Siberia—three weary months in leg irons and rough gray uniforms, fed on a few pennies a day, sleeping where they fell, or in jammed and fetid way stations. All to reach at last what Dostoyevsky had called "a house of the living dead"—a prison stockade in the primeval forest or on the empty tundra.[40] A low barracks with thirty men crammed together in noise and odor and airlessness. A narrow plank bed against the wall, inedible food, jeering criminals for comrades. And for many, hard labor too. An American who toured Siberia in the 1880's described convicts in the mines at Kara—many of them politicals—still wearing their leg irons, guarded by rifle-armed Cossacks, laboring through the dark, arctic days with crowbars and shovels in a frozen gravel pit.[41]

But whether they labored in the mines or merely stagnated in the wilderness, it was a wretched ending for any bright young Petersburg intellectual. A road that had begun in all-night student arguments and high idealism was ending in the brutalized, soul-destroying existence of Siberian exile.

For some few, the story of their lives had a still more unbelievable conclusion. An occasional erratically chosen martyr actually found himself jouncing dazedly across a crowded city square in an open prison cart, mounted Cossacks before and behind, a sign that said "State Criminal" around his neck, and the public gibbet looming up before him. He tried perhaps to shout some carefully conned, now half-remembered inspirational remarks, and was drowned out by the roll of drums and the noise of the close-pressing mob. He stood quietly then—there was nothing else to do—while his sentence was read and other last-minute preparations made. He felt the enveloping canvas robe thrust suddenly over his head, covering him in a shapeless white sack from head to foot. He felt the rough noose slipped deftly into place, the hemp knot hard against his ear. He had one last glimpse of the wooden platform, the vertical lances of the Cossacks, the faces of the people staring up at him in their suddenly silent thousands, the façades of buildings, and the open sky beyond.

There was no drop to speak of; the prisoner choked to death. The observant author of a French travel book who saw such an execution said the arms and legs jerked and flailed beneath the white canvas cloak for more than eleven minutes before the black-faced corpse was still, turning slowly, swaying slightly on the cord.[42]

The spiral of force and counterforce surged toward its final crest. Only one counterstroke now remained to the young revolutionaries.

On August 26, 1879, more than a year and a half after Vera Zasulich had fired the first terrorist pistol shot, the Executive Committee of the People's Will Society "sentenced" Tsar Alexander II to death for his crimes against the people.

4. *THE CRIME OF THE CENTURY*

The People's Will

The leaders of the People's Will were a striking group of revolutionaries. There was, for example, Alexander Mikhailov, the organizing brain, puritanical, business-like, meticulously security conscious. Efficiency, organization, and centralized control were his ideals. On his wall was a single motto: "Do not forget your duty." [43]

There was Nikolai Kibalchich, the bomb-maker. Kibalchich was a priest's son and an engineering student, brilliant, multilingual, dedicated to science. He had been converted to the cause of violent revolution after spending three years in prison for the crime of handing a forbidden book to an illiterate peasant.

Above all, there was the unlikely duo of Andrei Zhelyabov and Sophia Perovskaya. Zhelyabov was the son of a serf; Sophia Perovskaya was a daughter of the aristocracy. They met in prison, fellow martyrs to the cause of peasant liberation. Their lives together became the great romance of Russian revolutionary history. Their hands, more than any other's, guided the last campaign against the tsar.

Zhelyabov was one of those children of the lower orders who became increasingly prominent during the final stage of the *narodnik* generation's development. His story was typical. The offspring of a family of Crimean serfs, he had been admitted to the University of Odessa under the new, liberal policy of Alexander II's early years—and expelled soon thereafter for participating in a student demonstration. He had been swept up in the "To the People" movement, and had been imprisoned for his part therein. A person of no particular importance in the movement, he had emerged as a leader only after he had agreed to join the last great effort against the life of the tsar.

Zhelyabov was a big, full-bearded man, an indefatigable worker, a magnetic personality. He was given to vigorously optimistic maxims like: "History moves too slowly. It needs a push." [44] His fellow conspirators depended on his bluff confidence more than they knew —until he was gone.

Sophia Perovskaya was the delicately nurtured daughter of a former governor-general of St. Petersburg—an authoritarian, embittered man whom she detested. Elegant, slightly built, and slim, she had been arrested three times already for preaching sedition to the lower orders. In appearance, she was a workman's wife, her gentle breeding buried in a plain cotton dress, babushka, and no-nonsense man's boots. She tended to be realistic about the pace of history, which Zhelyabov seemed so confident of accelerating. For all their pushing, she declared, the revolution "will take two generations, and few of the terrorists will see it—but it will happen." [45] Yet she was a fanatically militant slip of a girl, tirelessly urging her comrades to action and more action.

These oddly mismatched lovers and comrades were both just over thirty in 1881—typical of the slightly older youth leader, many of whose troops were a good ten years younger than he. They represented that familiar phenomenon, the idealistic revolutionary driven to violence by his elders' obstinate refusal to make way for the new dispensation.

Their chosen weapon was dynamite. Guns had failed Karakosov and Soloviev in their attempts to kill the tsar. There was no chance of getting close enough to use a knife, as Kravchinsky had on the chief of the Third Section. So it was with high explosives, a weapon suitable in scale to so great a man as the emperor, that the People's Will hunted their anointed ruler.

They tried twice to dynamite the imperial train. They planted explosives under streets and bridges his majesty was expected to pass over. Each time, something went wrong. Sometimes the dynamite failed to explode. Sometimes the tsar did not show up.

In February of 1880, an agent of the People's Will planted large quantities of explosives in the Winter Palace itself, beneath the emperor's dining room. The blast shook the capital. Some fifty-six people were injured and eleven killed, most of them soldiers of the guard. But the tsar, who had been late for dinner, was unharmed.

The Bomb on the Catherine Canal

In 1880, Alexander made a final effort to return to the liberalism of his early years and to defuse the terrorist menace with a single bold stroke.

The "Dictatorship of the Heart" was an interim regime headed by Count Loris-Melikov, a moderate-minded administrator and a war hero. It was the best possible ploy under the deteriorating circumstances. There would be a warm hand henceforth for liberals—and an iron fist for revolutionaries. The uneasy alliance between the two groups, already badly weakened by the dynamite horrors, would be shattered, the terrorists left to face their fate alone.

At Loris-Melikov's orders, two young men caught in no more dangerous an activity than passing out subversive leaflets from an underground press were summarily hanged. Under his insistent urging, the security of the People's Will was broken wide open; its leaders began to be arrested. At the same time, some political prisoners were freed, censorship was eased, and the reactionary minister of education was dismissed. Most important of all, at least in its potential, was the so-called "Loris-Melikov Constitution." Had it been implemented, this document would have established an imperial advisory commission on reforms, a purely consultative body, of course—some of whose members would have been elected by a heavily class-weighted suffrage. It was a long way from parliamentary democracy, but it might have been a first step.

Alexander II signed a declaration of his intent to promulgate such a "constitution" for his people on the morning of March 1, 1881, just before he left the palace to attend a military review. It was a bright, snowy Sunday in the capital, and it was his regular practice to review the troops on Sunday afternoons. His wife of a few months urged him to avoid the crowded Nevsky Prospekt and go by the road along the Catherine Canal instead. It was a narrower street, little used, flanked by the canal and a walled garden; only government buildings overlooked it.

The tsar was apparently quite cheerful, feeling that he had taken a giant step in the right direction. He agreed to the tsarina's request as to the road he should take to and from the parade ground.

By the winter of 1880–81, the Executive Committee was only a tattered remnant. Mikhailov the organizer, usually so conscious of security, had imprudently left photos of two martyred comrades at a studio. When he called for them, he was taken into custody. Zhelyabov himself, working frantically, laughing too loudly, sometimes seeming almost in a trance, was clearly no longer the man he had been. He stopped by a friend's apartment one evening for a rare moment of relaxation; the police were waiting for him.

The remaining leaders knew it was only a matter of time before they, too, fell into the hands of their enemies. But Kibalchich had devised some new hand bombs to supplement the current mining operation. And Sophia Perovskaya, numb but determined, stepped into Zhelyabov's shoes as field commander of the operation. They were up all night long, fifteen hours straight, in a mood of near hysteria, pouring powder into their homemade hand grenades.

When the emperor set out that Sunday noon, there were four bomb-throwers in the field, and the Nevsky Prospekt itself was mined. Two of the young terrorists were waiting for him when he came back from the review, his carriage flanked by an honor guard of Cossacks, down the snowy road along the Catherine Canal.

A nineteen-year-old artisan named Rysakov, who had fallen under the spell of Zhelyabov's powerful personality, threw the first bomb. It exploded under the rear axle of the tsar's carriage, bringing down a mounted Cossack and terribly injuring a baker's boy who had stopped to watch the imperial cortege pass by. Horrified guardsmen quickly laid hands upon the bomb-thrower, while the carriage careened to a stop some distance down the road. The tsar emerged, apparently uninjured, from the damaged vehicle.

The emperor walked briskly back to the site of the explosion. He spoke sharply to the prisoner, looked compassionately at the injured. Yellow sulphur smoke still hovered in the air, and a small crowd was gathering. The tsar's security people urged him to hurry on, to get away at once. The mangled baker's boy was screaming all the time.

Tsar Alexander passed close by a young man leaning on the railing overlooking the canal. A faintly smiling, round-faced youth with a big fur hat and an awkward parcel in his hands—one of Kibalchich's five-pound hand grenades. The young man's name—for those last few seconds—was Grinevitsky, son of a small landowner, former engineering student. "I stand now with one foot in the grave," he had written soon after arising that morning. "History shows that the luxurious tree of freedom needs blood to quicken its roots." [46]

Grinevitsky flung the bomb at the tsar's feet from a range of perhaps six feet. A gout of flame and smoke and flying snow enveloped both the emperor and his assassin.

Through the thinning yellowish haze, Alexander became visible again, half-sitting against the railed parapet, his legs shattered, covered with blood. His anonymous young assassin lay close by, face down, also a welter of blood. Around them, some twenty others, dead or dying, lay scattered in the trampled snow.

Colonel Dvorzhitzky, the tsar's equerry, lying stunned and bleeding in the snow close by his master, heard Alexander speak. The voice was faint and blurred with shock, half-murmuring: "So cold . . . Help . . ." Moments later, as his grief-stricken brother, the Grand Duke Michael, knelt beside him, the emperor whispered his last royal order. "Home to the palace," he said in a barely audible voice, "to die there." [47]

The life of Alexander II flickered out in the Winter Palace about three-thirty that afternoon.

A dedicated young revolutionary named Vera Figner—a former populist who had once wept at the sight of the misery of the peasants—carried the news of their success home to what remained of the People's Will:

> I wept [she remembered many years later], many of us wept; that heavy nightmare which for ten years had strangled young Russia before our very eyes, had been brought to an end; the horrors of prison and exile, the violence, the executions . . . all were atoned for by this blood of the tsar shed by our hands. Now reaction must come to an end and give place to a new Russia. In this solemn moment, all our thoughts centered in the hope for a better future for our country.[48]

The Road to Revolution

What happened was very different, of course, and quite predictable to any but this messianic youth.

The official announcement of the emperor's death blamed the assassination on "the sacrilegious band . . . calling themselves nihilists . . ." Pobedonostsev, Procurator of the Holy Synod and strong man of the new reign, bitterly condemned "these adolescents and young men with subversive ideas . . . men dominated by the savage instinct for destruction . . ." Even comparatively liberal foreigners like the British, who twenty years before had had nothing but sympathy for the university rebels of 1861, condemned "this awful, unspeakable crime" as the work of "sinister maniacs." [49]

To the older generation of afflicted Russians, this was the final fruit of that youthful nihilism which they had condemned from the beginning. The reign of Alexander III, which began when his father breathed his last ragged breath that Sunday afternoon, was to vie with Nicholas I's as the most reactionary of the century.

The remnants of the populist-terrorist generation were quickly rounded up. Sophia Perovskaya was captured ten days after the assassination, Kibalchich a week later. Grinevitsky died only a few hours after his victim, without revealing so much as his name. Rysakov, the other bomb-thrower, confessed everything he knew, and wrote out reams of depositions implicating his comrades in the movement. Many others were hunted down, some guilty and some innocent, by a secret police now desperate to prove its competence.

Zhelyabov, Sophia Perovskaya, Kibalchich, and the two surviving bomb-throwers were tried and convicted within a month. On April 3, 1881, they were hanged in a public square in St. Petersburg, while some eighty thousand of the Russian people they had tried to liberate looked on. They mounted the scaffold with courage, embraced each other, and died unrepentant.

There had, of course, been no revolutionary upheaval on Alexander II's death. Many thousands of the peasantry had, in fact, passed reverently by the bier where the tsar emancipator lay in state, "making the sign of the cross and bowing." [50] Their open *muzhik* faces—especially, one of the honor guard remembered, the wrinkled faces of the old—were often full of grief.

The youth of the 1860's and 1870's were old men and women

themselves when the revolutions of 1905 and 1917 first shook, and finally toppled, the crumbling edifice of tsardom. But their contributions to the Russian revolutionary tradition, which thus bore fruit, were everywhere apparent in these two twentieth-century revolts.

The nihilists and the *narodniki* had not brought Marxism to Russia—that was left for the 1890's to do. But they had brought materialism, revolutionary socialism, and the notion of the Party as the vanguard of the people. They had developed the basic structure and most of the tactics of the Russian underground: cells and central committees, the underground press, agitation among peasantry and the working classes generally, political terrorism, and the dream of a mass uprising. They had taken an opposition movement that was little more than the drawing room conversation of enlightened aristocratic dilettantes and made it the business of hard-boiled, professional revolutionaries. The passionate extremism of these generations—sometimes saintly, sometimes brutal—had set Russia on the road to revolution.

Part III

THE GROWTH OF THE YOUTH REVOLUTION

7

"Youth! Youth! There Is Absolutely Nothing in the World but Youth!" *
Fin-de-Siècle *Youth in Ferment*
Europe, 1900

The nineteenth century saw the birth of the Youth Revolution. During that first hundred years after the Industrial and Democratic Revolutions, and the concomitant rise of literacy and leisure, all the main lines of the multifaceted revolt of the younger generation were laid down. Youthful ideological commitment and rejection of the adult world, student militance and Bohemian withdrawal, all were commonplace by the time the century turned.

New crusades would appear after 1900, of course, and new forms of alienation and rebellion among the young. But the fundamental patterns had been established. What, the historian is almost moved to ask, remained for the twentieth century to accomplish?

What remained was the fantastic growth and spread of the Youth Revolution. As the pace of economic and social change picked up around the world, as education spread, as unparalleled wars and rumors of wars, depression and unexampled affluence succeeded one another with bewildering rapidity, the conflict of generations leaped from class to class and continent to continent. Born in a handful of materially and ideologically developed European countries in the last century, the ongoing revolt of the younger generation would spread to every corner of the world before the present century was out.

It is this phenomenal *growth* of youthful disaffection with the modern world that will be chronicled in the next half-dozen chapters.

* Oscar Wilde, *The Picture of Dorian Gray* (London and New York, 1907), p. 48.

The great acceleration of the Youth Revolution was clear enough, even at the turn of the century. The years 1890–1914—oddly misnamed the "gay nineties"—and the tense years before World War I saw an unprecedented ferment of youth movements in politics, youthful schools of art and literature, and other ideological crusades that made a special appeal to the young. The younger generation was up in arms, not just in this country or that, but all across the Continent.

There was the *Wandervogel* movement in Germany—in some ways a remarkable prefiguring of the American hippie movement of the 1960's. The revolutionary generation of Lenin surged to the fore in tsarist Russia, building blindly toward the holocaust of 1917. Bohemia frothed and rollicked on in the Paris of Toulouse-Lautrec. Fabian socialists, militant feminists, and decadent young aesthetes pursued their radically divergent courses in the England of Victoria's declining years. Young Wales agitated for home rule, and the youthful Irish poet Yeats urged his contemporaries to rediscover the beauties of the Celtic twilight while they prepared their own demands for freedom now.

The demands of new generations were heard even on the far fringes of Europe. The Young Czechs pressed ever more militantly for autonomy in the superannuated empire of the Habsburgs, while Young Poland drowned its helpless bitterness against Romanov Russia in an ardent neo-romantic revival. The Spanish "generation of '98" fumbled its way toward new meanings in life and literature, and Futurism stirred the souls of young Italians. Far to the south and east, nationalistic student groups agitated in such unheard-of Balkan backwaters as Bosnia and Belgrade. On the very edge of Asia, the Young Turks—successors to the Young Ottomans of the later nineteenth century—labored to drag their collapsing country kicking and screaming into the modern world.

As the younger generation became increasingly visible, the West became more and more conscious of "the youth." G. Stanley Hall discovered adolescence as a stage of life in the nineties, and Freud presented his shocking theory of Oedipal conflict between fathers and sons soon thereafter. Writers as diverse as Oscar Wilde and A. E. Housman glorified youth, and *Bildungsromanen* like Joyce's *A Portrait of the Artist as a Young Man* became literary staples. Youth was everywhere in evidence, milling, turbulent, full of new ideas, and noisily discontented with the state of their parents' world.

As it happened, there was plenty to be discontented with in *fin-de-siècle* Europe.

1. *THE PROUD TOWER UNDER SIEGE*

A Smug, Successful Century

Looking back from beyond the carnage of the Great War, many people saw the decades around 1900 as a golden age, "misted over by a lovely sunset haze of peace and security." Those were the "Banquet Years," the Gilded Age, the *Belle Époque*. But, as Barbara Tuchman points out in her lush evocation of that vanished world before the wars, "it did not seem so golden when they were in the midst of it." [1]

It was the end of a smug, successful century. The solid older citizen of "1900 yesterday" could look back on a time of peace, prosperity, and growing power unparalleled in European history.[2] He must have been more than a little puzzled that the younger generation did not look with similar pride on all that had been done since Waterloo.

The century of relative peace that stretched from 1815 to 1914 was probably the longest span of minimal hostilities in Europe since the days of the Roman Empire. There had been wars, of course, but they had been for the most part short, and comparatively bloodless. Summer wars, six-week wars—the kind of *Blitzkrieg* Bismarck's generals were so good at engineering. Nothing on the scale of the Napoleonic Wars or World War I, the two holocausts that bounded this vast tract of Victorian peace. Britain ruled the waves, and the concert of nations seemed to have found a fundamental harmony in the affairs of states. International law, international business, the balance of power, the peace conferences that met so hopefully at the Hague—there were many who looked at these things and opined that peace was here to stay, that great wars were a thing of the past.

Prosperity also was a glittering reality for larger and larger numbers of Europeans. The Industrial Revolution, well past its painful take-off phase in most of the great powers, was raining unparalleled quantities of goods and services upon technology's favored children. Steel kings and coal barons lived in gilded palaces and dined out in splendor. The middle classes dressed their wives in moderate style and read the *Times* in comfort behind their solid brownstone fronts. Even the working man—the skilled worker, at least—was gaining the right to unionize and vote, and sometimes had a few *sous* or *pfennige* or pence left over for beer and tobacco of a Saturday night.

Peace, prosperity—and power. Europe in 1900 was, in a very real sense, the master of the globe. The "New Imperialism" of the late nineteenth century had, in less than the span of a single generation, chopped up Africa into colonies and Asia into "spheres of influence." Americans and Russians rolled west and east respectively, across the great plains of North America and the wastes of Siberia, carrying their dominion to the Pacific. The little island of Great Britain ruled a quarter of the world. Manchus and fuzzy-wuzzies, Apaches and Kalmucks, all bowed—or went down—before the new weaponry of a technological age. For one giddy moment, Western man was the undisputed master of the globe.

Who could reject such a heritage?

The Madman of Weimar

Many people could, apparently. People like the vocal idealists who denounced imperialism and condemned British excesses in the Boer War as vehemently as their descendants would condemn American intervention in Vietnam. People like the hordes of blue-collar workers who responded to a continuing down-swing in the European economy by pouring into Marxist political parties during the 1890's. People like the anarchists, who threw bombs into restaurants and crowded theaters, police stations and parliaments, and assassinated half a dozen kings, presidents, and prime ministers during the twenty years before World War I. People like the ideologically oriented youth in many lands who were stirred by these and other currents of revolt to take actions of their own scarcely less idealistic, extreme, and sometimes violent.

A prime cause of the alienation of the young seems to have been a feeling of hypocrisy, a sense of having been deceived. There was an inner fraudulence about those years to which the young seemed particularly sensitive.

Granted that few people starved to death in Europe anymore—but why should *anyone* have to struggle through life in the squalor of London's East End, or the slums of Paris or St. Petersburg, while a pampered few lived like Oriental potentates? Were the teeming masses of Asia and Africa really lesser breeds without the law—or was Tahiti, say, a far pleasanter place for a man like Gauguin to spend his life than some smoky, malodorous European metropolis? Was peace assured—or did the intensifying series of international confrontations that began in Morocco in 1905 presage a catastrophic conflict in the offing?

Something, so significant segments of the youth of many lands believed, was decidedly rotten somewhere in *fin-de-siècle* Europe. It showed in countless ways as the old century passed away and the new one came ominously on. A paralyzing dock strike in Britain; a devastating famine in Russia; the shocking "Panama scandal" that reached to the highest levels of French finance and government; the sensational trials of Oscar Wilde and Captain Dreyfus, which kept London agog for months, and divided all France throughout the later nineties; the stunning defeats of Spain by the United States in 1898 and Russia by Japan in 1905—first intimations that Europe's monopoly of power might not last forever.

Wealth that was built on poverty—imperial power that was more exploitation than *mission civilisatrice*—peace that was crumbling away even as the century turned. And among young people everywhere, the feeling that they had been duped. What had the dear father tsar done for his starving peasants, after all? What, for that matter, had the right to vote done for the East End? In Berlin, the stucco was already flaking off the fine new monuments to Bismarck's victories. In Paris, the nation of Voltaire and the Rights of Man was tearing itself apart trying to send a Jew to Devil's Island.

Victorian sentimentality tasted cloyingly saccharine to the new generations. The patriotic music had a brassy sound, and there was a smell of stale cigar smoke in the back rooms of the parliaments. The youthful revolutionary hunched over his dynamite and clockwork. The young *décadent* bent to his verses and his absinthe. They agreed on one thing only: beneath the continuing bustle of progress, there was a stench of corruption, an odor of decay.

The century turned. Europe rumbled down the road to the abyss.

In Weimar, Friedrich Nietzsche slouched in his shirt sleeves, staring with brooding eyes out over his huge mustache. Antichrist, idol-smasher, philosopher with a hammer, he had been hopelessly insane for a long decade when the old century expired. There were still places in the Europe of 1900—as Hermann Hesse noted in a youthful autobiographical novel—where it was possible to pass for educated "without knowing the speeches in *Zarathustra*." [3] But in Berlin, in Paris, in Madrid, wherever young minds quickened to new ideas in that mythical 1900 yesterday, the madman of Weimar was the prophet of the hour.

2. *AFTER US THE SAVAGE GOD*

Chocolate at the Moulin Rouge

The first night of *Ubu Roi*—December 11, 1896—made the first night of *Hernani* look like a picnic. Bohemia had come a long way in sixty-six years.

Alfred Jarry, the putative author, sat on the stage and lectured the audience about his play for awhile before the curtain went up.[4] Jarry was one of the uncrowned kings of the Left Bank: a stunted clown in a floor-length cape, a frilly woman's blouse, and a stovepipe hat, his face was painted chalk white, his long hair plastered down. He spoke in a weird mechanical voice, like an automaton. He lived in a colorful slum and was famous for his crude practical jokes (there were those who said that *Ubu Roi* was one of them). Jarry was twenty-three in 1896: in the course of the next decade, he would drift to the edge of madness and finally—like Toulouse-Lautrec—drink himself to death on absinthe and raw ether. He was one of the genuine culture heroes of the nineties, admired and imitated by half the young men in Bohemia.

Sitting on the stage that night before an excited crowd of friends and enemies, Alfred Jarry orated vaguely about marionettes and masks and the setting of the play—in Poland, that is, Nowhere, since Poland had long since been partitioned off the map of Europe. He called the audience's attention to the set, which he himself had helped to paint:

> You will see doors open on fields of snow under blue skies, fireplaces furnished with clocks and swinging wide to serve as doors, and palm trees growing at the foot of a bed so that little elephants standing on bookshelves can browse on them.[5]

Finally the chalk-faced little man skipped off the stage, the curtain rose, and King Ubu himself—a grotesquely padded, pear-shaped monstrosity—stepped forward to begin the play.

"Merdre!" he said: "Shit!" [6]

After that, it was *Hernani* all over again—*Hernani* and worse. It took fifteen minutes to quiet the audience enough to get on to the second line. People booed and hissed, clapped and cheered. There were fist fights in the orchestra. Some people, apparently unable to make up their minds how they felt about it, booed and clapped at the same time. The young Yeats, who spoke no French, was in the audience that night, and he probably got as much out of it as anyone:

> The players are supposed to be dolls, toys, marionettes, and now they are all hopping like wooden frogs, and I can see for myself that the chief personage, who is some kind of King, carries for Sceptre a brush of the kind that we use to clean a [water] closet.[7]

Young partisans of the piece hailed it for its "triumphant verve" and "superb buffoonery," seeing King Ubu as the incarnation of "all the grossness, the falseness, and the self-interested egoism" of the "vulgar bourgeois soul." It was clearly a deliberate assault on bourgeois sensibilities by the young "curly-haired aesthetes" of the Latin Quarter. A friendly critic—there were a few by this time—saw the nihilistic thrust of the piece, the hints of worse to come: "From this enormous figure of Ubu," he wrote, "blows the wind of destruction, the breath of contemporary youth which demolishes all traditional reverences . . ." Yeats cheered at the play, but he felt oddly melancholy that night, alone in his hotel room: "what more is possible?" he meditated. "After us the Savage God." [8]

Others of that famous first-night audience did not retire so early, or in so melancholy a mood. In the Paris of the Moulin Rouge and the Montmartre cabarets, where Aristide Bruant sang and Jane

Avril danced and "Chocolate," the black circus clown, entertained the patrons at the Irish and American Bar, there was always something to do after the show. Bohemian cafés and clubs abounded by this time—the notorious *Hippophage* Club, the Lapin Agile, the café Procope, and after the turn of the century the famous *Closerie des Lilas* which was mentioned in Baedeker's and became a tourist attraction even before the war. For many youthful denizens of the *quartier,* however, the evening typically ended in some less elegant bistro—something more on the order of Van Gogh's bare and bilious "Café at Arles," a shuddering little world of trembling lights and absinthe greens, all slouchy and askew, funneling finally into darkness and a gin-soaked table top.

This was the crowded street life of the turn of the century. A world of music halls and dance halls, cafés, bars, and brothels, of artistic anarchy and human misery, where desperate generations seemed to be trying their hardest to "destroy everything in themselves that might be of use to society." [9]

Guitars on the Roads of Germany

It was a life style that was no longer limited to Paris.

In London, Yeats himself attended the nightly soirees of the Rhymer's Club, a circle of self-styled "decadents" who met to argue over their wine at the Cheshire Cheese, an ancient, sand-floored restaurant in the Strand. More decorous gatherings than those of the Paris *Hippophages,* apparently. But Yeats himself characterized his contemporaries as "the Tragic Generation," and a considerable number of these devotees of the perverse drawings of Aubrey Beardsley did sink into drink and Continental-style dissipation. Many—like Beardsley—died young.

In Madrid, the new generation thronged the *Café de Madrid* or the *Café Ingles,* labored over journals like *The Spanish Soul* and *Youth* (Picasso was the artistic director), and argued far into the night over "the essential problem of this generation: Spain." [10] The youth of the *Café de Madrid* had grown up with a "golden legend" of Spain's ancient greatness, of the Catholic Kings and the conquistadors, only to be confronted with brute reality in 1898. Spain's catastrophic defeat at the hands of the United States shattered Spanish dreams of glory, stripped the country of her last vestiges of empire, and plunged her most sensitive youth into vales of despair. These Spanish "ninety-eighters" hailed the iconoclastic Nietzsche as the "ideological guide of this generation," marched on the halls of government to declare themselves "anarchists," and lost themselves nightly in the audacious rhythms of the dark-eyed dancer, Chelito, whose throbbing undulations epitomized for them the spirit of a decadent age.[11]

The German youth movement, perhaps the largest and most famous of all, followed a very different pattern.

The second half of the nineteenth century had seen German national unification, German military and diplomatic ascendancy, and the growth of an industrial powerhouse that challenged even Great Britain's. But the younger generation had no feel for these material triumphs. They shrugged off the "plush-upholstered comfort and respectability of the nineties" and turned their earnest attention to the realm of values instead. And here they found their elders totally lacking. For them, "parental religion was largely a sham, politics boastful and trivial, economics unscrupulous and deceitful," and the vaunted German educational system "stereotyped and lifeless," stifling the young psyche with cut-and-dried lectures and narrow specialization.[12]

Over against the strident materialism of the German present, the new generation set a gentle legend of the German past—a myth that had been fed to them since nursery days in pictures, songs, and stories. They harked back to the half-remembered *Biedermeier* time, "the dear dead days beyond recall," when family ties were close, when village life was still pure and unspoiled, and when romantic poets still wandered the dusty lanes of a simpler, greener land.[13] It was in a half-conscious attempt to recover those lost values of personal freedom, closeness to nature, and almost mystical *Gemeinschaft* and togetherness, that the *Wandervögel*—the "Wandering Birds"—came into existence in the years around 1900.

The *Wandervogel* movement was a youthful effort "to create an empirical environment in which their own value systems actually operate[d]," a "retreat from adult culture" that was "secessionist rather than direct actionist" in form.[14] It thus constituted—despite its obvious differences from the big-city Bohemias—a clear generational counter culture of the sort that has become so familiar over the last century and a half.

The Wandering Birds were bands of teen-age schoolboys—and later girls as well—who tramped the German countryside dressed in picturesque costumes, strumming guitars, singing folk songs, cooking over campfires, sleeping in barns or open fields. Sometimes they wandered as far as the Black Forest or the mountains of Bohemia, or even into foreign lands. Their rambling journeys gave them a great sense of renewed contact with Old Germany, the Germany of rolling pastures and hillsides ablaze with broom, of dark oak and evergreen forests, mossy rocks and trickling streams; the Germany of smiling girls in kerchief and dirndl, of peasants who still had time for a cheerful *"Grüss Gott"* when they passed you in the lane.[15]

There was a "romantic exaltation" in those long nights around the open fire, in the singing and the laughing, the comradely frankness and the closeness of experiences shared. Homosexual relations sometimes grew out of it: in many more cases, the *Wandervögel* provided a less intense but equally real escape from the inhuman efficiency and rigid formality of life in Wilhelmine Germany.[16]

The Revolt against Reason

There were ideas in plenty behind all this youthful Bohemianism, of course. There was the fundamental anti-bourgeois sentiment that had been part of the youth revolt from the beginning. There were the fecund influences of particular minds and works of art: Nietzsche's poetic apocalypses, for instance, or Huysman's perverse novel, *Against Nature (À Rebours),* and all the other seminal works of the avant-garde artists and Symbolist writers of the 1870's and 1880's.

One survey of the youthful literary schools of turn-of-the-century Paris alone discussed half a dozen *-isms* at some length—Simultanism, Impulsionism, Synchronism, Futurism, Paroxysm, and, unlikely as it may seem, Metabolism.[17] A similar tally of insurrectionary schools of art would be at least as long, including Cubism, Futurism in the visual arts, early Expressionism, the New Art *(Art Nouveau),* the Young Art *(Junge Kunst),* the Wild Beasts *(Fauves),* the Bridge, and the Blue Rider. Like rock groups in the 1960's, the turn-of-the-century *-isms* went in for colorful labels.

There is, however, an underlying oneness to all these turbulent withdrawals of the young, a common element that links these generations with their predecessors of the Romantic period and with their beat-hippie-existentialist descendants in our own time.

Historians often speak of a resurgence of romanticism at the end of the nineteenth century. Certainly the romantic concern with the emotions, from Wagner's stentorian enthusiasms to the refined sensibilities of Huysman's Des Esseintes, is evident in the later decades of the century. And if Freud was no romantic, the effect of his work was clearly to elevate the nonrational faculties to a new level of scientific validity.

A renewed passion for the mystic and the metaphysical was also self-evident in *fin-de-siècle* Europe—for truths that lay beyond the reach of reason. From Bergson on the level of high philosophy to Madame Blavatsky on the level of table-rapping and ouija boards, there was a new concern for the world of the spirit, the invisible realm that can only be known through intuition, poetic vision, or perhaps even religious ecstasy. Even the most hardheaded social scientists of the 1890's were "obsessed, almost intoxicated, with a rediscovery of the nonlogical . . . the inexplicable." [18]

It is sometimes called anti-intellectualism, irrationalism, or nonrationalism. Stuart Hughes puts it in a significant perspective for the Youth Revolution when he calls it a "revolt against positivism." [19] By which was meant—to break free at last from this tangle of *-isms* —a revolt against the claims of the empirical scientists to a monopoly on knowledge. There is—there must be—more to life than the materialistic, mechanistic men of science tell us, many thoughtful men of the late nineteenth century insisted. The youth emphatically agreed.

The penchant of the French *Fauves* and the German Expressionists for spilling their emotions across the canvas; the fertile despair of the Spanish "generation of '98" and the mystical absorption of the *Wandervögel* in nature and themselves; the Futurist passion for pure speed—the essence of the modern age, to be understood only with the nerve ends; the monstrous figure of Ubu himself, one of the grossest projections of pure id ever put upon the stage—all these reveal the younger generation's rejection of reason, their turning toward the emotions for salvation.

The metaphysical quest was equally strong among the ideologically oriented young. The Symbolist disciples of Mallarmé sought to reach the Absolute through words; the Cubists sought it through geometric forms. English decadents were notorious backsliders into Roman Catholicism, and Yeats groped his way through the Celtic twilight from Theosophy to Magic. In France, after 1905, Bergsonian metaphysics reigned supreme among young intellectuals, and the sons of the Dreyfusards became ardent champions of the Church. Beneath the veneer of absinthe and iconoclasm, in short, there was a renewed longing for the Absolute among the Bohemian youth of Europe.

It was a passion that baffled their elders, converts to Darwinism and dutiful admirers of each new technological marvel as it came out of the laboratory and off the assembly line (electric lights now, and horseless carriages). But it was a longing that would be echoed by many later generations of Zen seekers and followers of the Maharishi, of consciousness-expanding acid trippers and smiling Jesus freaks.

3. *WE THE YOUNGEST MUST MAKE A NEW HISTORY*

Djugashvili Has a Ticket to the Library!

There were those among the younger generation, however, who saw the pursuit of the Absolute as something less than essential. Were there no more immediate concerns, the militants demanded, in a Europe where most people were still poor, where whole nationalities languished in bondage, where fundamentally illiberal regimes continued to be more the rule than the exception?

Young Russian radicals, for example, never seemed to learn the futility of rebelling against the *status quo*.

"It appears," one of the monkish instructors at the Tiflis Theological Seminary noted in the Conduct Book on a November day in 1896, "that Djugashvili has a ticket to the Cheap [Lending] Library, from which he borrows books." "Confine him to the punishment cell for a prolonged period," the principal responded primly. "I have already warned him once about an unsanctioned book, *Ninety-Three* by Victor Hugo."[20] Nineteen-year-old Joseph Djugashvili was, in fact, caught reading such forbidden fare by candlelight in the dormitory, or behind the hymnbooks in chapel, no less than thirteen times in four months. He seemed incorrigible.

The grim, four-story seminary in the rapidly industrializing, south Russian city of Tiflis was used to student militants, however. Few students really enjoyed the school: "Locked in day and night within barrack walls," one of them recalled, "we felt like prisoners who must spend years there without being guilty of anything."[21] The year before Djugashvili matriculated, there had been a student strike, and eighty-seven students had been expelled. Ten years earlier, a seminarian thrown out for radical agitating had responded by assassinating the principal. The Tiflis Seminary seemed to be graduating more revolutionaries than priests.

Djugashvili, as it happened, was a more dangerous firebrand than the monks realized. He soon passed from Hugo's novel of the century-old French Revolution to socialist visions of the Russian Revolution yet to come. He was admitted to a circle of student radicals and began to slip out of the seminary after curfew to indoctrinate the weavers, printers, shoemakers, and horsecar drivers of Tiflis. He spent many long hours in dimly lit tenement rooms, crowded with men, reeking of sweat, tobacco, and boiled cabbage, laboring to kindle class-consciousness in Russia's new proletariat.

Djugashvili, a lean, slow-speaking, arrogant youth, found it increasingly hard to be an obedient student by day and a revolutionary agitator after hours. At the end of September, 1898, the monkish hand rasped irritably across the page of the Conduct Book: "At nine P.M. a group of students gathered in the dining hall around Joseph Djugashvili, who read them out of books not sanctioned by the Seminary authorities, in view of which the students were searched [for further literary contraband]." And again the following month: "in the course of a search of students . . . Joseph Djugashvili tried several times to enter into an argument . . . expressing dissatisfaction with the repeated searches. . . . Djugashvili is generally disrespectful and rude toward persons in authority . . ."[22]

Obviously, Djugashvili had to go: there was no place for trouble-makers like this in any Russian institution of higher learning. In the spring of 1899, the young student activist was peremptorily expelled for failing to submit to his examinations.

From that point on, his story was typical enough of his time and generation: the underground, arrest, Siberia, repeated escapes and reimprisonments. Along the way, he gave up the mouth-filling moniker his parents had saddled him with and adopted a series of catchier pseudonyms: "Koba" for awhile, and then "Ivanovich." He finally settled on "Stalin."

Vladimir and Nadya

They met at a *bliny* (pancake) party in St. Petersburg one spring night in 1894 and strolled home together afterward along the banks of the Neva. Not a very prepossessing couple, really. He was an apprentice lawyer, twenty-four, stocky, prematurely balding, with flattened, vaguely Tartar features, "a scanty reddish beard" and "squinting eyes [that] peered slyly from under his brows." [23] She was a schoolteacher, a year older than he, tall and plain, carelessly dressed in the venerable *nigilistka* tradition, short hair drawn tight in a bun behind her head. The sort of couple that might do for a genre *Marty*-style love story, perhaps—certainly nothing more glamorous.

Yet there was something about this Vladimir Ilyich, Nadya thought, as she strolled beside him along the river, listening to his quick, serious talk. Something aggressive, self-confident—and excitingly militant—that had aroused her instant admiration. Many years later, she remembered one remark of his in particular that had quickened her interest at that pre-Lent pancake party—really little more than a front for a Marxist meeting—where they had met:

> Someone was saying—I think it was Shevyagin—that what was important was to work in the Committee for Illiteracy. Vladimir Ilyich laughed, and somehow his laughter sounded laconic. . . . "Well," he said, "if anyone wants to save the fatherland in the Committee for Illiteracy, we won't stop him." [24]

Since Nadya, like hundreds of other young socialists in St. Petersburg in the 1890's, was deeply involved in night schools, Sunday schools, and other efforts to bring literacy to the masses, she should have been irritated by his arrogant, more-militant-than-thou air. Somehow she wasn't.

And so the walk along the Neva. A typical tell-me-about-yourself encounter, or as much of a one as could be managed within their common framework of larger radical concerns.

Vladimir Ilyich, it turned out, had his revolutionary credentials well in order. He had already written a pamphlet or two, including a scathing attack on the populist line still being preached by Mikhailovsky, the aging mentor of the *narodniki.* He had sat at the feet of some graying veterans of the People's Will terrorist society, absorbing underground lore about codes and police spies and "how to write with chemicals in books." [25] In his late 'teens, he had been expelled from the University of Kazan for taking part in a student demonstration. In 1887, his older brother Alexander had been executed for plotting to assassinate the tsar.

Clearly, the Illiteracy Committee was not the place for Vladimir Ilyich—"Baldy," as the members of his workers' study group called him—"Lenin," as he would later call himself.

Too much is sometimes made of the role of students *qua* students in the generational upheaval of our times. Lenin and Krupskaya were no college revolutionaries: they were, in fact, several years older than most of their comrades in the resurgent Petersburg underground of the nineties. But they were young and dedicated, and Lenin at least could be as ideologically dogmatic as any undergraduate. They were Marxists—in that decade of burgeoning industrial growth and commensurate growth of the oppressed proletariat, Marxism was the latest thing. But the Marxist circles had much in common with other branches of the continuing Russian revolutionary tradition: with the reviving populists, with the student rebels, with the younger, more enlightened professional men who were finally beginning to surface as a liberal force in Russia. Lenin certainly regarded himself as part of that broad spectrum of "revolutionary youth," as he himself described it, that was so vigorously in evidence in the Russian 1890's.[26]

Lenin and Krupskaya saw much of each other in the months and years that followed that chance meeting in 1894. They studied together and agitated among the workers together. They shared Siberian exile and flight to the West, the bitter disillusionment of 1905 and the dazzling triumph of 1917. Along the way, almost incidentally, they were married.

Lenin sleeps alone in his massive tomb in front of the Kremlin today, a tribute to his unique qualities. But Lenin was typical too, a highly developed type of the young ideological revolutionary that is the nineteenth century's special legacy to the twentieth.

One of Mrs. Pankhurst's

A young woman in shapeless prison clothes sat huddled on the bare plank bed, listening to the sobbing and the screaming from another cell, somewhere down the corridor. She was, no doubt, trembling, remembering what had happened to her, and knowing what was going to happen to her now.

Young women by the scores, by the hundreds, sat in cells all around her, biting their lips and waiting too. In the late summer of 1909, Pentonville Prison, Brixton, Aylesbury, Halloway—where the redoubtable Mrs. Pankhurst herself was locked up—were full of them. The WSPU, the Votes-for-Women militants, had been arrested in mass lots after their latest riotous march on the Parliament. The *Daily Mail* coyly called them "suffragettes," to distinguish the Women's Social and Political Union—the shouters, the rock-throwers, the Parliament "raiders"—from the more conservative women's suffrage groups. Even some of their sisters in the feminist movement objected to the escalating tactics of Emmeline Pankhurst's militant "prison volunteers."

They look rather quaint in the old photographs, these turn-of-the-century feminists with their wide, flowered hats and the heavy, square-shouldered gowns that swung to their sensible shoes. There is surely something lilac-scented and unreal, for instance, about the suffragette anthem:

> Shout, shout—up with your song,
> Cry with the wind, for the dawn is breaking.
> March, march, swing you along.
> Wide blows our banner and hope is waking.[27]

It might be somebody's forgotten alma mater, or perhaps a temperance hymn.

But there was nothing lilac-scented or unreal about sitting in a cell in Pentonville that August of 1909, listening to your sisters screaming down the hall.

There were older women among the suffragettes, of course: one "so old [that she] had to be wheeled to the House of Commons and lifted out." Mrs. Pankhurst herself was in her forties; her grown daughters marched with her in the van. But most of them were young women—"girls of fifteen," "girls at college," "young ladies

[sent] to street corners to demand the vote." [28] And their movement had all the religious fervor and the firm ideological foundation of the true youth crusade.

The suffragettes were a generation of young women. They had grown up with that restless discontent with Victorianism which characterized the 1890's. They had been stirred to new hope for the Women's Movement by the rise of dissent over the Boer War, by the rapid gains of the Labor Movement, and by the advent of a Liberal government in 1906. The years from 1906 to 1914 were to be the "heroic years" of the women's suffrage movement, and 1909 was the turning point in the tactics of these most militant crusaders for "the Cause."

The typical young woman in the Pentonville cells—and Brixton, and Halloway, and the rest of them—had seen it all.

She had perhaps nodded vigorous assent to John Stuart Mill's sagely reasoned strictures against *The Subjection of Women,* his urgent plea (fifty years old now) for the "social and political emancipation" of the female sex.[29] But what had sent the typical militant, first to the street corners and then into the streets themselves, was the loud clear voice of Mrs. Emmeline Pankhurst—daughter of a radical family, articulate widow of a left-wing barrister, and imperious organizer, six years earlier, of the militant wing of the suffrage movement. "Deeds, not words!" Mrs. Pankhurst had said. "They must give us the vote," she cried passionately after her tenth hunger strike, "or they must give us death." [30]

Moved by her oratory and by her readiness to put her own slender body on the line, hundreds, then thousands of gently nurtured women had followed Mrs. Pankhurst. They had done their picketing and marching and demonstrating, their speech-making and leafleting, their organizing, their petitioning, their political campaigning. The girl in the solitary cell perhaps remembered the "Mud March," that first nervous, rain-soaked procession through the streets of London—with men looking down from the windows of their clubs, laughing. She surely remembered other rallies these last three years: the ringing exhortations to action, the singing and the chanting, the "cries of 'Rise up, women!' and answering shouts of 'Now!' " [31]

She remembered the violence.

She remembered the party stewards throwing the suffragettes out of public meetings, Liberal and Conservative alike, when they demanded to know where the candidate stood on Votes for Women; the police lines, hundreds of helmeted bobbies deployed across Parliament Square to stop the march of the militant women, to bustle and chivy them into the waiting vans; and the crowds, the mobs of grinning males, the bowler-hatted toughs who loved a chance to rough up the women in the turmoil of a street confrontation.

And then the beginnings of violence by the young militants themselves.

"Men and Women!" shouted the handbill, *"help* the *Suffragettes* to *RUSH* the *House of Commons!"* [32] The first rocks were thrown, shattering the windows of government offices. Mrs. Pankhurst struck a police inspector at the entrance to the House. Arrested by the hundreds, the suffragettes announced that they were "political prisoners" and declared that they would no longer collaborate with prison regulations. A quarter of a century before Gandhi, they declared that they would go on hunger strike in English jails until they were released.

The government had responded firmly, that summer of 1909: prisoners who would not eat would be forcibly fed. The women would not eat: they fought. And so the scuffles and the screaming in cell after cell down the prison corridors as the warders and the prison doctors proceeded with their brutal work. It was feeding time in Pentonville.

They came for each proud, frightened, lonely girl in turn. After the exaltation and the excitement of the march, the pummeling in the streets, the arrest, the windowless prison van, the humiliating indignities had begun. But at least her sisters had been with her when they had all been herded into "a great room thronged with wardresses and other prisoners" to "strip and be searched," to undergo the filthy bath and be dressed in the patched and shapeless prison uniform.[33] The misery and fear had not begun until she was alone in her solitary cubicle with its cold cement floor, plank bed, and airless isolation. One day, two days, three days of gnawing hunger, growing weariness, sudden reasonless frights. And then the prison doctor with his sanitary apparatus, come to see to it that all prisoners consumed sufficient nutriments to keep body and soul together.

Guards would seize and hold her while the forcible feeding took place. Some form of nutritious liquid was used, often milk or beef tea. The food was poured into each girl through a "stomach tube," a length of flexible rubber tubing inserted through the mouth or nostrils. The young woman, weak from her fast, would resist as long as she could, writhing, screaming, often vomiting. The violence of her struggles after the tube was inserted could cause internal injuries.

When what was being done to the women became known outside the walls of the prisons, there was some protest. Keir Hardie, the Labor MP, called it "a horrible, beastly outrage!" Two editorial writers for the *Daily News* resigned in protest: "we cannot denounce torture in Russia and support it in Britain . . ." Other Englishmen objected to forcible feeding on less humanitarian grounds. "Some people," a biographer of Mrs. Pankhurst notes, "thought that the suffragettes in prison should . . . be allowed to starve to death." [34]

As far as the Women's Movement was concerned, the result of the novel form of police brutality was immediate and quite predictable. Their numbers swelled: from a march of three thousand in 1907 to a four-mile parade of forty thousand in 1911; from seventy suffrage organizations in 1909 to 305 in 1911.[35] The violence of their assault also increased. Window-smashing became a standard tactic, and government glass was followed by the panes of countless expensive West End shops—and even by the windows of those sacrosanct clubs from which the men had once looked down and laughed. Militant women began to resort to arson, to demolishing property with acid and axes, and even to dynamite. Lloyd George's new house in Surrey was blown up by a suffragette bomb.

"I incite this meeting to rebellion!" cried Mrs. Pankhurst. "Sedition! The Women's Revolution!" [36]

The Revolution did not come, of course: it almost never does. But in 1918, the women got the vote.

Gavro on the Apel Quai

It was a sultry Sunday morning in late July, and the streets of the old provincial capital were jammed. Flags waved. There was a babble of voices, German and Slavic dialects intermingled. Perspiring citizens shaded their eyes, peering up the Apel Quai, the central avenue of the city, straining after a first glimpse of their distinguished visitor.

The slight young man with the pistol in his pocket stared too.

He was short and slender, with a narrow jaw, deep-set blue eyes, and a pencil-thin mustache. He had been rejected for military service two years earlier with the contemptuous remark: "You are too small and weak"—an insult he never forgot.[37] For Gavrilo was an ardent South Slav nationalist who had longed to fight for his people in some more orthodox way than that upon which he was now embarked. He slid one sweaty hand inside his pocket and cradled the Browning revolver he had picked up several hours earlier at the pastry shop. He would show them all.

Gavrilo, at age nineteen, was a young man drunk on ideas. "Always a reader and always alone," an alienist who had a crack at him after the event recorded. "Books for me," he himself declared, "signify life." He had read anarchist and socialist tracts, but his guiding passion had always been nationalism. The South Slavs, and the Bosnian Serbs especially, must be free of the Habsburg yoke. "For freedom and fatherland . . . Gavro," he signed his letters. Gavrilo was, in short, a not untypical specimen of Young Bosnia, the vanguard of that "altogether different 'new generation' " which sprang up in the Bosnian provinces of the Habsburg Empire at the beginning of the twentieth century.[38]

Like many of his contemporaries, he had been stirred by the Russian Revolution of 1905, and by the anarchist "cult of the individual deed"—the cult of terrorism. He had been stunned when the Habsburg monarchy had annexed Bosnia outright in 1908. He had been inspired to new hope when his Serb kinsmen across the border had fought so heroically in the Balkan Wars of 1912. The world was spinning around him—anything seemed possible. Gavrilo dropped out of school, and plunged into the movement for Bosnian liberation and a greater South Slav union.

He was a personal disciple of the organizer of Young Bosnia, Vladimir Gratchinovich, and a passionate admirer of the first would-be Bosnian tyrannicide, Bogdan Zherajitch. Zherajitch had fired half a dozen shots at the Austrian governor of Bosnia—all of which missed—before taking his own life. The governor, according to the legend, had spurned the heroic student's body with his foot and ordered it buried in potter's field, surrounded by suicides and sneak thieves. Gavrilo had knelt more than once beside that grave, literally in tears, swearing vengeance.

Nor was he alone. Many young Bosnians made the emotional pilgrimage to the grave of Zherajitch. Many, like Gavro, had been mesmerized by the ecstatic words of the youth leader Gratchinovich, originally a student at the University of Vienna: "We, the youngest, must make a new history . . . we the messengers of new generations and new people." And again: "These young people, not yet awakened, will be our apostles, the creators and cross-bearers of new religions . . . and save the Serbian soul from vice and decay." [39] Once again the younger generation—the "prophetic minority"—was called upon to save the soul of a nation whose elders had failed to do it for themselves.

One authority on the Youth Revolution suggests Oedipal complexities in the Bosnian tyrannicides.[40] If so, theirs was a whole generation so afflicted. For the deed of Zherajitch and Gratchinovich's winged words galvanized students all across the Bosnian provinces of the Habsburg empire. There were student demonstrations and strikes. Police overreacted violently, and a student was shot dead in the street in front of the University of Zagreb. More violent demonstrations followed, and more police brutality. The student activists occupied the University Hall, unfurled the black flag, and held off police attacking with drawn sabers for a day and a half. After that the militants organized and went underground.

Gavrilo had helped to run student demonstrations, had been wounded in the streets, had been expelled and had vanished into the shapeless, ill-organized Bosnian underground. But he had not been alone.

He was not alone now, as he stood in the crowded, flag-decked streets of Sarajevo squinting into the heat that pulsed off the pavement of the Apel Quai, watching the approaching motorcade. Half a dozen comrades were in that crowd, armed, like him, with guns and bombs. The mob itself would hurl execrations after his victims when Gavro had done his work "for freedom and fatherland."

Six black cars chugged slowly up the avenue, returning from the formal welcome at the City Hall. In one of them, with the top down, waving and smiling somewhat nervously at the crowds, sat the unwelcome guest of honor—the heir apparent to the Habsburg throne. He wore a plumed helmet and a chestful of medals. Beside him sat a lady in a white dress and a wide summer hat.

The Archduke's car pulled up directly in front of Gavrilo

Princip. A wrong turn—some mix-up about the route—but it could not have been more perfect if it had been planned. The slight young man in the dark suit stepped forward and fired into the open car from a range of perhaps five feet.

It was almost dreamlike, as he recalled it later. The white heat pulsing off the street, the black car, the nodding plumes, the broad white hat.

> I drew the revolver . . . and raised it against the automobile without aiming. I even turned my head as I shot. . . . Where I aimed I do not know. But I know that I aimed at the Heir Apparent. I believe that I fired twice, perhaps more, because I was so excited. Whether I hit the victims or not, I cannot tell . . .[41]

A jumbled, slow-motion dream of unreal violence.

The night before, he had knelt once more at the martyr Zherajitch's grave: it seemed now, for an endless moment, as though Princip, too, had failed of his object. The man beneath the plumed helmet simply stared at him; the lady in the wide white hat hardly moved. Then the car picked up speed with a sudden jerk, and the lady swayed slowly forward and to one side, against her husband.

Gavro had shot the Archduke Franz Ferdinand in the neck, the Duchess in the stomach. Both were dead within minutes.

Within days after the assassinations at Sarajevo—to the bewilderment of Princip, who never understood the complex reverberations of his simple blow for fatherland and freedom—Europe was at war. The twentieth century, historically speaking, began that day in late July of 1914, with two shots from the pistol of this unhappy product of the Youth Revolution.

8

"You Are All a Lost Generation" *
The Age of Jazz and Dada
Europe and America, 1920

The preceding chapter has tried to show that by the end of the nineteenth century, the Youth Revolution had spread to significant segments of younger generations in many European countries. The numbers involved were often small, but the influence of an ideologically driven minority was frequently far greater than any mere head count would indicate. A handful of young writers or painters could reshape public taste for decades. A few hundred youthful revolutionaries—given a few historical breaks—could redirect their nation's history.

It was only after the Great War, however, that these small enclaves of youth in revolt began to coalesce into something resembling a mass movement, a large-scale revolt of the younger generation.

The 1920's saw the Bohemian counter culture burst out of the Bohemias of the West, leap the Atlantic, and begin the conquest of the sons and daughters of the bourgeoisie. The 1930's saw the revival of youthful political militance—again in both Europe and America—and the first major attempts by modern states to reintegrate activist, ideologically motivated youth back into society at large. This chapter and the next will offer brief glimpses of each of these events in turn.

A couple of caveats should, however, be offered before we begin.

The escapism of the "youth culture," in the first place, was not the only form the Youth Revolution took in the 1920's. Nor was

* Gertrude Stein, epigraph to *The Sun Also Rises.* See note 6 below.

political activism the sole mode of youthful dissent in the '30's. There were Leninists at large in the twenties, their hopes exalted beyond measure by the success of the Communist Revolution in Russia. There were Surrealists in the thirties, their Dadaist sense of the dark absurdity of life considerably enhanced by the same historic developments—the Great Depression, the rise of fascism—that stirred up so much militant activism in the Red Decade. The dominant motifs of the two inter-war decades do, however, seem to have been those stressed in these chapters: cultural alienation in the "age of jazz and dada," social and political activism in the Depression years.

Europe and America, finally, were not the only theaters of the expanding Youth Revolution in the earlier decades of this century. As far away as China, for instance, young people were in revolt, both culturally and politically, against their fathers' world. As in Russia in the nineteenth century, Westernized Chinese students took the lead in the modernizing of their ancient, tradition-bound, and materially backward country. Even before World War I, these "emancipated" young men had formed the cadres that launched Sun Yat-sen's Revolution of 1911. In 1919, China's humiliation at the Versailles Peace Conference and the resulting wave of anger against Western imperialists triggered the aggressive May Fourth Movement. Chinese secret societies, like the Russian nihilists, hurled Western science, materialism, and socialism in the faces of their Confucionist fathers, rather than turning to the Romantic non-rationalism of counter-cultures in developed bourgeois nations. But student marchers and demonstrators rioted in the streets and struck the universities of China just as their opposite numbers in Europe had so often done. Mao Tse-tung himself was a student leader in those years.

By and large, however, the Youth Revolution was limited to the Western nations and to the Romantic counter-cultural mode in the twenties. It is with these that the present chapter deals.

1. *WORLD'S END AND AFTERWARD*

Out to the Death Fields

"English Youth went out to the death fields," one young observer of the changing social scene wrote in 1921, "hundred thousand after hundred thousand, until four million men had gone that way. . . . Out of every four men who went out to the World War one did not come back again, and of those who came back many are maimed and blind and some are mad." Robert Graves, in his grim *Goodbye to All That,* noted that "at least one in three of my generation at school died. . . . The average life expectancy of an infantry subaltern on the Western Front was, at some stages of the war, only about three months . . ." [1] It was the beginning of what was to be called "the century of total war," and it scarred the lives of several generations of Western man.

Europe had experienced no war of comparable length and scope since the Industrial Revolution had begun to transform the life of the Continent a century before. The trench warfare of 1914–1918 was thus something new under the sun. It was technological warfare, a war of steel and chemicals and ever more ingenious new machines into which human flesh was fed, month after month and year after year, like hamburger into a meat grinder. Machine guns and barbed wire, poison gas and massive artillery barrages, airplanes and submarines and tanks, all had their chance at the Fritzes and Tommies and doughboys. The trench lines shifted forward a few hundred yards and back a few hundred yards, while the youth of the West sat there through the months and years, taking their inexplicable, mind-shredding punishment.

The Great War was a monstrous generational trauma from which no one escaped unscathed; all were spiritually, if not physically affected. "This ain't a war," marveled a character in one of the earliest war novels, "it's a goddam madhouse." Hemingway's more famous lines about the impact of the war on young ideals deserve to be quoted one more time:

> I was always embarrassed by the words "sacred," "glorious," and "sacrifice," and the expression "in vain." We had heard them sometimes standing in the rain almost out of earshot, so

> that only the shouted words came through, and read them, on proclamations that were slapped up by billposters over other proclamations now for a long time, and I had seen nothing sacred, and the things that were glorious had no glory, and the sacrifices were like the stockyards at Chicago if nothing was done with the meat except to bury it.[2]

Those who did not go to the war could read about it in this rash of 1920's war books. Books with titles like *Goodbye to All That, A Farewell to Arms, What Price Glory, The Four Horsemen of the Apocalypse, World's End*. "I think it is safe to say," wrote one contemporary historian of the decade, "that no book, play, or motion-picture, in any language, about the Great War, glorified it." [3]

World War I had been sold to the peoples as a great crusade for civilization, God and country—a "war to make the world safe for democracy"—*"Gott mit uns"—revanche* for 1870 and the "lost provinces"—and so on. The generation that survived it quickly came to see it as barbarous, ungodly, a disgrace to all flags. The result was a unique generational heritage, a revulsion against the war that rapidly expanded into a vast rejection of the civilization that had produced it.

The New Paganism

Other causal factors contributed also to the moral revolt of the younger generation and to the concomitant growth of a genuine "youth culture" in the Western World.

A great sense of liberation seems to have flooded the West in the decade after World War I. A feeling—sometimes joyful, sometimes angry—that all barriers were down, that the future was coming on with a rush, and that that future belonged to the young. It was a view that naturally appealed to the young themselves, and that was ruefully accepted by surprising numbers of their battered elders.

The very applied science that had made the war horrible seemed to be turning the peace that followed into an Aladdin's cave of technological wonders uniquely designed for the delectation of the young. The older generations, raised on the horse and buggy and the band concert in the park, struggled resignedly with gearshifts and wireless dials. The new generation grew up with the family car and the radio, with the phonograph and the movies and the telephone—all increasingly commonplace in the middle-class homes of the twenties. The parents had grown up in small towns and tended to stay there; the children hurried off to the glitter and bustle of the city, or traveled "student thirds" in the great ocean liners to play or even to live in foreign lands.

The minds of the new generation seemed to be as liberated as their bodies. The impact of popular culture on the young had perhaps never been so pervasive, reaching through movies and magazines down even to shopgirls and out to the most isolated provincial youth.

The aesthetic experimentation of the prewar "new schools" continued unabated in Paris and Weimar Germany and even in Soviet Russia during the pre-Stalinist NEP period. Names like Pound and Proust and Joyce, T. S. Eliot and Gertrude Stein were battlecries for youthful *cognoscenti* in their unending war against the Philistines. Far broader in their impact, however, were the subjects and sentiments of even the most unexperimental piece of postwar prose. The 1920's were the great age of popular debunking. The young took to the new cynicism—or "realism" as it was often called—with the enthusiasm of epigones exposing the gods.

Not only were patriotism, glory, and the war beneath contempt. So were religious dogma and social convention, hard work, free enterprise, political democracy, and all the other shibboleths of the prewar period. The most eminent Victorians, Lytton Strachey informed the youth, were pious frauds. The West was clearly declining, opined the Spenglerian popularizers: let it go, said the young. "I am persuaded," wrote Mencken in *The American Mercury,* widely read on American campuses in the twenties, "that hedonism is the only sound and practical doctrine of faith for the intelligent man." [4] He got very few arguments from people under thirty.

Science itself, after all, proved that inhibition was unhealthy, that the instincts should have free rein. For Freud, the most popularized of all the new prophets, had found a massive lay audience among the new generation. Warped Sunday-supplement accounts and cocktail-party conversation made the Viennese psychoanalyst the champion of a new morality—a "new paganism," their elders sometimes called it. And if "science itself" preached the emancipation of the id, what normally physical, newly mobile, militantly anti-Victorian youth was going to say science nay?

From the postwar Paris of the expatriates to Bertolt Brecht's decadent Berlin at the end of the decade, the Youth Revolution found new recruits everywhere for its countercultural withdrawal from the old order. The spreading contempt of the children for their fathers was a "general madness which seems to have overtaken all lands, like some medieval epidemic . . ." The many volumes of Galsworthy's *Forsyte Saga,* with its intricate conflicts of generations, appeared through the twenties, and in the Germany of the Expressionists, "the father-son conflict was demanded of every good young writer." [5] In America especially—which had, after all, some catching up to do—the revolt of the younger generation was the most astonishing phenomenon to come along since the war.

When Gertrude Stein told Ernest Hemingway, "You are all a lost generation," she was not referring merely to a handful of writers. The immediate object of the remark, it seems, was a French garage mechanic who had proved incompetent to handle even the simplest repair job on her model T.[6] The Paris expatriates were "lost," all right, as had been many similar small communities of the alienated over the preceding century. But from the viewpoint of the older generation, the label now fit a larger segment of middle-class youth, on both sides of the Atlantic, than ever before.

2. *THE DECADE OF THE YOUNG*

Flappers and Jelly Beans

One day after the war, America woke up to find itself confronted with "a first-class revolt against the accepted American order." Even in those days of the Palmer raids and the great Red Scare, furthermore, it was clear from the start that this was no Bolshevik plot. "The shock troops of the rebellion were not alien agitators, but the sons and daughters of well-to-do American families . . ." For the 1920's were "the decade of the young" in America, a time when, as Mark Sullivan saw it, "an emphasis was placed on the young, simply because they were young, that has probably never been equalled in the history of the world." [7] After all due allowances for provincial bias have been made, one thing was surely true: the Youth Revolution had reached America.

The pattern should have been familiar enough, if anyone had been looking for historical patterns. There was the distinctive generational costume, the shocking life style, the private language, the undergirding of half-formed ideas, the simmering spirit of generational revolt. The "flappers" and the "jelly beans" of fifty years ago —the grandparents of today's insurgent youth—had them all; all the trappings of their common ancestors, the *bousingos* of Balzac's day, alive and vigorous and vastly more numerous in the America of Harding and Silent Cal, of "normalcy," booster clubs, and rampant Babbittry.

You could see them on the streets of practically any town or city —if they were not plinking their mandolins on your own front porch. The young man with the bell-bottom trousers and the slicked-down "patent leather" hair, perhaps even sporting the famous raccoon coat with its ingenious hip-flask pockets. Or the young girl—the "flapper" as she was universally called, whether her galoshes flapped or not—in the short skirt, the brutally bobbed hair, the tight-fitting cloche hat, the cigarette poised, the quick "damn" ever ready on her painted lips. Or perhaps the two of them together, gyrating to the wild rhythms of the Charleston or swaying to the wail of the jazz saxophone, dancing "as if glued together, body to body, cheek to cheek" in a "syncopated embrace" that left their elders gasping.[8]

You could learn all about the shocking life style of this new generation from an avalanche of popular literature on the subject— if you could not observe it for yourself. Hundreds of magazine and newspaper features filled worried parents in on "the revolt of the youth," "what the younger generation thinks," "what the younger generation wants," and asked the plaintive question: "where have we failed our children?" [9] Scores of novels and movies and uncounted short stories depicted the outrageous behavior of the young under such suitably lurid rubrics as *Flaming Youth, Our Dancing Daughters, Dancers in the Dark, Unforbidden Fruit, The Plastic Age,* and of course Hemingway's more ambitious *The Sun Also Rises* and Scott Fitzgerald's trend-setting *This Side of Paradise, Tales of the Jazz Age,* and the rest. The younger generation had, as one wit put it, some fantastic press agents.

But there was considerable fire beneath all that smoke. Particularly on the female side, the 1920's did mark a "moral revolution" of the first order.

It was estimated in 1928 that "the amount of material required for a woman's complete costume (exclusive of her stockings) had declined from 19¼ yards to 7 yards" since 1914.[10] Young women cheerfully set aside their mothers' sweeping Victorian swathings in favor of skimpy knee-length rayon shifts. They abandoned corsets, rolled their stockings, cut off their hair, painted themselves with rouge and lipstick. They learned to smoke cigarettes and drink bootleg gin with the men. They joined emancipated youth of the opposite sex in jazz clubs, movies, midnight auto rides, cocktail parties, "petting parties." "Neck" became a verb.

How frequently they "went further" than necking and petting, we do not know: there were no Kinseys, no Masters and Johnsons then to reduce the matter to statistics. Certainly, there was a great deal of talk about sexual freedom, shedding inhibitions, and facing sex frankly and honestly, as a part of life. There was probably more talk than action. From the perspective of our own enlightened age, there is something touchingly naive and innocent about Fitzgerald's flirts and lovers. But there was some fire here too: "the prostitute," opined Frederick Lewis Allen, "was faced for the first time with an amateur competition of formidable proportions." [11]

It was, in any event, a hectic life the new youth led. The automobile, the hip flask, and the brazen call of the saxophone swept them on at a giddy pace that made the picnics and church socials of their parents' time seem remote indeed. Edna St. Vincent Millay summed up this first American fun culture in a quatrain that was quoted by flappers and their consorts from one end of the country to the other:

> My candle burns at both ends;
> It will not last the night;
> But, ah, my foes, and oh, my friends—
> It gives a lovely light.[12]

Practically a Total Loss

An important sociological subculture, clearly, in Babbitt's America—a slick, jazz-tempo, art-deco, new subculture of the young.

But a counter culture too: a conscious revolt against American Babbittry and boosterism, puritanical morals and the cult of material progress.

Dorothy Parker, in an article in the anti-Bohemian *Saturday Evening Post,* described the notorious disillusionment of the younger generation in less than sympathetic terms:

> They [the "professional youth" of the nation] are in an especially depressed state about America. . . . The country has turned out to be practically a total loss—no art, no literature, no folk dancing, no James Joyce, no appreciation, no native basketry, nothing; just so much real estate inhabited by a lot of people who follow the comic strips, present automobiles to baseball players, and keep conscientious track of what film will be shown at the local Bijou . . .

The new youth saw to the heart of all our problems, Miss Parker sardonically declared, and was totally disillusioned with the state of the world:

> They come clean with the news that war is a horrible thing, that injustice still exists in many parts of the globe even to this day, that the very rich are apt to sit appreciably prettier than the very poor. . . . They have even taken a calm look at this marriage thing, and they are there to report that it is not always a lifelong trip to Niagara Falls.[13]

The young themselves, of course, took their own alienation somewhat more to heart than the Philistine readers of the *Saturday Evening Post* did. The average flapper probably did not spend much time thinking about it; not thinking about "serious" matters was part of their withdrawal. But in the America of the Harding scandals and the Palmer raids, of postwar disillusionment and the amazing national folly called Prohibition, a certain cheerful contempt for adult society came naturally to the young.

The boys and girls who came of age around 1920 had, after all, grown up through one of the great reform periods of American history—the Progressive era of Teddy Roosevelt and Woodrow Wilson. They were too young to remember trust busting and TR's "bully pulpit." But they had been touched in their impressionable 'teens by Wilson's soaring oratory, by the New Freedom, and the war to end war, the fight for the League of Nations, the vote for women, and the triumph of the temperance movement: the last act of the great Progressive crusade—a great crusade gone sour. For the war and the peace that followed were disasters, the fight for the League was lost, the vote for women made no great difference in the quality of American governance, and the Prohibition Act turned half the country into instant lawbreakers. Wilson's mute, inglorious end and the national stampede back to Harding-style normalcy completed the debacle.

It was not an unfamiliar situation. As the failure of the Revolution of 1830 in France produced the first Bohemians, as the crippling compromises of the tsar emancipator's reforms of the 1860's spawned the Russian nihilist withdrawal, so the debacle of Progressivism in America generated the massive generational disaffiliation of the 1920's.

Leaky, Red Hot, Threatening To Blow Up

Scott Fitzgerald's *This Side of Paradise,* which rolled off the presses in the spring of 1920, summed up the sad situation of yet another younger generation cast ideologically adrift by the crumbling of their elders' crusades. We are, the golden boy of the twenties lamented in this famous first novel, "a new generation . . . grown up to find all gods dead, all wars fought, all faiths in man shaken." [14] By the middle of the decade, Mencken's acidulous cynicism was more to the taste of the worldly young: Let the boobocracy take care of itself—enlightened hedonism is the thinking man's philosophy. Whether romantic or "realistic" in tone, however, the message remained the same.

But the flaming youth of the 1920's had, by and large, no more use for Babbitt's America than the first Bohemians had for the France of Louis Philippe. A young man who graduated from Yale in 1920 spoke for many of the more thoughtful of his contemporaries when he lashed out at his elders in the pages of the *Atlantic Monthly:*

> . . . I would like to observe that the older generation had certainly pretty well ruined this world before passing it on to us. They give us this thing, knocked to pieces, leaky, red hot, threatening to blow up; and then they are surprised that we

don't accept it with the same attitude of pretty, decorous enthusiasm with which they received it back in the eighteen-nineties . . .[15]

Attempts to compile a "credo" for a generation in revolt—particularly for a counter-cultural generation—are seldom very satisfactory. A number of efforts to analyze the attitudes of the emancipated youth of the twenties were made, however, and these lists do at least indicate the direction in which the new thought was flowing.

Malcolm Cowley's creed of the younger generation, for instance, included such counter-cultural notions as "paganism," "living for the moment," "liberty," "self-expression," and, of course, freedom from sexual inhibition. In only two areas did Cowley touch on issues which could conceivably have interested a political activist: "female equality" and education. But female equality tended to mean social and sexual equality rather than political or economic parity. And the educational complaints of these generations boiled down to the not unfamiliar idea that the true potentialities of the young were being "crushed and destroyed by a standardized society and mechanical methods of teaching," and that children should be "encouraged to develop their own potentialities, to blossom freely like flowers . . ." The "new, free generation" of flower children which would result, Cowley suggested, might yet save the world.[16]

In general, however, the dissenting youth of the twenties had little enthusiasm for world-saving. Another draft code, this one for the younger intellectuals, put heavy emphasis on negative attitudes and offered few nostrums for the ailing society. The new intellectuals—according to Frederick Lewis Allen—despised Puritanism, Victorianism, fundamentalism and religion generally, and were firmly opposed to prohibition, censorship, and blue laws. They were of course full of the usual "scorn of the great bourgeois majority" and fearful of the soul-warping impact of "mass production and the machine. . . . Fordismus and the chain-store mind" on American life.[17]

The generations of the twenties seldom marched with the Wobblies or took to the streets for Sacco and Vanzetti. But there was a generalized distaste for the money-grubbing of Sinclair Lewis's *Main Street* and the puritanical philistinism of the Lynds' midwestern *Middletown* that, in itself, constituted a cultural revolution of startling proportions.

Most disturbing of all, the alienated youth were no longer merely colorful islands of nonconformity, the Sohos and the Latin Quarters of the Western World. America had its Bohemian communities, of course—in New York's Greenwich Village, in Chicago, on the West Coast. These vanguard groups, which had flourished even before the war, had been the first to discover the new gospel according to Freud, and to see sexual repression as the key to all the ills of their puritanically driven land. But the Freudian doctrines, the contempt for the bourgeoisie, and the new free style of life had quickly overflowed the Bohemian enclaves in the twenties. Youthful disdain for the alleged materialism, puritanism, and hypocrisy of the American way of life could now be found on campuses and in towns and cities all across the country.

Flaming youth remained a minority, of course, even among their own age-group and social class. But the young made themselves talked about. Some of their elders, the sort of liberals who prided themselves on their ability to empathize, even insisted that the youth had a point or two—that the war had been a horrible thing, that hypocrisy was a besetting sin of the older generation. And many more citizens, middle-aged and older, offered the insolently unconventional minority among their children the sincerest form of homage—they began to imitate them. It was a small-scale trend as yet, a mere matter of dress length and hair style, of public drinking and private sex. But it was a beginning.

Bohemia was invading Main Street, and the issue, as of 1929, was distinctly in doubt.

3. A WHIFF OF CHAOS FOR THE BOURGEOISIE

A Virgin Microbe

Every year tens and hundreds of thousands of prosperous Americans took ship for Europe. In 1928, 437,000 people sailed for the Old World—a great many of them young.[18] They went to live for a time the life of the expatriate, as glamorized for them by Fitzgerald and Hemingway. They went to Paris, to see what flaming youth was *really* like in the land of its birth. For when all was said and done, the Europeans were the old professionals at this business of being young and insurrectionary.

The youngest and most enthusiastically anti-social of all the European youth revolts of the early twenties was the dazzling, baffling, totally anarchistic phenomenon that went by the incomprehensible, oddly disturbing name of Dada.

DADA.

Dada? the most sophisticated young American in Paris might ask. What is Dada?

"Dada," he might be cheerfully informed, "is a virgin microbe."

Or: "Dada, acknowledging only instinct, condemns explanation a priori."

Or, more volubly, from the little Rumanian, Tristan Tzara, who seemed to be the international impresario of Dada: "Dada is life without carpet-slippers or parallels . . . without discipline or morality and we spit on humanity. Dada remains within the European frame of weaknesses it's shit after all but from now on we mean to shit in assorted colors . . ." [19]

Shitting in assorted colors was hardly Scott Fitzgerald's thing, or even Ernest Hemingway's. But it made a circus for the young of half the capitals of Europe for half a dozen years after the war to save civilization.

If you asked to be taken to their leader, you would be happily informed that "the Dadaist Movement has three hundred and ninety-one presidents and . . . anyone can become a president without the slightest trouble." [20]

If you asked for a Dada manifesto—all youth movements have manifestos, after all—you might be shepherded to the Dada demonstration at the Grand Palais des Champs Elysées, at which no less than six Dadaist manifestos were read aloud simultaneously to a grand chorus of boos, cheers, laughter, and inarticulate howls.

If, in desperation, you demanded to know the history of Dada, you might at least learn a few facts—trivial though such things seemed to the Dada masters. You might learn that the movement had been founded at the Café Voltaire in Zurich in 1916 by a handful of exiles from warring Europe; that it had reached Berlin in 1918 and Paris in 1920; that it also had representatives in Cologne, Hanover, the Netherlands, Italy, Spain, and New York.

And that Dada stood foursquare against "Honor, Fatherland, Morality, the Family, Art, Religion, Liberty, Brotherhood," and all the other allegedly sacred abstractions of the older generation.[21]

It was harder to find out just what Dada was *for*. Tzara included among the movement's goals "the abolition of logic" and "the abolition of the future." The painter Hans Arp, another of the founders, asserted that "Dada stands for art without sense. . . . Dada is without meaning, as Nature is," adding proudly: "The Dadaist gave the bourgeois a whiff of chaos." [22] More concretely, Dadaists indulged in painting without subject matter, poems without words, sculpture purchased "ready-made" at the hardware store, and, of course, their fantastic cabaret and concert performances, featuring completely cacophonous "noise" music, readings rendered totally inaudible by the continuous ringing of an electric bell, and countless other "happenings" of all sorts. They painted in a trance, composed poetry by scattering bits of newsprint at random over a table. In Paris, they regularly started riots in the theaters. In Germany, they were arrested for threatening to blow up Weimar.

If it was shit, it was certainly polychromatic shit. And young shit too: there was scarcely a single Dadaist over thirty.

A Fifth Wheel on the Common Grave

Dada, of course, was a protest, part and parcel of the youthful rejection of the shattered world, "leaky, red hot, threatening to blow up," their parents were foisting on the young.

America's contribution to the international revolt of the younger generation had been typical of America's contribution to most things in those days: it was a matter of sheer size. The American contingents, fueled by mass education and unparalleled affluence and leisure, quickly outnumbered all others. It was a purely quantitative contribution, the sort of thing Babbitt himself might have been proud of.

But for sheer depth of disgust at the way the world wagged, for depthless contempt for their elders' universe, European youth still held the edge. There was an abyss of bitterness in Brecht's Berlin, a savage glee in the Paris of the Surrealists that no American flapper, however hipped on Freud, could match. Above all, the war had scalded the psyche of bright young Europeans far more horribly than it had the fresh-faced youth of America. Compare Hemingway's quietly understated account of the devaluation of old values by the war, for instance, with Erich Maria Remarque's savage assault on the conventional wisdom that had sent his generation out to the death fields. Toward the end of *All Quiet on the Western Front,* Remarque describes a German military hospital, with its acres of smashed young bodies and unquantifiable fields of pain:

> . . . abdominal and spine cases, head wounds and double amputations . . . lung wounds, pelvis wounds, wounds in the joints, wounds in the testicles. . . . How senseless is everything that can ever be written, done, or thought, when such things are possible. It must all be lies and of no account when the culture of a thousand years could not prevent this stream of blood being poured out, these torture-chambers in their hundreds of thousands.[23]

It was this bitterness against the war and the Victorian blindness that had brought it on that powered the Dada assault upon the world at large.

The Dadaists, as they themselves have amply testified, were "revolted by the butchery of the 1914 World War"—"beside ourselves with rage and grief at the suffering and humiliation of mankind"—horrified at "four years of senseless slaughter, in which many friends had died on both sides . . ." It was not they who had gone mad, they giggled as they dribbled their bits of newspaper over the table top, but the nations of the world, "association[s] of psychopaths who, like the Germans, marched off with a volume of Goethe in their knapsacks to skewer Frenchmen and Russians on their bayonets." [24] That people who loved Goethe and Voltaire and Tolstoy could do such unspeakable things to each other proved one thing to these young anti-intellectual intellectuals and their youthful audiences: the world was totally senseless, without rhyme or reason, direction or indwelling purpose. Dada "gave the bourgeois a whiff of chaos" because, for Dadaists, "the principle of dissolution and anarchy" was the one great truth about the universe.[25] The world made no sense: why should art or ideology?

They tried to keep it light, like " 'Eggboard,' a sport and social pastime for the top ten thousand, in which the players, covered from head to foot with egg-yolk, leave the field of play . . ." Tristan

Tzara blasted his magic klaxon with its "three successive invisible echoes" at the audience, and the howling crowd responded with insults, eggs, pennies, and even raw beefsteaks.[26] It was the revolt against reason, the abolition of logic, Ubu and pure idiocy triumphant.

And yet, time and time again, even when they submitted to the directionless discipline of automatic writing, the thrust of their rejection would out:

> Their rubber hammer strikes the sea
> Down the black general so brave.
> With silken braid they deck him out
> As fifth wheel on the common grave.[27]

I Am Beginning To Be Bored—and That's Ghastly

Beneath Fitzgerald's gyrating flappers, beneath the giddy hilarity of the Jazz Age and the mad high jinks of Dada, there yawned a Baudelairean abyss. These were in a real sense spiritually crippled generations—castrated, like Hemingway's Jake; doomed creatures of enfeebled will, like Fitzgerald's Dick Diver of *Tender Is the Night*. The old-fashioned values they rejected now were, after all, the values they had themselves imbibed with their mothers' milk. The war, by destroying these values, had smashed a gaping hole in the psyche of the youth of the 1920's.

These were the generations of hollow men—crow's feet, stuffed with straw—whom T. S. Eliot described. Their febrile gaiety masked a clear vision of the Wasteland within:

> When lovely woman stoops to folly and
> Paces about her room again, alone,
> She smoothes her hair with automatic hand,
> And puts a record on the gramophone . . .
>
> O O O O that Shakespeherian rag—
> It's so elegant
> So intelligent
> "What shall I do now? What shall I do now?"
> "I shall rush out as I am, and walk the street
> "With my hair down, so. What shall we do tomorrow?
> "What shall we ever do?" [28]

Fitzgerald cracked up. Hemingway shot himself. Eliot clawed his way back to religion. Tristan Tzara ended by cramming his anarchistic soul into the rigid strait jacket of Communist Party discipline.

Less serious, less perceptive young people reacted less violently to the new vacuum in the realm of values—but they, too, felt the void, the emptiness at the heart of the fun culture. Hedonism might be the only philosophy for the thinking man, but it had its drawbacks too. "I've done all the things I've been told not to," sighed one vaguely perplexed young flapper, "and they aren't so amusing as they looked. There's a screw loose somewhere. I am beginning to be bored—and that's ghastly." [29]

They had launched a whole nation on the rocky road to sexual, social, and spiritual emancipation. They set America on the way to pre-eminence in the burgeoning Youth Revolution. But the psychic cost had been immense: the claim that sin was boring was surely a Freudian substitution for some far darker malaise.

Boredom was certainly going to be no problem for the youth of the next decade. The decade that began a year early, in 1929.

9

"Tomorrow the World!" *
Youth Crusaders on the March—
Totalitarian and Free
Europe and America, 1930

The numerical escalation of the Youth Revolution had begun with the wholesale rejection of old values by the youth of the 1920's. During the 1930's, that escalation spread to the militant stream of youthful insurgency. For the thirties saw a vigorous revival of that political activism which had spread to so many countries in the years before World War I. It was a revival—but a revival on a new scale and in new forms that gave disturbing promise of things to come.

In the Western democracies, particularly in the United States, it was the Red Decade. In the major totalitarian powers of Europe —Mussolini's Italy, Stalin's Russia, Hitler's Third Reich—it was a decade of unprecedented mobilization of youth for political action. Different as these two forms of youthful political involvement may seem, they clearly represented a single historic phenomenon: a massive new wave of socio-political involvement of the young. *Massive* was the operative word. Where a few hundred, perhaps a few thousand young people had rallied to the crusading banners of the nineteenth century, hundreds of thousands, in some cases millions, were swept up in the ideological wars of the 1930's.

But the thirties went even beyond the twenties in one crucial respect. The counter-cultural withdrawal of the Jazz Age had been numerically large, but lacking in organization or common direction. The decade of Hitler and Stalin, by contrast, saw the first major effort to *institutionalize* the Youth Revolution.

* Marching song of the Hitler Youth, in Walter Z. Laqueur, *Young Germany: A History of the German Youth Movement* (New York, 1962), p. 215.

The totalitarian powers, at least, recognized the immense potentialities of youth's restless energy in the grip of an idea. The new dictators sought to channel those energies into the service of the State. In so doing, however, they made a historic breakthrough. For the first time since the Industrial Revolution had begun the process of cutting youth off from the rest of society, a serious effort was made to reintegrate entire younger generations back into the body politic. The resulting surge of youth power might have given more people pause than it did in that hectic decade, when there were so many things to wonder at.

1. BREAD LINES, APPLE-SELLERS, BUMS

D'Ya Think Yuh'll Be Workin' By Next Year, Papa?

It was always a star-sprinkled summer night in Scott Fitzgerald's 1920's—or a spring evening at Princeton—or a hot morning on a Riviera beach. In the thirties, it always seems to have been a winter afternoon, gray and cold, with men in battered coats and shabby shoes slouching on park benches or shuffling aimlessly up snowy streets. The decade that began in 1929 was a dark and bitter one, "when humanity," as one who barely managed the transition grimly put it, "seemed to pass into a dark night of the soul." [1]

In *Life*—the old humor magazine, not the glossy new version that began in 1936—a whole new set of standard subjects for gags and cartoons intruded in the early thirties on such old stand-bys as prohibition, gangsters, and the absent-minded professor. Now began the long parade of jokes about impoverished millionaires, suicidally inclined stockbrokers, apple-sellers, pencil-sellers, bums and hobos, bread lines and park-bench philosophers. "Step up and buy, folks," called the street vendor of gew-gaws, knickknacks and dancing dolls. "Help keep the wheels of industry turning." [2] It was funny, after its grisly fashion, in 1930. It would be a lot less funny five years, or ten years, later.

The Great Depression of the 1930's was an international catastrophe as traumatic in its impact on the young as the Great War of 1914–1918 had been. Like the World War, the World Depression that began with the American stock-market crash of 1929 was the greatest in history to that time. Like the war, the Depression sucked nation after nation into the maelstrom: in 1932, there were almost four million unemployed in Britain, better than six million out of work in Germany, and well over twelve million jobless men in the United States of America.[3] It is not surprising that, like World War I, the Great Depression warped younger generations all across the Western World.

No one in Europe or America had to read about the Depression or see it in the movies. It was highly visible everywhere. Soup kitchens and bread lines and men sleeping under newspapers on park benches were not just cartoon conventions, they were daily realities. People did eat out of garbage cans and go without shoes in winter. There were beggars in considerable numbers on the streets of the richest nations in history.

There were real people like the ragged man and the very ragged boy in the *Life* cartoon, trudging past the gaily lighted shopwindow full of Christmas toys, the little boy looking up to ask wistfully: "D'ya think yuh'll be workin' by next year, Papa?" [4]

Youth Today Accepts Its Fate With Sheep-Like Apathy

Nineteen thirty was a bad year in which to be young. The young, lacking seniority and experience, found it doubly difficult to find work. Lacking work, they could not get married, raise families, take their places as adult members of society. They were stalled, stuck on square one in an endlessly prolonged adolescence.

Long-jawed young men in cloth caps lounged in the doorways of mining towns in the British Midlands, fags dangling from lower lips, smiling vacuously. They had, they explained, never worked at all: they had graduated from school directly onto the dole.

In Berlin, youths sucked at their steins in beer halls or cabarets, or browsed in bookstores full of some of the most exotic erotica in print. A parade or a political meeting might pull them out of their lethargy for a time, but it was no substitute for a job. Only a few of them belonged to the strong-arm squads that most of the political parties maintained in those last crumbling years of the Weimar Republic.

In America, the young man pumping gas who might have done

better, or the youths slouching around the filling station with nothing at all to do, seemed considerably less involved in politics. They didn't like the situation. But when asked why they didn't "organize and do something about it," these orphans of the Depression simply shrugged. "What's the use. The politicians run everything, the dirty crooks. . . . An' the big boys run the politicians. I'm wise, lady, I'm wise." You can't fight city hall.

"Youth today, we note with trepidation," concluded the inquiring girl reporter, "accepts its fate with sheep-like apathy." [5]

2. THE RED DECADE

Will the Communists Get Our Girls in College?

By the mid-thirties, apathy was hardly the word that leaped to the average newspaper-reader's mind when he contemplated the universities of America. On the West Coast, Senator John J. McNaboe, having uncovered not only the American Student Union but even the Young Communist League on the Cornell University campus, was fulminating that "Cornell is a center of revolutionary, communistic activity." In the great American heartland, Charles Walgreen, the drugstore magnate, was demanding an investigation of the University of Chicago, where his niece, he claimed, had been "required to read the *Communist Manifesto* and exposed to ideas of free love." In the East, the Hearst papers were embarked on their own exposé of Reds on campus, demanding in a front-page editorial: "Drive All Radical Professors and Students from University!" [6]

A provocative article in *Liberty* magazine raised a particularly disturbing question: "Will the Communists Get Our Girls in College?" Young radicals across the country guffawed when the girl in question, the author's daughter, angrily answered him in a *New Masses* piece entitled "My Father Is a Liar!" [7]

Something, it would seem, had happened to the "sheep-like apathy" of American youth.

It was not entirely a bolt from the blue, of course. As early as the turn of the century, a "small minority" of college students had become involved in "reformist political concerns" ranging from settlement work in the slums to avowed socialism. Even the essentially escapist 1920's had seen a certain amount of student activism, centering around the radical journal called *The New Student,* and a handful of radical issues like the Sacco-Vanzetti case.[8] But it was not until the 1930's that the real beginnings of a large-scale youth movement sprang up in the United States.

The Depression was the prime trigger, the first cause of the new militance in America. The 1920's had been a decade of exaggerated popular idolatry of the businessman, and of supreme confidence in the future prosperity of the nation. Admiration for tycoons and moguls, captains of industry and financial wizards was not new, of course; but, as one contemporary put it: "No previous President could have dared to say, as Calvin Coolidge did say, that 'the man who builds a factory builds a temple . . .' "[9] The big bull-market of the booming twenties, it was generally assumed, would go rolling on forever. And then the bottom dropped out.

> Our boys and girls [wrote one observer in the early thirties] have grown up in the belief that America is the Land of Promise. . . . As naturally as their voices broke and deepened, our young men grew up in the assurance that education and hard work were the Open Sesame to respectable jobs secured by reliability and perseverance, to homes of their own, and to honored places in the eyes of their fellow men.
>
> In the last few years many of them have found this is not true. The older generation has betrayed and deceived them.[10]

Even the emancipated minority that made the Jazz Age jazzy, however much its members despised Philistinism and Babbittry, believed in the sheer *power* of the captains of industry and the wizards of Wall Street. Their feeling of betrayal, of having had the props kicked out from under their world, was almost as great as that of their more orthodox contemporaries—especially when they found that even they, the college elite, were to be hard hit by the Depression. When in the early thirties some fifty to eighty-five per cent of college graduates were jobless; when even *Harper's* could describe "the post-1929 college graduate" as "an American tragedy . . . all dressed up with no place to go . . ." it is not surprising that university youth turned its back on the fun culture and took up protest instead.[11]

Add, finally, the exciting political atmosphere of the 1930's, full of schemes for social change, and the resulting youth revolt was practically inevitable. In the thirties, Upton Sinclair ran his EPIC campaign to *E*liminate *P*overty *I*n *C*alifornia. Huey Long was offering a flamboyant, new-model populist dictatorship in Louisiana. Father Coughlin, the Michigan "radio priest," spread his quasi-fascist gospel to millions over the airwaves. East Coast intellectuals, swamped by Eisenstein movies, "parties for Spain," and the latest literary accounts of how utopia was taking shape in the Soviet Union, all seemed to be Waiting for Lefty.

Washington, D. C., was full of bright young men—the "Brain Trust" they called them—new alphabet agencies, and the contagious enthusiasm of "that man" in the White House. FDR cocked his famous cigarette holder at a jaunty angle and informed the nation that this generation had a rendezvous with destiny. The college intellectual avant-garde, however little use they had for "Rooseveltian half-measures," were soon infected with the new passion for social change.

The New Militance

Once the dogs of youthful dissent were unleashed, they seem to have taken off in every direction at once.

There was a new militance in university newspaper offices, "editors hurling manifestoes at college administrators" with a vigor that would have done the 1960's proud.[12] Radical speakers of many persuasions, from the perennial Socialist Party Presidential candidate, Norman Thomas, to Communist leader Earl Browder, fanned out over the campuses. Radical student organizations cropped up everywhere: the Student League for Industrial Democracy (SLID], the Young People's Socialist League (YPSL, pronounced "Yipsel"), the Young Communist League (Stalinist), the Spartacus Youth League (Trotskyite), and the large, left-dominated National Student League, the first attempt at a genuine American students' union. All these groups were small, perhaps a few dozen or a few score members on even a good-sized campus. But they wielded a great deal more influence than their numbers seemed to warrant.

The new political and social activism took many forms. Here and there arose demands for purely campus-level reforms: for better teaching, later dormitory hours, an end to compulsory classroom attendance, better food in student cafeterias. In other places, the students moved off campus to offer their help to striking working men. Students from a handful of New York schools took a famous bus ride to Harlan County, Kentucky, site of a bloody miners' strike, only to be turned back by a mob. Students at Oberlin, Goucher, Amherst, Smith, Vassar, Columbia, and other schools offered moral support, money, and even help on the picket lines to strikers in nearby communities. As college youth of the 1960's "discovered" the plight of the Negro, so the "socially conscious" young people of the 1930's suddenly became aware of the hard lot of the working man in Depression-ridden America.

Probably the two most famous—and oddly contradictory—thrusts of the university revolt of the thirties, however, were demands for new directions in America's foreign policy.

Everything Seemed to Be Moving Toward Some Final Decision

The first and numerically most powerful of these foreign policy crusades was an anti-war movement that erupted in the middle of the decade.

In a sense, of course, the student pacifism of the thirties represented not so much a new direction as a demand for the continuation of America's post-World War I isolationism. Following widely publicized exposés of Allied propaganda during the war, and of the political machinations of arms manufacturers—"merchants of death"—America was, in fact, overwhelmingly opposed to any further entanglement with the quarrels of the Old World. But student anti-war sentiment soon went well beyond the America-First isolationism of their elders. College men organized the Veterans of Future Wars and sardonically demanded their veterans' benefits in advance. They attacked the ROTC on campus. In 1933, almost forty per cent of students polled declared that they would not fight in any American war.

Over the next three years, thousands of young people annually struck their universities in support of an American version of the notorious Oxford Oath, a formal refusal "to support the United States government in any war it may conduct." The numbers involved in these one-hour annual student strikes are somewhat debatable. Some idea of the growth of the movement may, however, be gleaned from the following set of figures. In 1934, perhaps 25,-000 walked out of classes across the country; in 1935, 175,000 struck; and in 1936, with liberal college administrators in the van, as many as 350,000 cut classes to march for peace.[13]

The second major trend of the youth movement, far less important numerically, but of much greater relevance to the realities of the 1930's, was the spread of anti-fascist militance among the young, especially during the latter half of the decade.

The influence of the Communist Party, whose youth cadres were the most tightly organized and disciplined of the movement's leadership, had much to do with this new direction. The CP-USA was now following the Communist International's new line of Popular Front support for the Soviet "workers' motherland" against fascism everywhere. At least as influential as the youthful agitprop experts, however, were the books and movies of the thirties—the Eisenstein films from Russia, Silone's accounts of exploited Italian peasants, Malraux's stark portrayal of Chinese Communists martyred by Chiang Kai-shek, and the flood of enthusiastic books about Soviet Russia by Westerners who had gone to see the Five Year Plans in action.

Finally, of course, there were the events of those fearful years themselves, as seen through the eyes of young men and women trying to make sense out of the oncoming apocalypse.

The new generation of activists had found their heroes early in the decade: the miners, factory hands, Okies, and other assorted proletarians and peasants whom Communists called the "workers of the world" and Carl Sandburg simply "The People—Yes!" But the villains shoved their way onto the stage only later in the thirties, when the march of fascism was well under way. Hitler's unopposed thrusts into the Rhineland, into Austria and Czechoslovakia, Mussolini's assault on Ethiopia, and Japan's invasion of Manchuria in defiance of the League were deplored by many Americans of all ages. So was General Franco's rebellion against the fledgling Spanish Republic and the Spanish Civil War that followed.

To the young activist, however, these aggressive moves on the international chessboard meant a good deal more than they did to his disturbed elders. To the young true believer, all these events were parts of a single vast conspiracy. These were all battles in the same titanic struggle between the People—whose sole champion seemed to be Soviet Russia—and the forces of international fascism. They were all part and parcel of a conflict that was being waged around the world—and on the picket lines of New Deal America as well.

> Everything [recalled one who was young in the thirties] seemed to be moving toward some final decision, for by now the Spanish Civil War had begun, and every day felt choked with struggle. It was as if the planet had locked in combat. In the same way . . . unrest and unemployment, the political struggles inside the New Deal, suddenly became part of the single pattern of struggle in Europe against Franco and his allies Hitler and Mussolini . . .

For the young and committed, the pattern was filled out by many less obviously anti-fascist struggles

> . . . in [Silone's] Fontamara and the Valley of the Ebro, in the Salinas Valley of California that Steinbeck was describing with love for the oppressed, in the boilers of Chinese locomotives [described by Malraux] where Chiang Kai-shek was burning the brave and sacrificial militants of the Chinese Communists. Wherever I went now, I felt the moral contagion of a single idea.[14]

Another who was young then described that single idea as "the myth of the thirties." [15] It was a typical generational world view, a dramatic structuring of political reality in glaring blacks and whites. The myth of that decade, for most of the young and dedicated, was rooted in the Marxist-Leninist dialectic of class struggle and coming world revolution. It was a vision of Armageddon just around the corner, a final clash in which the victory of the People over capitalism, fascism, and all their running dogs was guaranteed by the iron laws of history. It was a grim gospel for the ideologically driven minority who truly believed—like Turgenev's Bazarov in tsarist Russia—"that our [American] society was not merely doomed but undeserving of survival, [the few] to whom every one of its institutions seemed not just unworthy of preservation but crying out to be exterminated." [16]

Spain was the great testing ground for the myth of the thirties. Less than three thousand Americans went out to join their English, French, and other generational contemporaries in offering their homage to Catalonia, or to die in the trenches before Madrid. But many more volunteered than could get visas, or could get through the Allied blockade. And many times that many knew those who went, and they fought the great generational crusade vicariously through them.

> Remember with me [writes still another of these battered veterans of the thirties] the young student who stood in that softly-appointed living room, the tears rolling down his face and the mark of death on his brow, saying: "Okay. They asked for it. Now is our chance to get them, now is our chance to kill the bastards. They've been getting away with it, but now we can smash the bastards." He stood there among the necking couples and the quiet drinkers and the loud talkers, shaking with his tears and crying out, "What are we waiting for?" [17]

Less than half the young Americans who went to fight in the International Brigade or the Abraham Lincoln Brigade returned. Neither their faith, nor the generational revolt whose finest flower they were, survived the triple catastrophe that brought the decade to a close: the Moscow purge trials, the Stalinist purges of Anarchists, Trotskyites, and other deviationists in Spain itself, and the stunning duplicity of the Hitler-Stalin pact of 1939. What faith, after all, could survive a treaty of convenience between God and the Devil?

The generational debacle was complete. "I knew in my heart," wrote Richard Wright, remembering his own final break with the Party, "that I should never . . . again . . . be able to feel with that simple sharpness about life, should never again express such passionate hope, should never again make so total a commitment . . ." [18] Each generation, as Woodrow Wilson put it, has only one great adventure.

Fifteen Thousand at the Most

There has been much debate about just how red the Red Decade really was. The meager impact all the marching and demonstrating and youthful speech-making really had on the course of American history in the 1930's has been duly pointed out. The small membership of the militant campus organizations has been emphasized—as it was at the time by beleaguered college presidents. Considerable stress has been laid upon the large numbers of young would-be world-savers who quietly abandoned the great crusade after 1939 and ended as housewives or businessmen, perhaps even vaguely ashamed of their youthful enthusiasm for a cause.

From the point of view of the Youth Revolution, however, the young militants of the Red Decade cannot so easily be dismissed. For they did play their part in the history of the spreading revolt of the younger generation.

It may be granted that most of the activists lost their militance in later life. But this is a familiar feature of the typical youth revolt, once age and adult concerns have undercut early fervor. This tendency of generational energies to dissipate does not make the modern Youth Revolution any the less formidable while those energies are at the flood.

It may be granted also that there were few totally committed revolutionaries among the young, even at the height of the movement—less than fifteen thousand in all the radical youth groups of the thirties, according to one informal estimate.[19] But, as a student leader of those days subsequently pointed out: "For every one who joined there were perhaps two who agreed in the main with what the student movement was trying to do" and many more "who were ready to support most of the campaigns or actions which the student organizations might launch . . ." [20] There may have been only fifteen thousand committed rebels, but 350,000 struck for peace in 1937. It is a pattern as familiar to campus activists of the 1960's as to their predecessors of thirty years before.

And yet the final charge must be faced: the American youth movement of the 1930's did not change the course of American history. The New Deal was committed to aiding the "forgotten man" before most college activists discovered him. Student strikes and marches may have added some weight to an already overwhelming anti-war sentiment, but they did no more than that. FDR did eventually lead the country into the world-wide struggle against fascism—but the student movement hardly influenced his judgment in the matter. The youth revolt of the thirties was a beginning; but no more than that.

The militant stream of the Youth Revolution thus reached America at last; and it had a future here. But it was in Europe that the revolt of the younger generation took a giant step forward in the 1930's. And it took that step, surprisingly enough, under the most repressively totalitarian regimes of the decade.

3. THE PARTY OF THE YOUTH

Macht Platz, ihr Alten!

"National Socialism," declares the best-known historian of the German youth movement, "came to power as the party of youth." [21] There is every evidence that this is so. The Nazis, after all, made their first political breakthrough in the late twenties, among university students. Their astonishing gains in the Reichstag elections of 1930—from twelve to 107 seats—came in considerable part because of the Party's ability to win over large numbers of disgruntled younger voters. And the Party itself, from the original Brown Shirts to the Hitler Youth, seemed to be drawn largely from the younger generation.

The slogans of the National Socialist Party emphasized this claim to be, as Hitler himself repeatedly described it, "the young party." *"Macht Platz, ihr Alten!"* thundered the Nazis at the aging rulers of the Weimar Republic: "One side, old men!" "National Socialism," they declared, "is the organized will of youth." [22]

Berlin in 1933, during the months after Hitler's rise to power, looked to foreign reporters like a city surrendered to the younger generation. "Never before," marveled a *New York Times* correspondent, "had I been in a country where youth had taken the bit between its teeth and was running amok . . ." [23]

Many other groups besides "the youth" voted for Hitler in 1933, of course, and they voted for many reasons besides ideological rebelliousness. Resentment over inflation, depression, and the virtual paralysis of the Weimar government during its last two years moved Germans of all ages. Hatred of Jews and fear of Communists was at least as widespread among shopkeepers and professional men as it was among the youth. The growing conviction that Germany needed a leader, even a man on horseback, to pull her together again, was by no means limited to young romantics in search of a hero. But the younger generation did play a crucial role in the history of Nazi Germany. And the Youth Revolution itself did enter a new phase as a result of the rise of Adolf Hitler—and the other totalitarian rulers of the thirties—to power.

We'll Have Civil War in a Fortnight!

The reasons for the upsurge of militance among the German youth are many and complicated, but the World Depression clearly loomed large among them.

The Depression probably hit Germany, and German youth, harder than it did any other nation except the United States. Germany, furthermore, was in far worse shape than America was to handle such a setback. In 1918, the proud and prosperous Reich of the 1890's had given way to the Weimar Republic, Germany's first experiment in democracy. The new government was the heir to the humiliation of the Versailles peace and the ruinous inflation that followed. It was politically divided and seemed internationally impotent. After a long decade of Weimar ineffectuality and disillusionment, the Depression thus came, not as a stunning departure from the norm, as in America, but as the last straw to a people that had supped full of miseries.

The snows of the early thirties were falling, slow and smothering and hopeless, in Europe as well as in America. Homeless, jobless men slept on benches in the Berlin Tiergarten through those cold, dark winters, just as they did in New York's Central Park. But the mood was very different on the two sides of the Atlantic. When banks fell in Berlin, people did not shrug and mutter about "the big boys" and the politicians. "The milkman says," the German landlady excitedly informed Christopher Isherwood the morning after the National and the Darmstädter collapsed, "we'll have civil war in a fortnight! Whatever do you say to that?" [24]

To the young German generation of 1930, it must have seemed quite likely. And high time too.

The young man who put on the brown shirt and swastika armband in the late 1920's, or voted National Socialist in 1930, had been born only a few years before World War I broke out. His childhood, it has been suggested, was deeply scarred by the exigencies of the war years—the physical and emotional starvation, the loss of his father to the army and his mother to the defense industries, and the eventual return—if at all—of the authoritarian German paterfamilias as a defeated man. Such psychic traumata may well have molded a generation that was peculiarly susceptible to the second national catastrophe which struck Germany twelve years later. Insecure and Oedipally unsettled, this generation may in fact have regressed to "the search for an idealized father" that led them to the feet of Adolf Hitler.[25]

Other factors also played their part, however. During the decade between the war and the Depression, this generation had grown up. During their later childhood and their 'teens, they had seen revolution and the overthrow of the Kaiser, followed by a long series of riots, putsches, and even political assassinations. Ideological extremism and political violence were a normal—and exciting—part of the only politics these young Germans knew.

Youth organizations of all kinds, furthermore, were more highly developed in Weimar Germany than anywhere else in the world. The *Wandervögel* had proliferated fantastically in the postwar years. Adult groups of all sorts developed their own youth groups—religious denominations, political parties, even the Boy Scouts. The roads of Germany in the 1920's were thronged with guitar-strumming hikers of every description, many of them seeking not only to build sound bodies but to inculcate youthful allegiance to some set of ideals.

The haunted youth of 1930 finally found a leader who intuitively understood and eagerly catered to their needs. For Adolf Hitler, like Stalin and Mussolini, was himself an alumnus of the Youth Revolution.

Adolf Hitler: From Long-Hair to Rabblerouser

Hitler had been early alienated from society at large. He found his father, a minor Austrian official, "domineering," and early rejected the bureaucratic career the old man prescribed for him. He hated school, where dry-as-dust teachers "had no sympathy with youth" and relentlessly crushed "the slightest trace of originality" in order to "stuff our brains and turn us into erudite apes like themselves." Only one instructor was able to reach little Adolf: a history teacher deeply imbued with the spirit of German nationalism, who played upon "our youthful national fanaticism" so effectively that "we would sit there enraptured in enthusiasm, and there were even times when we were on the verge of tears." [26] The future demagogue was thus early exposed to the crucial role ideas can play in stirring the passions of the young.

Hitler actually participated in both the main streams of the Youth Revolution. During the prewar years, young Adolf sought to withdraw from society into a private world of art—of painting, architecture, Wagnerian opera. For a time, he "let his hair grow long and even developed a crop of whiskers," living in Bohemian destitution, first in Vienna and then in Munich's notorious Schwabing section, on the meager proceeds from his painting.[27] It was only after World War I that he found his true métier as a revolutionary activist, an organizer and agitator in the swirling world of Weimar opposition politics.

Hitler had a magnetism that drew the youth. His sense of drama, his apparent decisiveness, his shrill arm-waving eloquence, and the endless parades, songs, rallies, and other brilliantly staged spectacles all had a special appeal for adolescence and youth. Once in power, furthermore, Hitler, like his fellow totalitarian rulers, moved vigorously to channel the power of ideologically rebellious youth into the service of the Party and the State.

In 1932, the last year before Hitler's ascendancy to the Chancellorship, the National Socialist paramilitary youth auxiliary numbered something over 100,000. Six years later, the Hitler Youth, with its child and adolescent affiliates, included more than 7,700,000 young people.[28] Only the Russian Communist *Komsomol,* with its junior auxiliaries, exceeded the *Hitler-Jugend* in size, and none excelled it in moral and emotional impact on the young.

In Nazi Germany, as in New Deal America, there was a feeling of progress, of a nation on the move again. Vast public works projects and an immense program of national rearmament put millions back to work again. Industrial production doubled, food production was up, and the nation embarked on a dramatic program of synthetics research and development intended to make Germany self-sufficient, totally independent of the outside world. Above all, there seemed to be a vigorously decisive government in Berlin again. Hitler, they said, was not afraid to stand up for the fatherland against the conniving villains of Versailles.

For the young, in particular, there was an exhilarating sense of a new world coming to birth. There were the nationwide sports programs, the dirt-cheap vacations, and the rest of the famous "Strength through Joy" program designed to make this the finest generation of young Germans since Father Jahn's day. There was the new feeling of *Gemeinschaft* among the young, of national togetherness that overrode all barriers of class and caste. In the Hitler Youth, as in the *Wandervögel* and the *Burschenschaft* before them, bankers' and bricklayers' sons were equals and comrades. And the Hitler Youth, by 1939, included all the youth of Germany.

Concentration camps had already begun to sprout as early as 1933. But nobody noticed them then.

Red-Beating and Jew-Baiting

The Hitler Youth is often seen as merely another expression of the total power of the fascist state. What could be less idealistic and less insurrectionary, after all, than the brainwashed children of Nazi Germany? The *Hitler-Jugend* themselves, however, heard a very different story from the *Führer*.

They gathered every year at the great rallies to hear him, thousands and tens of thousands of them, phalanx after phalanx of serious young faces beneath the fluttering banners and the trim new uniforms. "My German Youth!" they heard the demigod on the rostrum high above them shout:

> Seldom in the history of Germany has a fairer destiny than yours fallen to the lot of a younger generation. You live, as the youth of Germany, in a youthful Reich . . . full of joyous life, full of strong hope, full of an indestructible confidence. You live in a Reich with youthful, new ideas, full of youthful new forces . . .

A state, in short, in which youth had a place. But a state also in which youth was needed, in which much was demanded of the young:

> What we ask of you now, my Youth, is this: we wish you to be first and foremost an idealistic youth . . . consciously idealistic, because we believe that only from this fundamental attitude of idealism can a real community of the people arise . . .[29]

The ideals, like all the other ideas in these young people's heads, would of course be provided by the ideologues of the National Socialist Party. But then, ideologically motivated youth movements have usually derived their ideas from their elders.

An ideological movement—and a revolutionary one as well. Even under this most totalitarian of modern governments, Nazi Germany retained much of the aura and excitement of a people mobilizing for a social revolution.

The young Nazis who marched to power under the swastika banners were, of course, self-proclaimed revolutionaries. Hitler himself had served a short stint in jail after the abortive Munich putsch of 1923. Young veterans of the Party's rise could remember with pride the revolutionary struggles of the twenties. One such recalled the stirring "election battles" of 1930, the year of the great breakthrough, when "we kept going day and night. During the day we distributed leaflets; at night, we stuck up our posters; in the evening, we were ordered to duty at meetings. If we slept much, it was for two hours on the bare floor of the Lion Inn."[30]

But the new generation that came of age in the thirties was promised its share of revolution too. The Nazis found plenty of un-German individuals, groups, and institutions that remained to be dealt with after Hitler's accession to the Chancellorship, and the young were encouraged to take these jobs on themselves.

International Jewry, the ring of financial giants who had "betrayed" Germany in the Great War and brought the blight of the Depression down upon her, remained to be driven from the citadels of money power. The schools and universities must be purged of the tyrannical pedants and the subversive books that had so long masked as "authorities" in an intellectually stifled Germany. Even beyond the frontiers of the fatherland, there would be revolutionary work to do—German nationals to be reclaimed, German lands to be recaptured. The new youth, the *Führer* assured them, would have their share in the demolition of the old order, within Germany and without.

"The students," an eyewitness reported, "took things into their own hands, howled down the few Jewish professors who had received exceptional treatment because of war service, raided libraries, denounced suspected liberals right and left." [31] They forced university administrators to resign, compelled the firing of faculty members, began on their own hook to repeat on a mass scale that historic book-burning on the Wartburg more than a century before. They were making the revolution too. And if ever the pace seemed to flag, if the heady air of crisis seemed to wane, there was always the Leader's magnetic oratory to remind them of the tasks ahead, the odds to be overcome, the glorious victories yet to be won.

Part of Hitler's secret lay in his skill and willingness to cultivate the endemic violence of youth. The continuing revolt of the younger generation has seen a good deal of violence, of course, along with much gentleness and love and beauty. In the Thousand-Year Reich, the brutal violence of the goon squad joined that of the barricade fighter and the assassin of an earlier century in the repertoire of the Youth Revolution.

The Brown Shirts of the 1920's, along with the private armies of other political parties, prowled the streets like young lions in search of a fight. They took their casualties; they savaged their enemies. By 1933, they had swept the field. The swastika flag flapped from every building, and SA men arrogantly patrolled the streets, beating up Jews and Communists wherever they met them, like kid gangs in some American slum brutalizing any alien who wandered onto their turf.

The new generations of the thirties found Hitler equally tolerant of their youthful proclivities for violence. In fact, the *Führer* encouraged "His Youth" to move violently against all enemies of the German *Volk*. The fury of Hitler's own blood purges of Jews, Socialists, and of his own SA formations provided vivid examples for the young. Truckloads of Storm Troopers roared through the darkness, machine guns at the ready, dragging enemies of the State out of their beds across the country in a single night. There was a spectacular dramatic quality to the Leader's style that set the blood to pounding in the young animal beneath the trim new uniform of the *Hitler-Jugend*.

And all this Jew-baiting and university-wrecking was merely the prologue. The great struggle for the fatherland was yet to come. Soon the youth of Germany was prowling the forests and fields in full battle gear, carrying rifles instead of guitars, playing war games, far removed from the gentle legend of the Wandering Birds.

Tomorrow the World

Everywhere in totalitarian Europe in the later 1930's, youth was on the march. In Communist Russia, the marching formation might be the Young Octobrists or the *Komsomol.* In Fascist Italy, they were called the Wolf Cubs, the *Avanguardisti,* the Young Fascists. In Germany, they were the Young Folk, the League of German Maidens, or the Hitler Youth. In the West, people shook their heads at the robot-like march of the youthful millions. They called them slaves of the swastika, or shuddered at stories of how Stalin was molding a generation of atheists.

Even the most unsympathetic reporters had to admit, however, that something was happening here. Radio reporter William L. Shirer, for example, shuddered at the ideological poison that was being pumped into the heads of German young people. But he admitted that "the boys and the girls, the young men and women, seemed immensely happy, filled with a zest for the life of a Hitler Youth. . . . The young in the Third Reich," he confessed, "were growing up to have strong and healthy bodies, faith in the future of their country and themselves, and a sense of fellowship and camaraderie that shattered all class and economic and social barriers." [32]

They swung along the roads of Germany to the tune of the "Horst Wessel Song," the hymn of the Party's chosen young martyr to the cause. But they sang their own anthem too, a ringing challenge to the world:

Und heute gehört uns Deutschland
Und morgen die ganze Welt.

Today all Germany belongs to us—
Tomorrow, all the world! [33]

Shirer saw them again in 1940, marching into Belgium in their sharp new *Wehrmacht* uniforms, and was impressed once more by "the contrast between the German soldiers, bronzed and clean-cut from a youth spent in the sunshine . . . and the first British war prisoners with their hollow chests, round shoulders, pasty complexions and bad teeth . . ." [34] In England, the grinning Midlands youth in the cloth cap had been given a dole—and nothing more. German youth had been given a faith to live by and a place in society at large, and had flourished like the green bay tree.

"Tomorrow the world!" they sang. They did not get it, obviously. Hitler's sun-bronzed legions were soon storming off across the snowy plains of Russia to confront other blond young warriors with a cause. And when Hitler's *Blitzkrieg* slammed into Stalin's artillery, lined up hub to hub around Stalingrad, another generation of European youth would be shredded into raw meat by the machinery of modern war. We saw the last of them in the old newsreels, hollow-cheeked and unshaven, stumbling in their battered greatcoats as they began their last long march to somewhere beyond the Urals. The bodies of many of their comrades, and of millions of young Russians too, were left behind them in the snow.

The *Führer* unleashed all that was worst, as well as much that was best, in the German youth of the 1930's. But the shrewd psychopath in Berlin—like the silent paranoid in the Kremlin—had hit upon a profound truth. Youth felt left out. The younger generation, untrained and inexperienced, had no place in complex modern society. The young, desperately trying to make sense out of a changing world, could get no enduring principles out of their harried parents. The state that would make a place for youth as a functioning part of the social order, and that could inspire the new generation with a vision of a better life, might yet unleash an immense new force upon the world.

10

*"I Saw the Best Minds of My Generation Starving Hysterical Naked . . ." * The Beats and the Angries Both Sides of the Iron Curtain, 1950*

The world staggered even more groggily out of the second global conflict of the century than it had out of the first. Things tasted a little better this time, at least on the winning side: the crimes of Hitler made it all seem worth while. But few sensitive people could look back with martial pride on the fire-bombing of Dresden or the atom bombs over Japan. John Hersey's grimly factual *Hiroshima* was soon required reading in many American high schools. In Europe and Asia, of course, winners and losers alike had their own ruins to dig out of. It was hard to feel very triumphant about it all, somehow, once the confetti had settled and the hangovers had faded away.

World War II, then, like World War I, left little energy and few ideals intact around which youthful militance might coalesce. Not surprisingly, however, this second postwar period of the century did see another wave of nonmilitant rejection of the *status quo* among the young—a second massive generational withdrawal comparable to that of the 1920's. This pervasive youthful alienation of the 1950's is the subject of this chapter.

This is not, of course, to say that there was no youthful militance, no political activism at all among the younger generations of the fifties.

The first word the world heard of the astonishing Hungarian revolt of 1956, for example, was a broadcast from Radio Budapest

* Allen Ginsberg, "Howl, Parts I and II," in Donald M. Allen, ed., *The New American Poetry 1945–1960* (New York and London), 1960, p. 182.

that began with a vivid vignette right out of an earlier century of the Youth Revolution:

> National flags, young people with rosettes of the national colors singing the Kossuth song, the Marseillaise, and the Internationale. . . . This afternoon a vast youth demonstration took place in our capital . . .

The rebellion was in fact far more a nineteenth-century nationalist revolt, of the sort in which youth had played so prominent a part, than it was an anti-Communist upheaval. And the instigators of this massive effort to drive the Russians from the soil of Hungary were once more "students of all the universities and high schools of Budapest . . ." [1]

Far larger than the scattered East European revolts against Russian hegemony, however, was the sweeping emancipation movement among the people of the far-flung European colonial empires in Asia and Africa. The generational element was clearly evident here as well. The leaders of these postwar struggles for national liberation were members of young generations "emancipated" from their African or Asian heritage by Western educations. Gripped by Western ideologies—nationalism, socialism, even liberalism—this new wave of youthful leadership rebelled against both European dominance and the "backward" traditional ideas and practices of their own fathers. They carved out half a hundred new nations, the nations of the so-called "Third World," in the process.

Yet the fifties were not a decade of notable militance among the young. The anti-Russian revolts were quickly and massively crushed —the Hungarian revolt, for instance, was broken in just thirteen days after that first astonishing "youth demonstration" behind the Iron Curtain. The national liberation struggles, on the other hand, were often all too easily won. European imperial powers, exhausted by World War II, let the peoples of the Third World go with comparatively little resistance—leaving the new generation of "mission-boy" leaders untested, the peoples themselves not yet molded into self-conscious nationhood by serious struggle.

In most places, finally, activism was hardly even considered in the demoralized fifties. It was, instead, a decade of withdrawal, a decade when youth drew back into its own subculture once more to lick its wounds—and accumulate new generational energies for the explosive resurgence of youthful militance that was to come.

1. *CHILDREN OF THE BOMB*

Hula Hoops and Higher Education

On the surface, the 1950's, like the 1920's, were a time of youthful escapism, when the young withdrew from political involvement into a gilded ghetto of their own. And never since the social and educational ghettoization of the younger generation began 150 years before had the private world of the youth been so golden—or so overpopulated.

The fun culture of the fifties made that of the twenties look almost Victorian by contrast. The new affluence of the United States was dazzling beyond anything in recorded history. The Marshal Plan and the "economic miracles" of Germany and Japan soon carried a considerable share of the new prosperity to other lands as well. Even behind the Iron Curtain, enough wealth accumulated to provide the new generation of the ruling elites with a self-indulgent life style that must have made Old Bolsheviks spin in their graves.

Everywhere, much of this new affluence went to the young. An international youth culture grew up, with a vast array of youth industries pandering to its needs. The Pepsi generation must have its blue jeans and hula hoops, its hi-fi and TV and surf boards, its motorbikes and cars. America set the tune, and the youth of the world danced to it. Political action was the furthest thing from the mind of these pampered generations.

How far the youth-oriented fun culture of the fifties—like that of the twenties—represented a subtle form of generational disaffiliation, we shall see presently.

Other factors, meanwhile, were shaping these postwar generations into growing and increasingly unified cohorts with their own peculiar views of the world. Perhaps most importantly, educational institutions enfolded vastly larger numbers of the young for longer and longer periods of their lives. During the decade 1952-1961, the global school enrollment at all levels more than doubled, from 220,000,000 to 447,000,000. The so-called *explosion scolaire* put almost forty percent of young people 18 to 21 years of age into some sort of educational institution, compared to half that number ten years earlier.[2] The Communist victory in China and the Red take-overs in Eastern Europe, furthermore, brought massive, totalitarian-style youth organizations into existence, comparable to those that still flourished in Soviet Russia.

Everywhere, in short, the older generation continued at an accelerated pace to institutionalize the ghettoization of their children. New generations thus segregated and, in most cases, rigidly cut off from significant involvement in the larger world around them, would emerge in the 1960's as a power bloc of unparalleled size and strength, with interests, attitudes, and styles of life totally at variance with the functioning values of society at large.

The extent to which this youth culture felt a real ideological alienation from their parents' world even in the nonmilitant fifties will be estimated in the pages that follow. For beneath the frivolous surface of the fun culture, many dark resentments flickered—and with good reason.

Double Bind and the Doomsday Machine

The youth of the 1950's were the children of cataclysm and the double bind. In ideological, emotional, spiritual terms, they formed a generation born to lose.

Cataclysms gathered like great birds of prey around their childhood and adolescent years. Yet somehow, the great wings scarcely seemed to touch the new generation directly. This in itself provided a special frustration for the young, who might have responded as passionately as their parents had to a concrete challenge, a simple black-and-white imperative like those of the 1930's. Lacking such simple choices, the postwar generation groped in a fog of complications and contradictions that seemed to leave them only one live option: psychic withdrawal from the system.

The youth of the fifties, for instance, could remember little of the Second World War and less of the Depression. These catastrophes did shape their generation indirectly, however—through their parents. An older generation who had lived through the greatest war in history, for example, was bound to be a bit nervous. People who had grown up in the jobless thirties were quite likely to be excessively preoccupied with money and material security. Such nervous, overly materialistic parents, in turn, would have their own peculiar effect on the next generation. The parents had eaten bitter fruit, and the children's teeth were on edge.

The Cold War and the crumbling of the great European world empires—the two most cataclysmic consequences of World War II—had a more direct impact upon the young. But these also failed to provide the satisfying sense of clear-cut issues and conflict for a cause that could mold a generation of militants. The Cold War, in particular, entangled the young of many lands in a bewildering mesh of pressures and counterpressures, of tarnished ideals and unsatisfying pragmatism that effectively stifled militant idealism.

In Germany and Japan, for instance, the crushing defeat of the older generations in World War II, coupled with the moral opprobrium the whole world heaped on the fascism and expansionist militarism of the thirties, had a profoundly alienating effect on the young. In their children's eyes, no "economic miracle" engineered by their elders could eradicate the stigma of having once been Nazis and militarists, and of having been humiliatingly defeated into the bargain. The resulting generational ambivalence toward the fathers was further intensified by the simple fact that, practically speaking, no youth crusade could be mounted against parental lapses which were, after all, past history, shadows beyond the reach of activism. Distaste and chafing discontent were there, but generational revolt was sheerly impossible.

Among the youth of the victorious Allies, all sense of triumph was quickly undercut by the upsurge of the Cold War. But here again, catastrophe could produce no clear-cut militant response on the part of the young.

American youth might bridle at the arrogance of Russian power politics in the take-over of East Europe, or in the Berlin blockade. But no liberal youth could approve of McCarthyism, and no humane one could find much to cheer about in the grubby, bloody "police action" in Korea. About the time the young potential radical found himself drifting back toward the pro-Russian politics of the thirties, however, he was brought up sharply by the shocking spectacle of Russian tanks rumbling into East Berlin or Budapest. It was a bind—bind and double bind. American sociologists like

Daniel Bell began to talk seriously about "the end of ideology" in the 1950's.

Russian youth, on the other hand, might work up a considerable head of steam over "capitalist encirclement" ("containment" we called it in the West). But the late forties and the early fifties were also the years of Stalin's last brutal purges—at least as uninspiring a time in Russia as in McCarthyite America. When Stalin died in 1953, of course, the young Russian might exult in the new freedom of the "thaw." But the shadow of their parents' complicity in Stalinism, of "Babi Yar" and *A Day in the Life of Ivan Denisovich,* lay heavy upon them even then. That, and the growing realization of just how limited the Khrushchev brand of "freedom" was going to be.

Among the European allies and satellites of the two Cold War giants, simmering discontent was also frustrated by the very circumstances which kindled it. In the Soviet satellite states, Russian hegemony was a bitter pill for the intensely nationalistic peoples of East Europe, many of whom had won their independence as recently as World War I. In Western Europe, many young people were glad enough to see the old empires go, however much their parents might lament the passing of European greatness. But these same young people joined their elders in resenting American business dominance and the continuing American military presence in Europe itself, not to mention the extent to which their governments clearly kowtowed to Washington. And yet—to cap the emotional confusion—these same young generations eagerly lapped up American pop culture—movies and music, costumes and fads—by the bale.

On both sides of the Iron Curtain, finally, there was the fundamental frustration of realizing that power did, in irreducible fact, reside in Washington and Moscow: that where so much sheer might was involved, young Europe's notions of what was merely right were simply irrelevant. A hard lesson for the young to learn, but one which they could hardly escape in postwar Europe.

Overarching all other concerns, finally, there was the Bomb and the Balance of Terror. The ever present threat of a nuclear Armageddon was new and horrifying to generations who could remember Hiroshima as a newspaper headline. The proliferation of superweapons—A-Bombs and H-Bombs, atomic submarines and intercontinental missiles—seemed to proceed with a nightmarish inevitability. The feeling was perfectly captured in the mad "Doomsday Machine" of *Dr. Strangelove*—man had created the ultimate catastrophe, and now he could not turn it off. A subsequent generation, sated with end-of-the-world movies and novels, has grown almost blasé about it. But it was all new and mind-warpingly unbelievable to these first-born children of the Bomb. Confronted with the sheer day-to-day reality of a lemming-like world plunging blindly toward its own destruction, the mind of youth veered wildly, battered its wings against the bars—and careened once more toward the total alienation of the Dada masters.

Many young people, of course, simply had fun because fun was there for the having. But there was a subtly muted tone, a tendency to irritable shrugs and sudden silences when larger questions came up, even among the most dedicated fun culturists. And the decade of the silent generation, it must be remembered, also saw the "Beat" revolt, the beginning of a whole new cycle of generational disaffiliation and rebellion.

2. *THE SUBTERRANEANS*

Howl

"Beat," declared Jack Kerouac, whose *On the Road* made the Beat Generation an American byword, "means beatific, it means you get the beat, it means . . . Zen, apple pie, Eisenhower—we dig it all. We're in the vanguard of the new religion." The husky Canuck and former footballer enthused over the "subterranean hip generation" with its "tendencies to silence, bohemian mystery, drugs, beard, semiholiness . . ." [3] For the involved minority of the youth, at least, the "beat mystique" was a whole new epiphany, a revelation of how things were, and of how they ought to be.

Like *Dada, Beat* seemed to be a word of a million definitions. "To be beat," wrote a sympathetic, sometime participant, "is to be at the bottom of your personality, looking up . . ." Norman Mailer, in his celebrated essay, *The White Negro,* described the beat youth as "the American existentialist"—

> the hipster, the man who knows that if our collective condition is to live with instant death by atomic war . . . or with a slow death by conformity with every creative and rebellious instinct stifled . . . why then the only life-giving answer is . . . to divorce oneself from society, to exist without roots, to set out on that uncharted journey into the rebellious imperatives of the self.

But it was probably Allen Ginsberg's savage and tender characterization of his contemporaries—in *Howl,* the *Wasteland* of the Beat Generation—that best defined them:

> I saw the best minds of my generation destroyed by madness,
> starving hysterical naked . . .
> angelheaded hipsters burning for the ancient heavenly connection to the starry dynamo in the machinery of night . . .
> who were expelled from the academies for crazy & publishing obscene odes on the windows of the skull,
> who cowered in unshaven rooms in underwear, burning their money in wastebaskets and listening to the Terror through the wall,
> who got busted in their pubic beards returning through Laredo with a belt of marijuana for New York,
> who . . . purgatoried their torsos night after night
> with dreams, with drugs, with waking nightmares, alcohol and cock and endless balls . . .

a restless, sensuous, spiritually hungry generation

> who lit cigarettes in boxcars boxcars boxcars racketing through snow toward lonesome farms in grandfather night,
> [and] studied Plotinus Poe St. John of the Cross telepathy and bop kaballa because the cosmos instinctively vibrated at their feet in Kansas . . .[4]

Experts used many words to describe them: alienation, anomie, lack of commitment, refusal to get "involved" in their parents' world. They were obviously a cohort of young dissenters. And they were on the move, though they might have been hard put to it to tell you where they were going.

A Society Which Is Rational But No Longer Sane

To the average American, however, the "beatnik" of the fifties was a journalistic stereotype much like the "hippie" of the sixties. He was long-haired and bearded, weirdly costumed, dirty, depraved, shiftless, and nihilistic. The female of the species, the beat "chick," was all of the above, except bearded. Both were fanatical devotees of jazz music, sexually hyperactive (promiscuously, homosexually, and even orgiastically), and devoted to every sort of intoxicant, from cheap wine through marijuana and peyote to the icy shores of heroin addiction. It was also generally suspected—Jack Kerouac to the contrary—that they did not love Eisenhower and apple pie.

There was much truth in this popular conception. There was also much that it left out.

Clearly, this was a self-contained subculture; almost as clearly, it was a counter culture on the by now hoary Bohemian model. As a separate subculture within American society, the beats had their own shabby "uniform," from beard to sandals. They had the usual private language—*hip, beat, square, cool, dig, crazy,* and so on. They had their scattered Bohemian enclaves, from Greenwich Village in New York to North Beach in San Francisco. They had of course their in-group mores—the music, the drugs, the sex, and the rest of it.

They had their beat "quest" too, a rambling search rather similar to that of the *Wandervögel* of fifty years before. Like the German "Wandering Birds," the beats went in search of the *real* homeland they had been raised to love, and had not found when they grew to man's estate. In their quest for that real America, many beats followed Kerouac West, out of the Eastern cities into the mythic America of Western movie and novel and comic book. They rediscovered the big sky, the ocean, the mountains and deserts, Big Sur and Mexico.

As a subculture, they also had their own ethos, an existential code well suited to these raw-nerved generations of the fifties. The virtues they tried at least to live by included such youthful imperatives as honesty, freedom, a determined if sometimes rather desperate effort to communicate, and a passion to live and experience everything—to dig it all. At the heart of this generational code lay an ecstatic irrationalism that would have been familiar enough to many preceding generations of romantic outcasts. Their Dionysiac enthusiasm for Charlie "Bird" Parker's brand of jazz, for Reichian sex, for grass and cheap wine and Zen Buddhism, all reflected this rejection of sterile intellection in favor of intense visceral experience. So, paradoxically, did the traditional "cool" stance of the full-blown hipster, the pose of total emotional catatonia. The complete cool cat—ideally a heroin addict entirely withdrawn into his own inner world—rejected both rational discourse *and* emotional commitment with his frigid "I'm hip, man." His was a frozen, private ecstasy, very different from the screaming, foot-stomping jazz orgies of his cohorts; but the addict's withdrawal certainly brooked no futile cerebration either.

There was an outside world, of course: they knew it well. It was the place where they washed dishes for a living, or drew their unemployment checks. They had a highly developed contempt for it. For this was a counter culture too.

Some of the things they rejected were, of course, the "names of violence and disaster" that had made them what they were: "Fascism, Nazism, Communism, Spain . . . Hitler-Stalin nonaggression pact . . . Dachau, Hiroshima, Hungary, Suez . . ." They were horrified at the thought of the atomic bomb as an instrument of national policy, rebelling violently against "a society which is only rational *but no longer sane,* a society which, because it has divorced man from his intuitive self, can talk calmly of waging nuclear war." [5]

On a day-to-day basis, however, the new Bohemians rebelled most consistently and completely against the bourgeois life style and the middle-class values in which most of them had been raised. The catalogue of bourgeois vices they posted was not unfamiliar. It included the crass materialism and futile ambition, the phony morality and false patriotism that were the older generation's heritage from a war and a depression the new youth had never experienced. It included also the hopeless lack of spontaneity and feeling, the soul-stifling conformity, intolerance, and inhibition that every generation from the flappers back to the first Bohemians had condemned in Western bourgeois society. And it included the self-defeating optimism and plain stupidity of Ike Eisenhower and the suburban millions who voted for him. The world blows up, lamented the beat poet Ferlinghetti, but golf goes on at Burning Tree.

In the fifties, there was some surprised comment on the strange affinity many beatniks felt for Adlai Stevenson, the polished, articulate intellectual who tried to "talk sense to the American people" and was twice defeated for President. From the beat point of view, the similarities were obvious: both the sophisticated gentleman from Libertyville and the scruffy Bohemians from nowhere in particular were prophets. And both he and they were without honor in their own country.

No Leaves in Their Hair

The other side of the American coin, at least according to the conventional wisdom of the 1950's, was the so-called "silent generation." This vast majority of the young—so it was said—was totally sold on the system. They sported crew cuts and button-down shirts. Their goals in life were limited to a gray flannel suit, a slot in the corporate hierarchy, and the proverbial split level in the suburbs, complete with tidy green lawn, barbecue out back, three and a half children (the official average), a dog, and a canary. *Security* was their highest ideal. It was generally assumed that they despised Reds, blacks, and beatniks, and voted a straight Republican ticket.

It does not seem to have been quite that way.

A conservative poll of college opinion, for example, concluded that "the dominant mood" among students was "permissive, antireligious, and relativist in the realm of ethics; statist [New Dealish] in the realm of politics; anti-anti-Communist in the crisis which grips our age. In a word, it is liberal." The Yale psychologist, Kenneth Keniston, found a number of short-haired Yalies who were every bit as alienated as their ostentatiously beat contemporaries. One of them, asked to list his dislikes, responded simply: "nearly everything, and everyone that's complacently middle-class." Another declared that "I have come to experience horror at the good American way of life, namely the comfortable, middle-class existence . . ." [6] The catalogue of detestable bourgeois qualities which these uncommitted Ivy Leaguers compiled was a carbon copy of the hipster's bitter litany.

Straight youth, in and out of college, lapped up films like Brando's *The Wild One* and James Dean's *Rebel Without a Cause.* The West Coast "Hell's Angels" and other outlaw motorcycle gangs, the violent nihilists of the road, became furtive folk heroes among the young. The more intellectually inclined pored over such mid-century classics of alienation as Colin Wilson's *The Outsider,* Camus' *The Rebel* and *The Stranger,* and the plays of Sartre, especially *No Exit.* They discovered the Absurdist school of drama—Ionesco and Genet, the early Albee, Pinter, Beckett's *Endgame* and *Waiting for Godot,* and all those other hilarious, horrifying psychodramas of a squirrel-cage world going nowhere. *Yes,* breathed many a bespectacled young man on his way to the corporate slot and the split level, *yes, that's how it is!*

Beat protest poetry sold like hot cakes in the most sedate city and college bookstores. Tourists and "weekend beats" swarmed into the Bohemian ghettos, eager to make the scene, dig it all, *live*—for a few hours, anyway. Many young people who did not dare to make the break, to go On the Road with Kerouac—the Easy Rider of his generation—sighed nonetheless over verses like Lawrence Ferlinghetti's "Junkman's Obbligato":

> Let's go
> Come on
> Let's go
> Empty out our pockets
> and disappear.
> Missing all our appointments
> and turning up unshaven
> years later
> old cigarette papers
> stuck to our pants
> leaves in our hair.

Jack Kerouac's wide readership—once he found a publisher at all—came not from his "spontaneous bop prosody," but precisely from the fact that he *had* dared to break away from the all-powerful System. When Ferlinghetti urged:

> Let us go then you and I
> leaving our neckties behind on lampposts

Take up the full beard
of walking anarchy
looking like Walt Whitman
a home made bomb in the pocket

there were many more who longed to join him than dared to admit it, even to themselves.[7]

A great many intelligent young people, in short, were really very unhappy with life in Ike's America. Both the beardy-weirdy and the button-down young conformist, furthermore, chose the same basic way of dealing with this unpalatable situation: withdrawal, escape into a private world of their own. For the beatnik, it was the quiet, dimly lit little world of the coffee house or the anarchic freedom of the open road. For the square, it was the highly touted "togetherness" of the suburban, red-brick rancher, where he could cling to wife and children for warmth, grill steaks in the back yard, and let the world go hang. They said the beatnik was alienated. "Privatism," was a word much used to describe the suburban phenomenon.

There was, in short, very little "booster" talk among the youth of the fifties, on either side of the respectability line. The silent generation accepted the System because they saw no viable alternatives and no hope anyway of toppling big business, big labor, and big government from their awesome pedestals of power. What could one man do against city hall? The most anarchistic beat sadly echoed these sentiments:

Where does one stand who contends
a stand taken is a fall invited?

asked Gregory Corso.[8] The fullfledged hipster merely grunted "I'm hip" and froze into a silence deeper and more ominous than the most uptight square's.

In the next decade, a handful of black Southern college kids would show them what the individual could do. But for the young generations of the 1950's, beat or button-down, there was only one solution: find someplace to hide.

3. *STYLE-CHASERS AND SPIRITUAL BARBARIANS*

Slouching Toward Byzantium

During the 1950's, as in the 1920's, Americans crossed the Atlantic in record numbers to travel, work, and study in the Old World. Young people of all sorts made the pilgrimage, from students doing their "junior year abroad" to GI's assigned to America's NATO contingent. One increasingly prominent type of the later fifties, however, was the new American Bohemian, replete with rucksack and desert boots, scraggly beard, "Jesus cut," and holy madness in the eyes.

One saw them everywhere: drowsing away an afternoon under the bridges of Paris, cadging handouts on the Via Veneto, digging the Acropolis, thumbing eastward on the road to Istanbul. Everywhere, they stood out, and people stared and wondered. Obviously this strange, shaggy new breed of trans-Atlantic Bohemian had nothing more to learn from the Europeans in that line.

It marked, in fact, a clear shift in the radiant center of the Youth Revolution. In the twenties, Hemingway had made a beeline for the Montmartre cafés already famous in the nineties. Malcolm Cowley had made special trips to Paris to see what this strange new madness called Dada might be all about. In the fifties, however, Allen Ginsberg or Gregory Corso had only to slouch onto the scene to become the cynosure of all eyes. Bohemianism, American style, like American music, movies, soft drinks, and comic books, was clearly in the vanguard.

But Europe had its own brands of anti-social youth too.

Long-haired young people lounged at the café tables of the *Deux Magots,* staring bleakly out at a France without glory or even *civilisation,* sunk in a Sartrean existential funk. Indigenous beards met the tourist buses in Warsaw, bright-eyed and voluble, hands extended. Even in the British welfare state and the Soviet workers' paradise, dissident young people seeemd to be "dropping out" in their own special ways. A glance at a couple of these European-style youth revolts will serve to round out our picture of the great generational withdrawal of the fifties.

Scum

In Britain, the welfare state inaugurated after the great Labor victory of 1945 spawned its own special discontents. Ironically, these discontents were strongest among the sons of the very laboring men who were the main beneficiaries of the new order.

Youthful disaffection ran the gamut in England, from the street-fighting juvenile delinquents called "Teddy Boys" to the youthful literary protesters internationally known as the "angry young men." By and large, they had in common a working-class background and a strong feeling of having been "sold" by the celebrated socialist reforms of the later forties. Labor's great victory and the institutionalization of many of the wild notions of the Fabian youth of fifty years before had simply not brought Utopia to Britain after all. "Phony" was, in fact, one of the key words in this strangely apolitical revolt of the nation's alienated blue-collar youth.

Their elders, Laborite and Conservative alike, couldn't understand it. The meager dole of the thirties had expanded in the post-war years into the National Health Service, public housing, a raft of new grammar schools and "red-brick" universities for the sons of the laboring man. The welfare state was here: "Cradle to the grave" security was a reality. And still the new generation was not happy!

The voices of these dissenting children of a socialized Britain were the so-called angry young men. Sons of the working classes, educated far beyond their parents' reach, yet still clearly excluded from the Oxbridge circles that remained the nation's unchallenged elite, these writers spoke for many less articulate than they who were caught in a similar bind. Such authors as John Osborne, John Wain, Kingsley Amis, and Allen Sillitoe brought a new protagonist to English fiction, films, and the stage:

> A new hero [wrote one critic] has risen among us. Is he the intellectual tough or the tough intellectual? He is consciously, even conscientiously, graceless. His face, when not dead pan, is set in a snarl of exasperation. He has one skin too few . . . it is the phoney to which his nerve-ends are tremblingly exposed, and at the least suspicion of the phoney he goes tough.[9]

This hard-boiled new anti-hero was a lineal descendant of the Russian nihilists of the 1860's, and a cousin to all the overeducated native elites in the vanishing European empires of their own time. Like Bazarov or Kwame Nkrumah, the "angry" had been educated out of his own class without being admitted to the higher orders. He was the *raznochinets* of the British fifties.

Sometimes he tried and failed ignominiously to make the move up, like Kingsley Amis's ill-fated Lucky Jim. Less frequently, he actually succeeded in marrying the boss's daughter and winning a place at the apex, like John Braine's Harry Lampton of *Room at the Top*. Either way, he lost. He was never really accepted by the chinless wonders who ran the country, yet he could not go home again to the cluttered, working-class flat of his childhood. Thanks to the 1944 Education Act, he had done intellectually in a single decade what had formerly taken two or three generations to accomplish. It was a leap that simply couldn't be duplicated in society at large.

His response, despite the rubric "angry" with which the school was tagged, was not militant in any politically activist sense. He had no program for social change. The traditional lower-class animus toward "all the pig-faced snotty-nosed dukes and ladies—who can't add two and two together and would mess themselves like loonies if they didn't have slavies to beck-and-call" remained strong in the new generation.[10] But it had almost as little use for the Labor party: It was "reform," after all, that had created the present agonizing contretemps.

The wide-ranging contempt of the "tough intellectuals" was, of course, reciprocated. Laborites shrugged them off as useless; self-styled literary aristocrats like Somerset Maugham called them "scum."[11]

Perhaps the most eloquent incarnation of this spirit of alienation was John Osborne's Jimmy Porter of *Look Back in Anger,* the play that changed the face of British theater in 1956. Jimmy Porter is the long-haired, insurgent son of a proletarian hero of the thirties, one of those who demonstrated the futility of militance by dying wretchedly for a lost and tainted cause in Spain. Jimmy himself has been to university, and has married the cultivated daughter of one of Britain's few surviving imperial proconsuls. He is a piercingly intelligent, brutally honest young man with a "sort of genius for love and friendship"—on his own absolute terms. In the phony world of postwar Britain, he is a "spiritual barbarian."[12] He can find nothing better to do with his frustrated existence than savage his aristocratic wife, fight with his working-class friend, blow his heart out on the trumpet, and while away the days running a candy stall in Soho.

Dirt and Boogie Woogie

The youth scene in Khrushchev's Russia was an odd mélange of 1930's *Komsomol* enthusiasm, widespread 1950's apathy, and some uniquely Russian forms of youthful dissent. Beneath the apparent diversity, however, a unifying spirit of restless alienation percolated. In their own muted way, Soviet youth was dropping out too.

The Communist Youth League, the *Komsomol,* of course still survived in Russia, the last of the great totalitarian youth organizations of the thirties. Tens of millions of young Russians participated in its practical instruction, its sports and cultural programs, and its Party indoctrination. And in the mid-fifties, hundreds of thousands of these were given a unique opportunity to make the experience an exciting, challenging, truly revolutionary one. They were asked to help change the face and reshape the economy of their country.

Khrushchev's "virgin lands" scheme to bring vast tracts of Russian Central Asia under the plow for the first time may have had its economic drawbacks, but it was just the sort of challenge to kindle the imagination of the young. Shrewdly, the cunning old peasant in the Kremlin made the massive pioneering venture the special responsibility of the Communist Youth.

> I saw them in Moscow [wrote a foreign Communist visiting in Russia] at the building of the Komsomol, which seemed transformed into a partisan headquarters of revolutionary days, with that air of confusion and improvisation which accompanies the feverish hours before extraordinary events.

Like Hitler in the 1930's, like Mao in the sixties, Khrushchev was offering the new generation a chance to relive the revolution, to taste for themselves "the difficulties, the sacrifices, the fighting enthusiasms amid which the new society was born."

> I saw them a few months later [wrote the same admittedly not unbiased witness] on the steppes of the Kulunda, between the Altai and Kazakhstan, where they lived in tent colonies and in freight cars. . . . There was about them a marked personality,

> a maturity, a tone of self-assurance which exists in the boy who has assumed the responsibilities of a man.[13]

The virgin lands program was a large-scale generational crusade, ideologically informed and imaginatively stirring. For the student of the history of the Youth Revolution, the project provides an interesting example of the extent to which youthful energies can be channeled into socially constructive paths—without, in this case, the endemic violence associated with the Hitler Youth.

But the most widely heralded event of the Russian fifties was not a recapitulation of things past, but what seemed at least to be a sharp break with "Stalin's iron age." Stalin died in 1953, a sickly, suspicious old man, totally unmourned by the Party leaders who had cowered for years in his shadow. The famous "thaw" began almost at once, with the purging of the secret police. Three years later, the anti-Stalinist campaign reached its climax with Khrushchev's celebrated "secret speech" at the Party Congress of 1956, exposing the crimes of the dead dictator.

Through the middle fifties, then, Stalinist tyranny was attacked, the secret police downgraded still further, numerous enemies of the Soviet State "rehabilitated" and—if they were still alive—brought back from Siberia. Party politics and bureaucratic inefficiency and arrogance were roundly denounced. Writers were allowed a greater freedom than they had known for thirty years. And young writers—particularly the younger poets and the new novelists—seized the opportunity to express themselves and to criticize Soviet reality with a new frankness. The result was an era of muckraking unparalleled in Soviet Russia's short history.

Novels like Ehrenburg's *Thaw,* Dudintsev's *Not by Bread Alone,* and, somewhat later, Solzhenitsyn's autobiographical account of life in a Stalinist slave camp, *One Day in the Life of Ivan Denisovich Zhukov,* were devoured by the younger generation. Like the American beat poets across the Atlantic, young Russian poets gave public readings which drew enthusiastic audiences of young people in turtle necks and sneakers in cities like Moscow and Leningrad. The language of Yevtushenko—damned by Party critics as the "ideological leader of the juvenile delinquents"—and of his even younger comrades was less lurid than that of Ginsberg and Corso, but their verses stirred the same rebellious chords in the new generation:

> You say in your presence we couldn't see dirt?
> We want to see dirt!
> Do you hear?
> It is time!
> We want to know in what corners it lay hidden,
> to look into the contorted faces of our foes,
> that we may twist their arms,
> that we may wring their necks.[14]

While older Russians struggled painfully to comprehend "de-Stalinization," the reversal of all they had been taught for three decades, this "literary opposition" and its youthful readership seized upon it avidly. The Great Patriotic War was a fading memory for them, after all, and the first Five Year Plans something you read about in schoolbooks. These great crusades of their elders' lives—of which "dear comrade Stalin" had been the official guiding genius—meant little to the young. When Yevtushenko—the lanky, mop-haired prince of the new poets—told the old folks in the provinces that Stalin had indeed been a tyrant (and, by implication, all their sufferings in vain), tears filled their eyes. But bright-eyed young Muscovites could inform foreign visitors with unhesitating passion that the great war leader and architect of the Soviet State had been "a vampire in the uniform of a generalissimo." [15]

Like the angry young Englishmen, they talked a militant game; but they did nothing. They had no program for a better Russia either.

Most young Russians of the fifties, however, neither flung themselves heart and soul into *Komsomol* crusades nor hoarded the famous typewritten manuscripts of the more unpublishable "thaw" poetry. Most seem to have been a thoroughly disillusioned lot. Apathy, and even a Western-style fun culture, were serious problems even in the puritanically work-oriented, ideologically saturated Russia of the 1950's.

Many young people, baffled by the sudden reversals of the "thaw" and bored to tears by official ideologizing, simply "turned off" on all political questions. They told busybody local *Komsomol* leaders to leave their private lives alone. They thronged to plays and devoured short stories that dealt with *human* problems—like love—rather than the eternal social-realist preachments about heroic collective farmers making their quotas in the nick of time. They shrugged off the required Marxist-Leninist lectures and demanded to know about Hemingway and Picasso instead.

For many Russian young people, Russian "people's democracy" was more of a wry joke than anything else. A Scandinavian exchange student picked up the following "typical comment on Soviet society" at a Saturday-night party at the University of Moscow:

> Three friends sat together in a railway compartment. After a long spell of silence, one of them said "Yes." Pause. The next one said "Yes." Pause. And then the third one said: "Oh, why don't we stop talking politics?" [16]

Some young people were so totally disillusioned that they turned their backs, not only on Marxism and "politics," but even on patriotism, on that love of Mother Russia that had carried their parents through so many trials. These extreme examples of Soviet alienation were called *Nibonicho,* "Nonbelievers." To John Gunther, who was "inside" Russia for the second time in the 1950's, this turned-off youth "resembled strikingly the nihilistic youngsters of the lost generation in Paris after World War I . . ." [17]

The most notorious of all these seceders from Soviet orthodoxy were the much-discussed *Stilyagi*—"style-chasers" or "dandies," also known as "jet setters" or the "golden youth" in the editorial diatribes against them which filled the Russian press. These were the sons and daughters of Russia's new elite—industrial managers, bureaucrats, generals, Party bigwigs—who took advantage of their privileged position to create their own hedonistic subculture in the heart of the workers' state. They bootlegged American hot jazz records and pored over *Vogue* and *The New Yorker* in search of the latest fashions—though they themselves usually ended up sporting 1940's zoot suits and dancing the boogie woogie. Some of them drank too much, stole when their allowances were not adequate to their style of life, and were alleged to be sexually promiscuous. They were aped by their social inferiors, the much-censured "hoodlums," "drunks," and the sideburned Russian "Teddy Boys."

> Who is not familiar [railed *Komsomolskaya Pravda*] with these utterly repulsive young men, with their ultramodish jackets, their ultratight and ultrashort trousers, and their eccentric

> neckties in all colors of the rainbow. . . . Or with the even more disgusting girls, with their . . . pitiful bristles of cropped hair, and their shoes that remind one of caterpillar tractors.[18]

The *Stilyagi* came from the opposite end of the social spectrum from the British angries, and they would certainly have looked somewhat dated to the disheveled, long-haired American beats. But they represented a mood quite similar to that which loomed so large among the younger generation on the other side of the Iron Curtain. The beats dropped out of capitalist society; the angries rejected the welfare state; the *Stilyagi* ostentatiously withdrew from the Communist workers' paradise. Almost everywhere in the fifties, apathy and withdrawal were the order of the day.

11

"We Are Inventing a New and Original World. Imagination Is Seizing Power!" * *The World-Wide Youth Revolution 1960 and After*

The 1960's unleashed one of the great explosions of the Youth Revolution. During the last decade, and into the present one, one of the great pandemics of youthful militance—like those of 1848, or of the years around 1900, or of the 1930's—raged across the nations. Not coincidentally, this period also saw one of the most colorful counter cultural withdrawals of modern times. The bomb-throwers and the Bohemians were everywhere, filling the newspapers and the TV screens with their violent objections to the *status quo.*

In essence, none of it was new, of course. Details might differ, but the basic patterns of generational withdrawal and rebellion had been laid down well over a century ago.

What *was* new, even for the twentieth century, was the sheer size of the thing. The scale of this youth revolt, the lineal descendant of so many others over the past 150 years, was vastly greater than anything we have seen before. It was a global outbreak, and one in which the young moved in larger numbers, and with less adult direction, than ever before. It was far and away the grandest climacteric yet in this history of the escalating revolt of the younger generation.

Many reasons have been suggested for this sudden upheaval: postwar affluence, freeing millions of young people for other than purely material concerns; the fantastic expansion of the university systems and of public education generally, producing the dehumanized "knowledge factory" and the resulting student discontent; the dehumanization and lack of community characteristic of modern technological-bureaucratic society generally; the failure of the

* Poster on the main door of the Sorbonne, May, 1968.

modern world to generate a convincing creed for the young to believe in; the influence of a handful of thinkers and even pop idols —from Marcuse to the Beatles—whose views of life *do* seem relevant to the young; the gap between intellectually "emancipated" youth and more traditional older generations; the permissiveness of parental generations who were themselves "emancipated" in earlier years and hence have no authoritative message for their offspring; the Oedipal aggressiveness of the young against their elders; and many others. To these, the generational historian might add the simple fact that 1960 saw the advent of the first generation that had not been psychically and spiritually scarred by the disillusionments of the late thirties and the horrors of World War II—i. e., the first generation that was ripe once more for holy wars.

The brief montage that follows, however, aims at no detailed analysis of the insurrectionary movements of the sixties. There is, in fact, no room even to mention all of them. The goal here is simply to communicate some sense of the amazing variety, the quickening pace, and the sheer massiveness of the world-wide youth revolt of the last decade. Thus grasped, the intercontinental generational upheaval of the 1960's takes its place as an awesome acceleration of the Youth Revolution of the past century and a half. It is with this problem, the place of the youth revolts of our own time in the broad sweep of history, that the last three chapters of this book are concerned.

1. *THE PROMISE OF THE SIXTIES*

Why They Liked Ike

Time magazine's "man of the year," smiling benevolently from the cover of the first January number for 1960, was a living symbol of the decade just ended. It was President Dwight Eisenhower, recently returned from a triumphal 'round-the-world tour. Eisenhower, leader of the United States' second Crusade in Europe and twice-elected President, was quoted as extolling friendship, freedom, world peace, "a sound dollar," and "the glory of America." Ordinary citizens, asked why they "liked Ike," answered simply: "he's a good (or decent, or honest) man," or "we can trust him."

In other national news, Governor Rockefeller's withdrawal from contention for the Republican Presidential nomination seemed to leave Ike's Vice President, Richard Nixon, with a clear shot at "lead[ing] the US into the fabulous promise of the . . . sixties."

The Education section of that same issue cheerfully predicted that "the number of Americans aged 18 to 21 will rise 57%" during the next decade, "and almost half of them will go to college." As a result, "by 1970, college enrollment will nearly double . . ." No larger political or cultural conclusions at all were drawn from this.

An article ominously entitled "Thunder on the Left" turned out —naturally—to deal with a rising young hockey star.[1]

As If a Dam Had Burst

Twelve months later, the last number of *Time* for 1960 had a rather different flavor. The cover story of that December issue focused on President John F. Kennedy's choice of a Cabinet: men selected to provide "the kind of 'vigah' that Kennedy had long promised 'to get America moving again.' " The story began with a picture of JFK and his brother Bobby, the controversial new Attorney General. Two smiling young men, confidently confronting the sixties.

A few pages further on, the Foreign News began with a vividly illustrated two-page spread on the resurgent Arab revolt in Algiers. Across the top of the page, a pretty young girl leaned and shouted, waving the crescent banner of the FLN over a mob of screaming Moslem demonstrators. At the bottom of the same page, a still-smoldering car lay on its side and a policeman sprawled in the street, his throat slit by the rioters. "Starting as a shout, the silent Casbah sprang to life last week . . ." the piece began. "It was as if a dam had burst."

President Charles de Gaulle had just completed a tour of France's Algerian colony that week. This authentic hero of another war, now twenty years in the past, had spoken ruefully to his assembled Army officers just before he left:

> "This insurrection . . . takes place in a new world, in a world which is not at all like that which I knew myself when I was young. There is," De Gaulle added sadly but resolutely, "a

> whole context of emancipation which is sweeping the world from one end to the other . . ." [2]

It looked that way to a lot of people that year. Particularly to the young.

The world in 1960 was ruled by old men and conservative establishments. Men like Eisenhower and de Gaulle and Adenauer, in Germany—the eighty-four-year-old Chancellor they called *der Alte* —the Old One; ill-defined but widely recognized power elites like the Japanese "Regime of 1955" or Sukarno's "Generation of '45" in Indonesia, the aging liberators of the nation. By and large, they were the men and movements that had made the postwar settlement fifteen years before; they had been running it ever since.

They had done great things in their time, these graying men of the 1940's. They had fought the greatest war in history, liberated the new nations of the Third World, established totally new regimes over large parts of the globe—as in Red China—or brought shattered nations back from the grave—as in the "economic miracles" of Germany and Japan. But they had been around a long time: some people were saying it was time for a change. Most of the malcontents were young.

Harold Macmillan, Britain's Conservative Prime Minister, might join de Gaulle in admitting publicly that "winds of change" were blowing in the world. But it was John Kennedy who spoke for the young, eagerly accepting the challenge of changing times. Like all inspirers of youth movements, from Father Jahn to Chairman Mao, Kennedy had a knack for seeing the world in terms of challenge, struggle, achievement, and a great day dawning:

> In the long history of the world, only a few generations have been granted the role of defending freedom in its hour of maximum danger. . . . I do not believe that any of us would exchange places with any other people or any other generation. The energy, the faith, and the devotion which we bring to this endeavor will light our country . . . and . . . can truly light the world.[3]

New generations of educated, alienated youth everywhere shared the American mood of 1960. It was time once more for youth to have its say in the world.

2. *CRUSADERS AGAIN, OPEN AND UNABASHED*

Confrontation in Korea

Most of the early action in that decade of youthful rebellion took place neither in America nor Europe, but in the emerging nations of the Third World. In Asia, in Africa, and in Latin America, student demonstrators and youthful guerrillas made some sensational news in 1960. Repeatedly, they stood up almost alone against authoritarian regimes; and repeatedly, to everyone's astonishment, they ended up on the winning side. A new image was being created, a new model set, that would soon stir the imagination of the younger generation in America and the Old World as well. It was a model of youth in revolt—and winning!

The confrontation was particularly glaring in Korea.

Syngman Rhee, the little country's American-sponsored president, was eighty-five years old in 1960, the very incarnation of gerontocracy. He had been born in 1875—the year before Queen Victoria became Empress of India—when mandarins still ruled the medieval "hermit kingdom" of Korea. Since his accession to power after World War II, the lemon-faced little autocrat had no doubt done his best, behind a façade of democracy, to modernize his country. But political corruption and police brutality were rampant as the new decade began, and Rhee himself, the last of the mandarins, seemed to be on the verge of senility.

The Korean university generation of 1960, by contrast, had been born as recently as 1940 in a Japanese-occupied Korea that was being dragged, head over heels, into the twentieth century. They had grown up in a divided, war-torn country where up-to-date American influences were paramount, a country, incidentally, in the grip of "an age of youth groups," most of them political, adjuncts of every adult faction from the Communists to Syngman Rhee himself.[4] The one ideal these young people had heard endlessly dinned into them—however little of it they had seen in practice—was "democracy," the great guiding principle of America, the omni-present superpower that had liberated them from the Japanese and protected them from the Communists. By 1960, fifteen years after World War II and half a dozen years after the Korean conflict, many educated young people thought it was time to see some democracy in Korea.

As election day, March 15, 1960, approached, students in many cities organized secret societies emotionally dedicated to "saving democracy" from the aging Rhee and his reputedly corrupt running mate, Yi Ki-bung. There was police violence on election day, and apparently a good deal of ballot-box stuffing. Then, a month later, the discovery of "the mutilated body of a high school boy with part of a police tear-gas grenade driven into his skull" set off student rioting across Korea.[5]

On April 18 and 19, university students marched in Seoul, demanding new elections and an end to police brutality. On the first day, they were attacked by police-inspired toughs. On the second, as tens of thousands of them advanced on the Presidential Palace, they were fired on by the police. More than a hundred were killed. "The blood of the fallen students"—here as in the Vienna of 1848—"turned demonstration into revolution." [6]

The results rocked the country. The troops went over to the students. Within a week, President Rhee, like Metternich, had resigned and fled into exile. The disgraced Vice President, Yi Ki-bung, committed suicide. The ruling Liberal Party collapsed, and a new regime dedicated to democracy took the helm.

A year later, the Korean military would take power into its own hands. But in that dazzling spring of 1960, when soldiers and students danced together in the streets, there was nothing to dim the luster of this clear triumph of idealistic youth over anachronistic age.

Turkey: Freedom! Freedom!

Ten days after the massive confrontation in the streets of Seoul, the chief cities of Turkey, at the other end of Asia, were convulsed in their turn by student violence.

"My subject today is the Constitution," declared the law professor at the University of Istanbul. "But it is forbidden, and being violated, so you are all dismissed." [7] The students, angrily discussing the repressive politics of the Menderes government, to which their professor had alluded, were milling around in front of the university gates when the police arrived. They declined to disperse. Fighting broke out. Jeeps were driven zigzag through the mob, cavalry charged them, there was gunfire. Miraculously, there was only one fatality, though many students were injured and more arrested. Martial law was promptly declared.

Menderes' Democratic Party (DP) had ruled Turkey for ten years. To many of the nation's educated elite, the DP seemed to be betraying the great principles of Kemal Ataturk, the founder of the modern Turkish state. By 1960, the press was heavily censored, the leader of the opposition had been denied his seat in the legislature, and Menderes was clearly ignoring the country's Westernized elite in favor of backward peasants and old-time Moslem religion. The students comprised the most volatile part of that elite of progressive "natural leaders." And had not Ataturk himself declared that "youth is 'the owner and guardian of the revolution' "? [8]

Istanbul University blew up on April 28. The next morning, students at the University of Ankara, in the nation's capital, brazenly defied orders to disperse. Police and troops took the political science building by storm, and the government shut down both universities for a month.

The students responded with practically daily riots in the downtown section of the capital. "Freedom, freedom, Menderes resign!" they chanted as they marched up the main thoroughfares of Ankara at the height of the rush hour.[9] The police gassed them and arrested them, but they always came back. By May 21, even the cadets of the Military Academy were in the streets, marching on the Presidential Mansion.

The military coup that toppled Menderes on May 27 probably would have come whether the students had risen or not. But the youth, who had taken action publicly and openly while others grumbled or plotted in secret, certainly saw themselves as leaders of the revolution. Like the French barricade fighters of 1830, they took to the streets repeatedly during the years that followed the overthrow of the Menderes regime, demanding their need of influence in the shaping of the new state. To the outside world, undoubtedly, student power seemed to be a reality on the Golden Horn.

Algeria: Yu! Yu! Yu! Yu!

The Algerian Revolution had been dragging along for six bloody years by 1960. The interminable struggle, coming close on the heels of the futile seven-year war in Indochina, had sapped France's national will, brought down the Fourth Republic, and propelled General de Gaulle to autocratic power. But during the later fifties, a massive French Army of 400,000 had all but crushed the guerrillas in the field. And the FLN (National Liberation Front) had never been able to rally the open support of the Algerian masses. To many, the war, costly though it had been, seemed almost over.

Then, in November and December, 1960, the missing Algerian popular support for the FLN suddenly and dramatically materialized.

On November 3, French colonial students in Algiers demonstrated against de Gaulle's policy of compromise with the FLN—and Moslem students, to everyone's amazement, defiantly counter-demonstrated! Europeans shouted threats and imprecations as the Arab youths moved through the streets, but they did not stop the demonstration. It was "perhaps the first time an organized group of Moslem civilians openly resisted the *colon* . . ." [10]

Early in December, angry colonials rioted against de Gaulle in downtown Algiers. Another challenge—and once again it was taken up. On December 11 came the great explosion out of the Casbah. Club-swinging young Moslem demonstrators, angrily flourishing the forbidden FLN banner, poured out of the ancient native quarter. Shouting *"Vive de Gaulle!"* and then *"Vive le FLN!"* they crashed through the barricades into the European sections. Young women in green blouses and green ribbons—the FLN colors—led the way, raising for the first time in a political demonstration that weird ululating chant—rendered in the Western press as *"Yu! Yu! Yu! Yu!"*—that was to echo so often through the streets of the sixties.[11]

The delirious march carried the inflamed young Arabs to disaster. In the French quarters, troops, police, and colonials, firing from roofs and balconies, slaughtered as many as ninety of them at a cost of less than half a dozen of their own.

Once again, however, final victory seemed to go to the young. December 11 was "the Dien-Bien-Phu of the official propaganda line," "a psychological jolt that was enormous." Henceforth it was impossible for the French colonists to claim that the FLN did not have the support of the Moslem masses of Algeria. The wild march of December 11 was, according to most French historians, "the turning point of the entire Algerian war." [12]

Cuba: The Kids Take Over

The biggest winners of all, however—and the most glamorous representatives of the new generation in the waves of unrest that seemed to be building around the world—were already celebrating the first anniversary of their triumph in 1960. If you really wanted evidence that the winds of change were blowing, you had only to take a look at Fidel Castro and his young Cuban guerrillas, come down from the Sierra Maestra to conquer their country—and challenge the most powerful nation in the world to do something about it.

Fidel, his black-bereted brother Raúl, and his flamboyant lieutenant, "Che" Guevara, were already becoming internationally known symbols in the first year of the new decade. The bearded young rebels had ridden into Havana on New Year's Day, 1959, in the wake of the fleeing dictator, Batista. Since then, their jaunty jungle fatigues, their bristling beards, the self-confident jut of their cigars, and their sheer youthful *élan* had seemed, to many people, to offer a jaded world the promise of a new and brighter day dawning.

To most older Americans, hardened by decades of Stalinism and Cold War crises, Castro was just another Red dictator—this one, to their horror, "only ninety miles off our shores." Castro fed their phobias by defiantly tweaking the nose of the "Octopus of the North" at every opportunity. He attacked the United States verbally and in print, nationalized hundreds of millions of dollars' worth of American-owned sugar mills and oil refineries, invited the Russians into Cuba, and was blamed for every guerrilla outrage in Latin America. To the typical middle-aged, middle-class American, the militant Cuban nationalist with his Marxist veneer was a bewhiskered Red thug, pure and simple.

But there was a special exuberance, an easygoing humanity about the victorious guerrillas in Havana that excited the younger generation. The young learned about Fidel from their own culture heroes—unconventional commentators like the radical American sociologist C. Wright Mills, the young Russian poet Yevtushenko, and the aging dean of French existentialists, Jean-Paul Sartre. What they learned excited them still further. "The greatest scandal of the Cuban Revolution," marveled Sartre, "isn't that it expropriated the plantations, but that it brought children to power." There were, he declared in a chapter on "The Kids Take Over," no older men at all among the new leaders. "Only the young had enough anger and anguish to attempt [the Revolution], enough integrity to succeed." [13]

Youth had conquered the island; youth, wide open to new ideas and new ways, ruled there. What might this insurrectionary young generation not bring to the Western hemisphere—to the world? A "third way," perhaps, neither Communist nor capitalist? [14] A new humanism in politics, free of bureaucracy and doctrinaire jargon? From Moscow to San Francisco, young would-be radicals and weary leftist survivors of the 1930's alike perked up at what they read about this fresh wind from Havana.

That summer of 1960, thousands of American students went south to see for themselves. Thousands of South American youths flooded in too, for the First Latin-American Youth Congress, in August. Most of them liked what they saw. Here was a revolutionary regime that still wore combat fatigues and did government business over café tables or in the open street. A thirty-three-year-old leader who, according to rumor, really wanted "to retreat into the hills to write poetry . . . and meditate." A revolutionary with a sense of style, who could speak grandly of turning the Andes into the Sierra Maestra of all South America. "I am leader of an American Revolution," said Fidel, "not [merely] chief of a small country's government." [15] In a symbolic sense, at least, young liberals everywhere seemed disposed to believe him—and to think that he might just win!

3. ASIA: MILLIONS ON THE MARCH

The Youth Revolution East of Suez

A beginning had been made. Through the decade that followed, much of the world seethed with generational unrest. No continent was spared, no system of governance seemed to be immune. Communist nations and capitalist ones, advanced and underdeveloped countries all felt the sudden, half-conscious surge of youth power. Wherever the hurtling pace of social change produced generational disjunction, wherever a sizable number of young people were exposed to the exciting influence of new ideas—there the war between the generations burst into flame. In many places, the challenge to the *status quo* and the strain on the body politic were even greater than they were in the United States—hard though that might be for embattled over-thirty Americans to believe.

Certainly, this was so in Asia, the largest and most populous of continents, where the velocity of change proceeded at a rate unexcelled anywhere on earth. Let us glance briefly at some of the Asian versions of the global rampage of the youth.

Japan: As Though They Had Been Bombed by Hand Grenades

The famous *Zengakuren,* Japan's radicalized equivalent of a national student union, came into existence in the years after World War II. The organization grew rapidly in the fifties, especially after it broke with the Japanese Communist Party, which it quickly left far behind in militance. By 1960, when their aggressive activism helped bring down a Cabinet and prevented a state visit by the President of the United States, the *Zengakuren* was the most famous student movement in the world.

In the sixties, the Japanese students were certainly among the most violent, as well. The bobbing, zigzagging lines of helmeted, stick-wielding students, raising "the chant of their ancient folk ritual, 'Wassho! Wassho!' " became a familiar fixture of the television news in many lands.[16] The *Zengakuren* fought police in the streets, protected by hard hats, special shields, and heavy cotton gloves, and armed with rocks, iron bars, "fire bottles" filled with gasoline, and the long, thick, wooden staves that became their trademark.

They were much better organized than most youth movements. They were also more "serious," theoretically—students of Marx's earlier, more humanistic writings, of Lenin's hard-core Party theories, and of some, at least, of Mao. But they fought over many of the same issues that stirred youth in other countries—university reform, nuclear weapons, the Vietnam War, and America's hegemony of the "Free World."

They had their own power elite to battle, of course: the Japanese "Regime of 1955," a conservative alliance that included big labor as well as big business and big government, and that had effectively muffled the official left opposition as well. And they had their own special emphasis. They demanded "direct democracy" and "violent direct action" and swore to expose "the 'capitalist deception' behind the . . . mass-consumer society" of the affluent, new, postwar Japan.[17]

The *Zengakuren* flourished particularly at the beginning and the end of the decade. During the middle sixties, as so often happens, they split into many factions and fought each other in the streets. But they were never long out of sight, or out of the mind of the world-wide Youth Revolution. When the Yippies came to Chicago in August of 1968, they cheerfully snake-danced through the parks chanting "Wassho! Wassho!" in preparation for their great "attack" on the Democratic National Convention.

Fighting, clearly, was the *Zengakuren*'s thing, and their violent defiance inspired youthful revolutionaries in many places. No one in the West, however, could mobilize tens of thousands of armed street fighters as the *Zengakuren* could. No one else could strike a major university for a solid year, as they did in Tokyo, holding professors and administrators prisoner, and violently resisting eight thousand policemen for two days when the crackdown finally came. No American campus occupation left university buildings looking, as they did in Kyoto in 1969, "almost as though they had been bombed by hand grenades . . . buildings in which virtually no doors remained on hinges and every window had been smashed."[18]

Indonesia: Platoons of Sweet-Faced Schoolgirls

In the sprawling Southeast Asian kingdom of Indonesia, student rebels played a major role in one of the bloodiest outbreaks of mass violence of the decade: the 1965 massacre of more than 300,000 Communists by their outraged fellow citizens.

The holocaust was set off by the Reds' murder of six Indonesian generals, and was therefore spearheaded by the Army. Much of the lynching was the work of fanatical, back-country Moslems, who declared a holy war against the unbeliever. But the students played a crucial gadfly role in the upheaval, spurring the Army on to greater militance and doing their share of the bloodletting too.

Few Western reporters were on hand for the sudden explosion of popular discontent that brought down President Sukarno (the new nation's liberator of twenty years before), his Communist supporters, and the whole corrupt, inept, and undemocratic "Generation of '45" that had come to power with him. The few Western observers who were in Indonesia at the time, however, agreed in viewing the massive student demonstrations of 1965 and 1966 as prime causes of the downfall of the regime.

Tens of thousands of students, directed by KAMI, their own Action Command, paralyzed Jakarta that winter. They created monster traffic jams that brought the capital literally to a standstill. They seized and occupied the Ministry of Education for their own headquarters. They rampaged through the Foreign Ministry, swarming over the building like ants, inside and out, covering the walls with insulting pictures, smashing windows, reducing top-secret papers to confetti, and emptying filing cabinets out the windows in search of an alleged "Secret Canton Pact" which was supposed to have "sold Indonesia to Peking." At one point, they even charged the Presidential Palace, only to be repulsed by gunfire. In other parts of Indonesia, students joined the Army in rounding up and executing Reds. In one city, "university students . . . slew 2,000, usually by bullets in the neck, before the Army called off the slaughter." [19]

To put it in an American context: it was as if one of the great Washington peace marches of the later sixties had run amuck, occupied Health, Education and Welfare, captured and sacked the State Department, charged the White House, and then fanned out through the suburbs shooting hard hats and people with American-flag lapel pins on sight.

There is no space here to trace the escalation of what began as one of the most gentle of children's crusades into a key contributor to a blood bath. One thing is sure, however. Whether they were stopping traffic, smashing windows, charging the Presidential Palace, or shooting their enemies down, these "platoons of sweet-faced schoolgirls and tousle-headed college boys" did become in a very few months what a *New York Times* man on the scene described as "one of the country's most powerful political forces." [20]

China: We Are the Critics of the Old World: We Are the Builders of the New

The whole world watched in disbelief what happened in China in 1966 and 1967.

Chairman Mao called it the Great Cultural Revolution. The prime instruments of the new revolution were to be the youth of the nation, banded together into new *ad hoc* groupings called the Red Guards. The goal: to save Red China from creeping capitalism —"bourgeois survivals and tendencies," as Mao Tse-tung put it; to save the Communist Party itself from "revisionism," bureaucratic careerism, and all the other vices so shockingly epitomized by China's great rival, the Soviet Union; and to save the much-discussed "Third Generation" of young Chinese, who had never known the hardening experience of revolution, from losing their zeal and going soft in peace and (comparative) prosperity; and not so incidentally, to mobilize a militant body of support for the Chairman himself against his political enemies in the Party machine.[21]

All very clear, as foreign analysts explained it. And yet somehow totally unbelievable as hints of the concrete reality seeped out.

Well over twenty million Red Guardsmen—college kids, high school kids, and many even younger—surged through the streets of China's countless villages and swarming cities. Almost twelve million of them marched on Peking itself, where they were "reviewed in batches of a million by Mao . . ." [22] Red Guard speeches, rallies, and wall posters attacked everyone from unpopular local teachers to "the Number One Party Person"—China's President, the aging Communist veteran Liu Shao-chi.

There were parades everywhere—drums and gongs, the red streamers, the giant pictures of Chairman Mao, the waving forests of "Little Red Books," the revolutionary songs and chanted slogans. The world could hardly believe the spectacle of eminent Party men and venerable officials sitting in dunce caps before jeering crowds of students, submitting to vigorously guided self-criticism sessions. Even the Chinese must have been dismayed by the rapid drift toward anarchy that followed: peasants and working men joining local Party cadres to resist the zeal of the adolescent Cultural Revolutionaries—Red Guardsmen holding up military arsenals to steal weapons—Red Guard factions turning on each other, fighting with clubs and knives until the river downstream from Canton was littered with floating bodies.

Mao Tse-tung, like Khrushchev and Hitler before him, urged the new generation to relive the revolutionary past of the Party, to develop revolutionary consciousness by making a revolution. The Red Guards were to become "courageous and daring pathbreakers," carrying the whole nation forward with them. The youth responded with an ardor typical of young ideological revolutionaries gripped by the vision of a better world. Marching through Peking in August, 1966, the Red Guard hordes bore aloft "great banners with the words: 'We are the critics of the old world; we are the builders of the new world.' "[23] Unfortunately, in rekindling the revolutionary zeal of the May Fourth Movement and the Long March, Mao also unleashed so much of youth's latent capacity for violence that in many places the army had to be called out to keep the rebellious younger generation from tearing the country apart.

That such a thing could happen in one of the most powerful totalitarian states in the world was striking evidence of the potential power of the Youth Revolution.

4. EUROPE: THE YEAR OF THE YOUNG REBELS

1848 All Over Again?

In 1968, the "incredible year" of political violence in America, the virus of revolt fastened with particular fury upon Europe.

Thus far into the sixties, European youth had seemed unable to pull themselves out of the acquiescent torpor of the postwar decades. Metaphysical alienation and sheer fun-culture escapism were as close as European youth dared come to expressing discontent with the system. "The year of the young rebels," as one European observer called it, changed all that.[24] If Americans saw their whole way of life violently challenged during the sixties, there were nations in Europe that literally tottered on the brink of revolution before that single tumultuous year was over.

Nineteen sixty-eight brought the Youth Revolution home with a vengeance to the Old World that had spawned it. Before that year was over, there were those who thought that the revolutionary year 1848 had come round again.

England: A Quiet Year on Campus

Nothing much seemed to be happening among the politically conscious youth of Great Britain in the late sixties. Everyone was very cool and very British. Learned English authorities on "student revolt" pursed their lips when an American student radical referred to a university president as a "motherfucker"—"surely the most remarkable crudity ever to be uttered by people claiming membership of an intellectual elite," a British expert sniffed.[25] Observers more sympathetic to the young dissidents tried to compare what little was happening in England to the gaudy doings across the Channel. But it wouldn't wash, somehow: London was not Paris, no matter how you strained the analogies.

So—sanity reigned in this sceptered isle, at least? Only comparatively speaking.

In England in 1967 and 1968, there were "serious incidents of direct student action" at twenty-three colleges and universities, Oxford and Cambridge included. These "incidents" included ten sit-ins, three occupations of college buildings, and ten cases of "universities where visiting speakers were subjected to violence or . . . violent demonstrations . . ." There were rallies, marches, and other actions against the Vietnam War, the exploitation of the working classes, and the unsatisfactory condition of higher education in Britain. The London School of Economics, the prestigious, left-leaning institution founded by the Fabian Socialists, was closed down by angry students, with consequent "violence and some damage at the school . . " A highly placed government official—Laborite, not Tory—declared that the student rebels "have set as their ultimate objective not merely the reform of LSE, but the destruction of the Wilson government and representative democracy in Great Britain." [26]

That was a quiet year in staid, stolid old England.

Italy: An Outstanding Student Victory

Nineteen sixty-eight was a much bigger year in Italy. Students struck universities, occupied buildings, fought police in the streets from Turin to Rome. They demonstrated over Vietnam, over germ-warfare research on campus, and—as usual—over the deplorable state of higher education. They marched in support of their German confreres on the occasion of the attempted assassination of one of their leaders, and in support of their French co-generationists on the occasion of the revolt in Paris.

Like students in many places, young Italians rejected not only the conservative establishment but the established left—including the Italian Communist Party—as well. They had no more use for Soviet intervention in Czechoslovakia than they did for American involvement in Vietnam. "Down with Russian *and* American imperialism!" proclaimed a banner swinging above an occupied building at the University of Rome. A plague on both your houses.

In Italy, as elsewhere in that spring of 1968, youthful militance intensified rapidly. As the demonstrations grew more violent, furthermore, the student notion of the limits of legitimate dissent grew correspondingly more extreme. In February, for instance, three hundred University of Rome students occupied the "faculties" of letters, philosophy, physics, and architecture, held them until the end of the month, and escaped without significant losses. They regarded the occupation as "a failure." Later that spring, seeking revenge on the police for beating some of their fellow demonstrators, "thousands of angry students" openly attacked police in Valle Giulia park, burned several police cars, and injured many people. Many of their own were injured also, and 250 were arrested. This display of head-busting, if suicidal, militance was widely hailed as "an outstanding student victory . . ." [27]

This was no year for cleverly staged demonstrations. This was a year for violence.

Germany: Demonstrators Filled the Streets

In the late afternoon of Thursday, April 11, 1968, "Red Rudi" Dutschke was shot in the head as he walked out of the German SDS headquarters in Berlin. Dutschke, the internationally known leader of Germany's most radical student group, did not die. The man who shot him turned out to be an unaffiliated nut—an artist, a Hitler fanatic, and a hater of Communists—who collected clippings on the assassinations of John Kennedy and Martin Luther King. But the student reaction was immediate and violent nonetheless.

They went for the Springer press.

Rudi Dutschke, an articulate East German escapee doubly disillusioned with the West, was probably the most powerful spokesman the German youth movement had. But he was by no means the only shrewd young man in the movement. German student radicals were often called the best-read and best-organized in Europe. German SDSers actually *read* Marx and Marcuse, Mao and Trotsky, and even Freud. They had studied the tactics of the Japanese *Zangakuren* and the American Civil Rights Movement. As contemporary issues stirred them, and gave them the levers to rouse others to action, the German SDS grew phenomenally in the later 1960's.

They began to demonstrate in favor of university reform and against oppression around the world as early as 1964. In 1966, their marches against the Vietnam War regularly ended in clashes with the police. Most of the action, however, was still limited to the great Free University of Berlin, and to the streets of that isolated city. In June, 1967, however, while hurling tomatoes, eggs, and smoke bombs at the visiting Shah of Iran, student demonstrators were surrounded and badly beaten up by exasperated police. One student was shot to death in the melee. Everywhere in Germany, students rose in sudden anger: "Demonstrators filled the streets of dozens of cities." [28] It was small potatoes compared to what was to happen a year later, when Dutschke fell. But the significance of the incident was immediately clear: at one blow, the Berlin police had made SDS a national force.

Older Germans, haunted by memories of the SA and the Hitler Youth, had never had much use for the SDS and their fellow travelers. This widespread dislike for the Free University radicals had been supported—and in many cases, no doubt, stimulated—by one man more than any other: Axel Springer, the newspaper baron. Since Springer's publishing empire accounted for more than seventy per cent of the newspaper-and-magazine circulation in Berlin, and more than forty per cent of that in all of West Germany, he undoubtedly had considerable influence on public opinion. All of this influence had been brought to bear against the nascent youth movement in Germany. Students, the Springer press told its readers, were "outsiders" and "terrorists," social parasites and probably sexual perverts as well. The Free University SDS leaders were Communists pure and simple, and Maoists at that—the "FU Chinese," Springer papers called them. Something should clearly be done about this subversive minority in a law-abiding nation.[29]

Axel Springer seemed to many young Germans to enjoy a one-man monopoly on access to the public mind. If the good citizens of West Germany despised the SDS, it was Springer's fault. When a deluded fanatic shot Red Rudi down, Germany's radicalized youth knew whom to blame. They also knew what to do about it: "we had to explain to the Berlin people," as one SDS girl put it, "our own democratic demands . . ." [30]

They went for the Springer press the way Karl Sand had gone after another corrupter of the German mind a century and a half before. But in 1968, the insurrectionary youth moved on a scale undreamed of in 1819.

"Spontaneously, tens of thousands of students all over Germany descended on the Springer plants." [31] They burned newspapers on the streets, overturned delivery trucks, blockaded printing presses. The police responded with tear gas, police dogs, water cannon and clubs. Two people were killed in Munich, probably by student rock-throwers. Barbed wire ringed the offices of Springer publications, and police rode shotgun on his delivery trucks for weeks.

The riotous Easter Weekend that followed the shooting of Rudi Dutschke "transform[ed] the tranquillity of West German society to a degree unknown since the end of World War II." [32] As recently as 1966, a quiet, nondisruptive sit-in by three thousand students at the Free University was an amazing achievement. In 1968, student radicals, opposing government efforts to arrogate new "emergency powers" to itself, could stage strikes, occupations, and demonstrations at practically every university in the country, and still have plenty left over to pour seventy thousand demonstrators into the streets of Bonn.

France: The Night of the Barricades

"Libérez nos camarades!" The chant went up from fifteen thousand young revolutionaries milling in a Paris square: "Let our comrades go!" [33]

It was the answer of the Youth Revolution to the French government's first offer of concessions in the escalating conflict between an angry studentry and the magisterial regime of Charles de Gaulle. The government was willing to withdraw the occupying police forces from the Sorbonne, and to permit the university itself to reopen—two of the three initial student demands. But student revolutionaries are not given to compromise. Their answer was a thunderous reaffirmation of the crucial point remaining: the freeing of their fellows expelled, arrested, or otherwise penalized over the preceding week of marching and rioting. "Let our comrades go!" And then the mob began to move.

The militants marched in the van, arms linked, crash helmets firmly in place. Behind them came a motley array of university and secondary-school *(lycée)* students from all over Paris. There were delegations from other cities too—Bordeaux, Toulouse, Nantes, Rouen, Grenoble, Montpelier, and other provincial universities had supported the Paris core with strikes and demonstrations of their own for most of the week. There were Germans, Italians, and young activists from other countries, youths who had dropped everything and come when the electrifying news had spread across Europe that young Paris was up in arms. Since 1789, Paris had been the motherland of revolution. However many tens of thousands might march in Berlin, however furiously they fought in the streets of Rome, Paris was still the big one—the place to be when the cobblestones began to fly.

And this was the big day, though no one knew it yet: Friday, May 10, 1968—the eve of the Night of the Barricades and all that would come thereafter.

Much had gone before. It had begun at Nanterre, the ultramodern, totally unlivable, new university extension in the Paris suburbs. The *enragés* of Nanterre, of whom Daniel Cohn-Bendit was the most colorful leader, had been challenging the system over educational reform, Vietnam, and the administration's repressive response to all such protests for months. The rebels were few, a handful of ideological activists organized in feuding groups with such impressive titles as the Federation of Revolutionary Students, the Union of Communist Youth (Marxist-Leninist), and the Communist Revolutionary Youth (Trotskyite—though they supported Cohn-Bendit, who called himself an Anarchist). *Groupuscules,* the authorities contemptuously called them: "little groups"; or as an American college president might say, "a small minority."

At Nanterre, aggressive action by the *groupuscules* had stimulated repressive response by the college administration, with the inevitable result—rapid growth in the numerical strength of the militants. When the administration had closed down the university the week before, rather than permit a radical rally, the *enragés* had led their growing cohort downtown to the Sorbonne to rouse their fellow students there. And when the police fell upon both the Nanterre contingent and the *Sorbonnistes* in the streets of the Latin Quarter, the final explosion had begun.

It had been building for a long, wild week. The police had occupied the Sorbonne, and the Sorbonne had moved en masse into the streets. The prestigious grandes écoles, the provincial universities, the *lycées* had joined them in striking and demonstrating. Day after day, tens of thousands of young men and women had paraded the boulevards of Paris, clashing with police, conferring ominously with underpaid working men, and raising to the roof tops of an apprehensive capital the mocking chant: *"Nous sommes un groupuscule"* —"We're just a small minority . . ." [34]

By Friday, May 10, the charge was laid, the flash point reached.

Tough French riot police, wearing shining, black leather uniforms and swinging truncheons, turned the chanting marchers at the Seine, blocking the bridges with vans and police cars bumper to bumper. They pushed the mob back into the Latin Quarter—back toward the occupied Sorbonne. The helmeted leadership knew it could not accept this kind of setback on its own home ground. "Like a flash," reporters who were on the scene recalled, "the word went out: 'The *quartier* must be ours at whatever cost!' " The march broke up as "the demonstrators fanned out through the familiar labyrinth of student Paris, like guerrillas on their home terrain." [35] And suddenly, spontaneously, the idea spread like a flickering brush fire from narrow lane to alleyway to darkest cul-de-sac—and the barricades began to go up.

More than sixty of them were thrown up in a few hours that wild night. It was an astonishing spectacle: "They tore up paving stones and piled them as though they were rebuilding memories of 1789, 1848, 1870." [36] They ripped up grilles and manhole covers, chopped down trees, turned parked cars over into the growing barriers. Packing crates, boxes, trash, chunks of wood, and more paving stones raised the obstacles still higher in the close-pressing streets. And when the police charged, masked and goggled, hurling gas and swinging truncheons, they got still more of the hefty, three-pound *pavés*—hurled into their faces, dropped on their heads. The student street fighters emptied gas tanks to make Molotov cocktails. Some overturned cars and trucks were set on fire as the *flics* rushed the barricades, turning them into unbreachable walls of flame.

In the long night of fighting that followed, hundreds were injured, hundreds more arrested. A visiting leader from the International in Brussels clambered up on a barricade and gave the flame-lit jungle of the Latin Quarter a passionate blessing: "How beautiful it is! It's the Revolution!" Daniel Cohn-Bendit, whose troops were fighting from those same barricades, offered a more precise commentary: "what is happening in the street tonight is a whole generation rising . . ." [37]

The heavily armed riot cops emerged bloodily victorious: by morning the smoking streets were quiet. But too many people had seen the fury of their charges—too many innocent bystanders had gone down under their flailing clubs. Like the "police riots" in Chicago a few months later, the Night of the Barricades was a Pyrrhic victory for the government.

Intellectuals, the press, the unions, and ordinary citizens were shocked at a government that could not maintain law and order except by "the fiercest street-fighting since the liberation of Paris." The Latin Quarter, said a visitor, "looked like a newly occupied colony: boarded-up store-fronts, gutted cafés, the pitted streets, all well patrolled by squads of police armed with submachine guns." [38]

Public outrage coalesced into a gigantic protest march the following Monday. Perhaps as many as 800,000 Frenchmen poured through the streets of Paris, with Cohn-Bendit and the student street fighters at their head. And the next day, workers who had struck in protest on Monday decided this would be a fine time to press their own long unanswered demands for better wages and working conditions. Instead of returning to work, they began to occupy their factories. Before the week was out, ten million workers were on strike—two thirds of the labor force. France was paralyzed. The kids—thanks to luck, their own daring, and too many social needs too long unmet—had shut the country down!

Only two forces stood against the revolution now: the Gaullist bureaucrats, and the Communist Party, who contemptuously dismissed "the kids" as "leftist adventurists." The leaders of the Youth Revolution shrugged off the Communist defection—yesterday's rebels, toothless tigers now. "The Communist Party?" said Cohn-Bendit after Monday's mass march: "Nothing gave me greater pleasure than to be at the head of a demonstration with all that Stalinist filth in the rear." [39]

The students turned the Sorbonne into a Soviet, placarded Paris with their demands, their intentions, their most whimsical notions. It was a glorious, unreal time, a moment of total liberation that none of them would ever forget. The graffiti of that "Almost Revolution" have become famous:

> Society will not be free until the last capitalist has been hanged with the entrails of the last bureaucrat.
>
> The more I make love, the more I make the revolution: the more I make the revolution, the more I make love.
>
> We are inventing a new and original world. Imagination is seizing power.[40]

Nobody seized power in France, of course. De Gaulle majestically took charge of political reform. The union leaders negotiated better wages for their people, and the Communists sent them back to work. Imagination in the Latin Quarter was reoccupied by *flics* with submachine guns.

The end—or the beginning?

12

"One More War—Reh-volution!" * *The Youth Revolution in America 1960 and After*

In the United States, as in the rest of the world, strange things were happening in 1960, and an astonishing confrontation between the generations was shaping up.

Let us slow the pace now, and narrow the focus for a comparatively detailed case study of one developing youth revolt of the 1960's—that which took place in our own country. Let us examine the American youth revolt of the sixties in slow motion, stage by stage, from the first confrontations to the final *kamikaze* charge. Here as in the Russia of the 1860's, let us concentrate on the sequence of generations itself.

This abandonment of the broad panoramic approach of the last chapter in favor of an emphasis on the vertical dimension, on development through time, may tell us a good deal about the sheer dynamics of generational conflict. It may tell us more about how a youth revolt comes about, and how it escalates into the familiar crescendo of violence and repression, than any amount of abstract generalizing.

A detailed generational analysis, in the first place, seems to reveal not one but three "younger generations" in succession loose in America in the 1960's. Similarly detailed probes of other insurrectionary decades—of the 1920's or the 1930's, for instance—would no doubt reveal similarly complex generational situations. Social generations follow each other with such bewildering rapidity in recent times that they often seem to come two or three to the decade.[1] I could not count the number of students, for example, who

* Street chant of the later 1960's.

have told me that they simply can't "reach" their younger siblings still in high school—all of three or four years younger than they. "If you think I'm radical," as Fidel reputedly put it, "wait till you see my little brother!"

The American Youth Revolution of the sixties began in 1960, with a cup of coffee in a Southern five and dime. It ended—it seems safe to say—with the arrest of twelve thousand young people in the streets of Washington, D.C., in the spring of 1971. The following chapter will attempt to trace the sequence of generations that lay between these two events. It will try to fit these generations in revolt into the larger context of forces—political, social, economic—that shaped the history of that turbulent decade. Above all, it will seek to re-create, in some sort, the psychological and intellectual milieu, the historically conditioned enthusiasms and desperations that lie at the heart of any youth revolt.

1. *YOUTH AND ENERGY AND NOBLE PURPOSE*

A Ripple of Pressure Beginning

Perhaps the most widely recognized symbol of generational confrontation in 1960 America was, as we have seen, the political campaign that was waged across the country that year. Journalists repeatedly took note of the striking contrast between Ike Eisenhower, the departing Republican President, and Jack Kennedy, the Democratic aspirant. It was not merely a contrast between conservatism and liberalism. Ike was the man of the fifties, the cherished symbol of stability and reassurance in a troubled world—and the oldest President in US history. Kennedy and his "Irish Mafia" were the brash, energetic apostles of movement, activism, a new surge forward: and John Kennedy would become the youngest President in our history.

Young people of all sorts, from mindless, totally apolitical teeny-boppers to developing radicals who would soon be considerably to the left of JFK, were stirred by the Kennedy campaign.

> One remembers being in a Kennedy crowd [wrote T. H. White in his first quadrennial *The Making of the President* book] and suddenly sensing far off on the edge of it a ripple of pressure

> beginning, and the ripple . . . would grow like a wave, surging forward as it gathered strength, until it would squeeze the front rank of the crowd against the wooden barricade, and the barricade would begin to splinter . . .
>
> One remembers . . . the jumpers . . . teen-age girls who would bounce, jounce and jump as the cavalcade passed, squealing "I seen him, I seen him." Gradually . . . their jumping seemed to grow more rhythmic . . . in a thoroughly sexy oscillation . . .[2]

That was the silly celebrity bit, of course, the famous Kennedy "glamour." But the charisma, the excitement, the sudden intoxicating thought that youth and energy and noble purpose might actually be about to win in America reached many more serious young people too.

The handsome young President-elect declared that the generation of the sixties, like that FDR had summoned in the thirties, had a rendezvous with destiny. He announced the Peace Corps to channel the energies of youth into building a better future for the world. And the young began to listen. College newspaper editors began to replace their blasé worldly wise 1950's pieces about "playing it cool" with cautious columns on the possibility of commitment, of being, as Camus said, *engagé*. Other young people, to the astonishment of their elders, were already beginning to act on this central radical impulse of the new American generation—the urge to take action for a cause.

We Are the People of This Generation

It was an amazing spring, those warm early months of 1960. The first black sit-ins were held in Greensboro, North Carolina, as early as February. The black Student Nonviolent Coordinating Committee (SNCC, pronounced "Snick") was organized in April. The Fair Play for Cuba Committee was set up that April too, in the San Francisco Bay area, to win a hearing for Castro. In May, the widely publicized anti-HUAC (House Un-American Activities Committee) riots further inflamed the Bay area. All this was perhaps not too surprising, in that already radicalized corner of the land, home of Berkeley and the Beat Generation. But by autumn, the notorious HUAC film, *Operation Abolition,* with its vivid shots of helmeted riot cops dragging dripping demonstrators down the courthouse steps, was unintentionally creating potential radicals on campuses all across the country.

In the background of that amazing spring in America loomed the Chessman case (anti-capital punishment), the growing anti-nuclear weapons movement in this country, the Aldermaston "ban-the-bomb" march in Britain, the toppling of the governments in Korea and Turkey. And in June, with little fanfare but considerable thought, a new group calling itself Students for a Democratic Society —SDS—was established at a leftist youth convention in New York.

The famous "Port Huron Statement" of the SDS was mostly the work of a young University of Michigan graduate student named Tom Hayden. It was not drawn up until two years after the founding of the organization. But this crucial document in the shaping of the New Left summed up much of the feeling of that earlier spring of 1960, when to be young and radically inclined—as Wordsworth wrote of another revolutionary dawn—was very heaven.

"We are people of this generation," the Port Huron Statement began, "bred in at least moderate comfort, housed now in universities, looking uncomfortably to the world we inherit." [3] The paragraphs that followed clearly traced the spiritual growth of the new generation of young radicals in America. "When we were kids," the manifesto continues, "the United States was the wealthiest and strongest country in the world," a nation dedicated to world peace and the United Nations, to "freedom and equality" for all. Or so it seemed, before the process of erosion began.

As the ideologically oriented among the generation of 1960 grew up, these childish assumptions were shattered one by one.

A freedom-loving people? The "southern struggle against racial bigotry" came as a revelation. The oppression of the Negro in America made all talk of freedom and equality ring hollow to Hayden and other civil rights activists who went South in the wake of the Greensboro sit-ins.

A peace-loving nation? "The proclaimed peaceful intentions of the United States," as the SDS founders saw it, "contradicted its economic and military investments in the Cold War status quo." It was a reasonable enough conclusion for a generation that had early absorbed C. Wright Mills' strictures on the "military-industrial complex"—and that had never known Stalin.

Wealth? America's vaunted standard of living began to seem almost shameful: "While two-thirds of mankind suffers undernourishment, our own upper classes revel amid superfluous abundance."

Power? Even America's vast power began to seem illusory in the face of "a world-wide outbreak of revolution against colonialism and imperialism, the entrenchment of totalitarian states, the menace of war, overpopulation, international disorder, supertechnology," and all the other problems that the older generation had somehow failed to solve. Like their beat predecessors of the preceding decade, the New Left militants of the early sixties thus came to believe that they were living, not in an "American golden age," but in "the decline of an era."

The Capacity to Believe

The difference—the crucial difference—was that the new generation saw hope for a better future beyond the rumble of oncoming disaster. The failures and fanaticisms of the 1930's were far enough behind them to carry little emotional weight with young people born around 1940. When their teachers told them how the Red "god" had failed the youth of the thirties, or reminded them that the Nazis had been true believers too, they simply shrugged their shoulders. A dry diet of pragmatism and hip refusal to get involved was no longer enough for them. Like so many generations before them, they thirsted for the cool waters of ideological salvation.

They possessed what the youth of the fifties had so pre-eminently lacked: the capacity to believe in a better world. For their elders, "doubt [had] replaced hopefulness: to be idealistic [was] to be considered . . . deluded." The youth of the sixties had no such hang-ups. They were frankly idealistic and increasingly ideological (however leery they remained of sentimentality and system-building). They were crusaders again, open and unashamed.

The ideals they espoused had the familiar ring of exaltation that commonly dominates insurrectionary generational creeds. They believed, according to the Port Huron Statement, that man is "infinitely precious and possessed of unfulfilled capacities for reason, freedom, and love." That "*human relations* should involve fraternity and honesty," real community and brotherhood as opposed to the prevailing "loneliness, estrangement and isolation . . ." That "participatory democracy" should be the foundation stone of politics. That the economic system should provide work for all which would be "creative" and "self-directed" and would impart "a sense of dignity" to the worker. They believed that the prevailing sin of "apathy" must be overcome among the young, and that the people themselves must take in hand the building of a better future.

To many older observers, something new seemed to be loose in the land—and in the world—that spring of 1960. Spring—dawn—fresh winds—new waves—they strained their metaphors describing it. But more and more frequently they called it simply: *the new generation.*

2. *THE EARLY SIXTIES: THE CIVIL RIGHTS GENERATION*

Nonviolent Direct Action

The first generation of "the Movement," as it came to be called early in that tumultuous decade, was a generation devoted overwhelmingly to a single burning issue: civil rights, meaning the rights of the black man in America. It was mostly a black movement, and its maximum leaders—men like Martin Luther King, James Farmer of CORE, James Foreman and John Lewis of SNCC—were black, though whites sometimes wielded a disproportionate amount of influence at the local level. It was mostly a Southern movement, with its battlefields in far-off, sweltering Southern places like Greensboro, North Carolina; Oxford, Mississippi; and Selma, Alabama. It was reformist, nonviolent, sometimes naive to the point of saintliness, and often—to everyone's astonishment—victorious. We may date it roughly from 1960 to 1963 or 1964, from the first sit-ins to the March on Washington, or the "Mississippi Summer."

The Reverend Dr. Martin Luther King, Jr., Atlanta-bred and Boston-educated, had shown the way as early as 1956 with his headline-grabbing—and successful—Montgomery bus boycott. The way for the Negro to win his rights in America, said King, was "nonviolent direct action."

> We will take direct action against injustice [he wrote] without waiting for other agencies to act. We will not obey unjust laws or submit to unjust practices. We will do this peacefully,

> openly, cheerfully because our aim is to persuade. We adopt the means of nonviolence because our end is a community at peace with itself.

Nonviolence, he admitted, meant "a willingness to suffer and sacrifice," a willingness to face jail or death for the cause. But in the end, he believed, "the oppressor will find, as oppressors have always found, that he is glutted with his own barbarity." Meanwhile, he said, in the rolling religious cadences that were to become familiar across the land, "This is a great hour for the Negro. . . . To become the instruments of a great idea is a privilege that history gives only occasionally . . ." [4]

Early in 1960, the great hour struck. One hot morning at the beginning of February, half a dozen black college students walked into a Woolworth's five and dime in Greensboro, sat down at the lunch counter, and ordered coffee. It took them six months to get it —but they got it. And across the South a Movement was born.

They sat in, stood in, waded in, prayed in, picketed, boycotted, marched, freedom-rode. Restaurants, theaters, stores, barber shops, public washrooms, swimming pools, universities, and churches that had traditionally excluded "niggers" were methodically desegregated. The Civil Rights marchers appeared on the streets of one Southern city after another, neatly dressed, carrying their hand-printed signs, singing their strangely moving battle hymns:

> Like a tree that is planted by the wa-a-ter
> We—shall not—be moved . . .

And:

> Ain't nobody gone turn me round—
> turn me round—
> turn me round—

And of course:

> Deep in my heart—
> I do believe—
> We shall overcome—
> Some day.

Bit by bit, they seemed to be doing it.

Like any mass movement, the Civil Rights crusade had its shock troops. There were the black, and white, militants of CORE—the Congress of Racial Equality—who began to tackle the tougher nuts of the Northern cities, where ghetto poverty complicated the issue. The crisp little *Freedom-NOW* buttons that CORE people wore sent a tingle down the spines of lesser folk. There were the legendary heroes of SNCC, almost all black, who plunged alone into the Deep South, risking beatings or worse every day to run the voter-registration drives that threatened the white power-structure itself. Names of SNCC saints like Bob Moses were spoken with awe in the Movement.

These were the totally committed ones, the full-time agitators and organizers who would as soon go to jail as take a drink of water. But the Movement itself was more than that: it was "the kids"—a whole generation on the march.

Plenty of Room in the Jail

They had grown up in the homes of the black bourgeoisie, raised in the same patriotic pieties referred to in the Port Huron Statement: America is the greatest, richest, freest and most peaceable of nations, dedicated to liberty and justice for all. Reality had tarnished the pieties somewhat, but it had not destroyed the faith of these black middle-class children in America. They didn't start out to make a revolution—they only wanted to make the system work the way it was supposed to work. Their campaigns were pointed toward Supreme Court decisions, Civil Rights acts, voter registration, executive orders, the simple enforcement of the Constitution. These young people set out to be the conscience of the nation—with an occasional whack at the nation's pocketbook, via the boycott route. If a man had the courage to put his body on the line, they believed, the nation would reform itself.

Southern whites couldn't understand the new generation of young blacks.

"All right," said Birmingham Police Commissioner "Bull" Connor, watching his policemen hustle hundreds of youthful demonstrators into police vans and school buses, "you-all send them on over there. I got plenty of room in the jail."

Connor, in shirt sleeves and with a straw hat cocked over

one eye, watched the eager young marchers, some of whom ran to the waiting patrol wagons.

"Boy, if that's religion, I don't want any," he said.

"Freedom! Freedom! Freedom!" chanted the Negro girls and boys as the school buses swept by the commissioner on the way to jail.[5]

It wasn't all fun and demonstrations: the Civil Rights crusaders suffered for their cause. They were beaten and jailed by hundreds and thousands over those four or five years. Their churches and schools were burned and bombed. Cattle prods and police dogs were used on them. Medgar Evers, the young leader of the NAACP in Mississippi, was shot in the back on his own front porch. Four little girls were killed by a bomb in a Birmingham Sunday school. Three young Civil Rights volunteers were lynched by a mob during the Mississippi Summer of '64. But they kept on coming.

They became, for rising generations of young Americans, the heroes of their time, the marching saints who would redeem America. Politicians praised their dedication. The media gave their campaigns full and sympathetic coverage—many reporters had had their own troubles with Southern mobs. Liberals everywhere, as has so often been the case, rallied to the support of these young people who dared to act on their beliefs. It was easy enough for the liberal establishment to take this line, of course, since all the action was in the South, a region widely known through the novels of Faulkner, the plays of Tennessee Williams, and countless films, as a dark and backward land of Jukeses and Snopeses, brutal rednecks and decaying aristocracy. A dubious vision, evidently: but it had its effect. A whole generation, white as well as black, grew up with the image of the young militant as hero—and with the notion that "the system" was vulnerable after all.

In 1963 and 1964, finally, another and oddly contrasting element was added to the legacy of this first wave of youthful militance: the element of failure. This, too, had its impact on generations yet to come.

The massive Civil Rights March on Washington of August, 1963, was the climax of this first generation's efforts. Two hundred thousand people, the majority of them young, gave Martin Luther King a rolling ovation that leafy summer day when he told them, from the steps of the Lincoln Memorial, that he had a dream. But the dream was already clouding over. There were a couple of more years' worth of Civil Rights bills left in the government, but the country at large, the middle-aged, middle-class establishment, was growing weary of black activism. More hazardous still, the Movement was shifting its focus to the North, and running into all the intransigent social and economic complexities of the urban ghetto. The Northern Movement was not genteel and nonviolent, like the Southern one. It was ghetto-bred, impatient, smoldering with potential violence.

The first rebellious younger generation of the sixties, then, proved that militance was still relevant, that a few individuals in the grip of a great idea could compel even Big Government and Big Business to take action. But the Civil Rights Movement also showed that single-issue reformism, however dedicated, was not enough to change the face of America. From these lessons, the next generation was to draw even more revolutionary conclusions.

3. *THE MIDDLE SIXTIES: THE FSM GENERATION*

Put Your Bodies on the Gears

That next generation of young American dissenters, the generation of the middle sixties, represented what we might almost call the "classic" phase of this cluster of rebellious younger generations. After the primitive innocence of the early Civil Rights days—single-issue, reformist, focused on the South—came an immensely more sophisticated, multifaceted, nation-wide youth revolt. In the hands of this new generation, and of some of the surviving leaders of earlier years, the Movement grew rapidly, radicalized, and broadened its attack into a wide range of shrewd, savage, sometimes antic, but always passionate assaults on society at large.

Call it the FSM Generation, the generation that made its debut at the Berkeley Free Speech Movement in the fall of 1964. For it was this more than any other single event that made it clear that there was "something new" on the youth scene—something that went beyond the single issue of civil rights to attack the system as a whole, the American Way of Life itself. Mario Savio, the Berkeley youth leader, spoke passionately for the new militance as he led some fifteen hundred students in a massive occupation of the University of California's Sproul Hall:

> There is a time when the operation of the machine becomes so odious, makes you so sick at heart, that you can't take part: you can't even passively take part, and you've got to put your bodies upon the gears and upon the wheels, upon the levers, upon all the apparatus and you've got to make it stop.[6]

The demand for free speech at Berkeley—really, for the right to politicize the campus—announced the sweeping new militance to the world. A few months later, on that same campus, a new countercultural revival spoke its piece when a handful of cheerful anarchists decided that freedom of speech ought to extend well beyond the realm of politics. One of them got himself arrested much less spectacularly than Savio and his hundreds of friends by simply sitting on the steps of the Student Union holding a sign with a single word lettered on it: "FUCK." [7]

Something new was happening.

They carried the American flag still at FSM rallies—not the Viet Cong flag—and they sang "The Star-Spangled Banner" before presenting their demands. But they had clearly turned a corner since black preachers led black children into the streets of the South.

The generation that occupied center stage between the Free Speech Movement of 1964 and the 1967 March on the Pentagon was what we might call a split generation. We have seen such split generations before—in Russia in the 1860's, for instance, and, more briefly, in the France of the 1830's.[8] The various cohorts of such a generation, building on a common generational background, draw radically different conclusions from that shared experience. Confronting the same massive challenges of the times, they respond in startlingly different ways. The resulting "generation units"—to use the sociologist Karl Mannheim's term—sometimes seem to have so little in common that it is hard to see the ties that bind them at all.[9]

In the present case, for example, there was the new cry of "Black Power" raised in the ghetto, and the surge of black riots that filled the "long, hot summers" of the middle sixties. But there was also the busy, bustling New Left, developing its multipronged attack on poverty, war, the universities, and many other aspects of what some of them had come to see as a thoroughly corrupted society. And there was the amazing hippie withdrawal, deluging the country with rock, drugs, and their own eager quest for love, freedom, a new community, and perhaps a peek at God. What could such a wild array have in common? Only what are perhaps the deepest of all ties in modern times—the ties of generationhood.

This new generation, which flowed into the colleges (or, if they were black, into the job market) in the middle sixties, had passed through their crucial last years before adulthood in the glow of early civil rights victories and liberal admiration for the new activism of the young. But they had also seen things going rapidly awry—JFK shot dead in Dallas, growing talk of "white backlash," a War on Poverty that looked increasingly like a losing skirmish, and the escalating war in Vietnam. The young of those middle years responded in many ways: by mindless violence, by another round of Bohemian withdrawal, by a brilliantly creative period of radical activism. But they formed a single generation nonetheless, and between them they shaped the full-blown "golden age" of the American youth revolt of the 1960's.

Burn, Baby, Burn

The most massive and insurrectionary section of this generation in revolt was the black ghetto youth of the North. Their response to the common challenge was simple and brutally direct.

Summer after summer through the middle years of the decade, the slums that ringed the great Northern cities went up in flames: Harlem in 1964; Watts in 1965; Chicago and Cleveland in 1966; Newark, Detroit, and many other cities in 1967. Between 1963 and 1968, almost fifty thousand people were arrested in "Negro riots and disturbances," and there were better than eight thousand casualties, including more than 190 killed in the streets of American cities. Blocks of tenements went up; stores were looted en masse; police and hastily mobilized National Guardsmen poured into the ghettos, often shooting as they came. And evidence soon showed that "a major proportion of riot participants were youths." [10]

The tinder had been piling up for many generations, of course. The socio-economic causes of "urban unrest," as the experts politely called it, were well known: the skin-color discrimination, the lack of education and skills, the joblessness, the broken homes, the dope, the rats, the crime in the streets, the cops on the take, the amorality and mangled psyches. The result was an inflammable mass of jobless, futureless, aimless young blacks, "young people with nothing to do and nothing to lose," as a SNCC organizer described them—the *classes dangereuses* of twentieth-century America.[11] But all these things had been as true of the sullen fifties as they were in the insurrectionary sixties. The unique experience that set this generation in motion was the Civil Rights Movement, with its concomitant rise in black race pride, resentment of white oppression, and demands for "Freedom Now!" among the young.

The typical rioters, statistics proved, were usually "late teenagers or young adults," no worse off economically than their neighbors, but—significantly—somewhat better educated. They were also "substantially better informed about politics," filled with "pride in [their] race" and with the newly kindled belief that "in some respects Negroes are superior to whites." They had picked up some of the hatred of the White Devil preached through the early sixties by Black Muslim militants like Malcolm X. They had heard what Stokely Carmichael, the young apostle of Black Power, had to say about violence:

> For God's sake, I don't understand how the white West can ever talk against violence. They are the most violent people on the face of the earth. They have used violence to get everything they have. . . . We have never lynched a white man, we have never burned their churches, we have never bombed their houses, we have never beaten them in the streets.[12]

Thus inflamed by the new ideas, black slum youths began to look upon their tenement world with new and angry eyes. They became walking time bombs ticking toward an explosion. The next time a policeman beat up a black cab driver for "tail-gating," or shot a "burglary suspect" to death, the new youth were primed and ready.

> "Hey, fuzz! The way you look, your mother was a monkey's whore!" a fifteen-year-old boy screamed . . .
>
> "For a bunch that keeps hollering about civil rights, they don't look so civil to me!" [murmured one policeman.]

Other officers slapped their riot sticks—"nigger-knockers," they called them—against their palms:

> "Let's move these black bastards out of here!" "Knock a few heads together and teach 'em a lesson!" [13]

The old challenge, but a new response from a new black generation in the streets. And then Watts was going up in sheets of orange flame.

The cities burned, while the kids kicked in the windows, cut hoses, and danced in the streets. The nation watched them on the evening news, black faces shining in the glare of fires, grinning as they passed TV's and cases of liquor out through the broken windows—scattering down dark streets—falling occasionally to a guardsman's shot. And their elders, whites, and many blacks as well, shuddered at the nihilistic new litany that welled up now in place of "We Shall Overcome":

Burn, Baby, Burn!

Turn On—Tune In—Drop Out

By the time Watts burned, in the summer of 1965, a wild new generational experiment in living was already going full blast just up the coast in San Francisco. In many ways, it seemed to be the direct opposite of the firestorm in the black suburb of Los Angeles. The new thing was overwhelmingly white, not black; it exalted love, not hate; and it was clearly more a withdrawal from, than a rebellion against, straight society. Its maxim was not *Burn, Baby, Burn,* but, in the words of one of its most celebrated prophets: *Turn On, Tune In, Drop Out.*

They were called the hippies, the flower children, the love generation. They churned up a storm of horror and indignation among their elders through the middle sixties, not only in San Francisco but all across the country. Like the looting and the burning in the ghettos, the hippie love festivals represented a natural, gut reaction to the successes and the failures—mostly the failures—of the youth of the Kennedy era. The blacks lashed out at the America that had raised and then dashed their hopes: the hippies simply turned away. "You see," explained a head-shop operator in New York, "they're so disillusioned and so disgusted with it all that they turn their backs on it." [14]

Withdrawal, it was called. It had been happening for 150 years, ever since that first, long-forgotten Bohemia; though never before, it must be confessed, on such a scale.

The hippies were also, of course, the heirs of the beat generation—though again, they seldom acknowledged the debt. The beat mystique of the fifties had largely evaporated—even in San Francisco—when King and the Kennedys brought new hope to the generation of 1960. By 1964, however, all that was over with for many young people. Some of them began to pick up on the beatnik idea again, to thumb through Kerouac's *Dharma Bums* for Zen, or some of the little white City Lights paperbacks for beat poetry. And there were still some hairy Bohemians here and there, in San Francisco and New York and elsewhere, to provide the nucleus for the new generational secession.

But the hippie phenomenon was a good deal more than a revival of the beat mystique.

The flower children had their own Bohemias—Haight-Ashbury instead of North Beach, the East Village instead of the West. They had their own new language, bizarre new words and phrases like *turn on, too much, far out, blow your mind, groovy, freaky, head, trip,* and *wow!* plus a liberal sprinkling of cheerful *fucks* and *shits.* They had their own costumes and hair styles—an eye-popping kaleidoscope that shifted restlessly from Indian garb to beads and bell bottoms, to total, gorgeous, free-choice anarchy—before settling down in the next generation to the grim denims and jeans favored by the end-of-the-decade street fighters. They had their own music—not jazz or quiet folk songs, but rock, the hard, acid, electronic San Francisco rock of the Jefferson Airplane, the Grateful Dead, Big Brother and the Holding Company, Country Joe and the Fish, the "new" Beatles, the Stones, the Fugs, and all the other weirdly named and wildly costumed new groups that flourished in those years.

Most important of all their subcultural, counter-cultural folkways, the hippies had the new drugs. New chemical escape hatches to replace the cheap wine and escalate the marijuana of the beats: seeds, dexies, bennies, hash, mescaline, methedrine, STP, and, of course, LSD, the wonder drug that started it all.

The new psychedelic drugs made the hippie counter culture what it was. The drugs set them off from outsiders, made them outlaws—and gave them that special messianic glow that comes from having ventured into realms of experience that no straight citizen could share. Sometimes it was pure silliness, like the Dada lyrics of one of Ken Kesey's Merry Pranksters, "zonked out of her mind," declaiming happily:

> Methinks you need a gulp of grass
> And so it quickly came to pass
> You fell to earth with eely shrieking
> Wooing my heart, freely freaking!

Occasionally, to the delectation of prudent straights, it really was an orgy:

> On methedrine, boys and girls became hopped up hell-cats, pouring out their thoughts like speeded up Mort Sahl records, driving themselves wild in frenzied folk rock dances, balling each other for six hours nonstop.

Sometimes it was much more than that. "The LSD trip," Dr. Timothy Leary assured the young, "is a religious pilgrimage." For some, these journeys into inner space brought a wider awareness, even a spiritual peace they had not known before. But always, silly, sexy, or spiritual, it was their thing, their trip, the defining experience that set tens, even hundreds of thousands of young people off from their elders.

> I looked down . . . at my crossed legs. Black pants, black socks, black shoes. The only trouble was, the legs weren't mine. . . . I'm about one quarter-inch outside myself now. . . . I'm sitting here, but I've also moved about a quarter-inch outside my body. . . . In the darkness of my mind I [see] a technicolor display of weird-looking growths waving about, like plants in a current at the bottom of the sea. There [are] stalks and sponges and fan-shaped objects: pink and green and purple.

And then the surge of Gargantuan laughter, pure joy bursting the lungs. Or the darkening, shrinking world, the panic-fear, the thick dry sobs curled up in a corner rocking, rocking, and sobbing. But either way, walking in space or deep in a wracking bummer, their own thing. They were indeed, as one young girl put it, "the psychedelic generation, the hallucination generation." [15]

The Age of Aquarius

A totally personal adventure, and almost totally unintellectualized. These children of McLuhan were not readers, nor particularly articulate talkers. Nevertheless, like all their predecessors, they had their own gurus and their own new ideological emphases.

Many of their ideas came to them entirely without benefit of books—from each other, from their music, from their own unique generational experience as outlaw tribes in America. But they had some spiritual guides at least. A few holdovers from beat days, like the poet Allen Ginsberg, back now from the mystic East, long-haired and bearded, *OM*-chanting, full of new Zen and Hindu insights for the new generation. And a few new names: Tim Leary, fired from Harvard for feeding students LSD, founder of the New York-based *L*eague for *S*piritual *D*iscovery and high priest of "consciousness expansion" through a variable mix of lysergic acid and Oriental mysticism. Ken Kesey, husky, hairy-chested young West Coast "black humor" novelist, pioneer of LSD, electronic supersounds and strobe-light shows, the master of the "Acid Test," free-form psychedelic dance orgies.

From this casual conglomeration of sources—a song lyric, a public lecture, a word going the rounds—the flower children assembled a rough creed to live by. The ideas were simple, often derivative, but devoutly held by the young believers.

The new tribes of the mid-sixties, like almost all their Bohemian predecessors in the West, stood foursquare against all the bourgeois vices: other-directed conformity, uptightness and sexual inhibition, the work ethic, the cult of success, moral and religious hypocrisy, the middle-class hunger for security and material things, and so on. They put special stress on such relevant American failings as racism (conscious or unconscious) and chauvinistic nationalism (i.e., support of the rapidly escalating war in Vietnam).

On the positive side, they generated their own unique forms of nonrationalism—again, a common enough phenomenon among Bohemian drop-outs of the past. All their group festivals, from the quiet pot party to the mind-blowing, rock-and-light orgy or the full-fledged acid trip, were directed toward emotional catharsis. Their religious impulses, whether based on Eastern faiths or drug-induced pilgrimages beyond the gates of perception, all aimed at ecstasy and mystical, nonrational comprehension of the nature of things.

Above all, the love ethic, the need to be close to each other and to all men, clearly carried them beyond the reach of logic and rational self-interest. They could be almost sententious about it sometimes: "This is sharing, this is love," explained a nineteen-year-old boy who had just been handed a sandwich by a long-haired total stranger. "She's giving me part of her food because she wants to share part of herself with me, and it doesn't have to be sex. This is an act of giving. We're all one." [16] Yet this overwhelming emphasis on love and true community—*Gemeinschaft,* the Wandering Birds had called it—surely expressed, most poignantly of all, the hunger of this generation for some warm, deep truth that lies beyond the reach of intellect.

One more quality, finally, distinguished the new Bohemian generation from their beat predecessors. Many of the new youth really thought they were going to win. With flowers and kisses, bells and incense, they would yet overcome the cold, hard world of money and guns, bureaucrats and brutal "common sense." A new age of love and peace and true humanity was dawning—the Age of Aquarius:

> . . . these young bohemians [explained one sympathetic interpreter] are the would-be utopian pioneers of the world that lies beyond intellectual rejection of the Great Society. They seek . . . to discover new types of community, new family patterns, new sexual mores, new kinds of livelihood, new esthetic forms, new personal identities on the far side of power politics, the bourgeois home, and the consumer society.

Or, as the internationally celebrated rock musical *Hair* put it:

> Harmony and understanding
> Sympathy and trust abounding
> No more falsehoods or derisions
> Golden living dreams of visions
> Mystic crystal revelation
> And the mind's true liberation

The golden Age of Aquarius had begun, the age when guns will be beaten into plowshares, when grass will grow in Wall Street, when at long last

> . . . Peace will guide the planets
> And love will steer the stars [17]

A New Kind of Politics

It was a glorious vision. There were those in this dissenting young generation, however, who were not so sure that the Peaceable Kingdom was at hand. Nor, on the other hand, did they see much use in the mindless black rage of the ghetto. These most direct inheritors of the ingenuity and direct-action purposefulness of the Civil Rights Movement set themselves as determinedly against the American Way of Life as any of their more colorfully insurrectionary contemporaries, only more rationally, more calculatedly. During the middle sixties, they came to call themselves the New Left.

New Left radicals shared the young black man's "new anger," his demand for "a politics of insurgent protest." Many white radicals like Tom Hayden had been through the civil rights wars themselves and had come to believe that "behind local segregation there lies a far more pervasive pattern of national political, economic, and social oppression . . ." These radical activists also shared the hippies' emotional moral revulsion at all the sins of bourgeois America—"war, bureaucracy, guilt-producing affluence, racism, hypocrisy, moral rot." They shared the flower child's deeply felt need for "a new way of looking at the world and a vision of a new kind of politics." [18] But in the answers they found to these problems, in the tactics adopted and the specific ends aimed at, these young white activists differed from all their generational contemporaries.

Like the other wings of their generation, they had their precursors. As the black riots were, in part, a by-product of the civil rights agitation of the early sixties; as the new Bohemian tribes borrowed some notions at least from the beats of the fifties; so the New Left went back far more than they cared to acknowledge to the despised "Old Left" of the 1930's.

They were much more organized and organization-minded, for one thing, than any other cohort of the FSM generation. Through the middle sixties, the New Left blossomed forth in a swarm of enigmatic new names and initials that easily rivaled the jumble of committees, clubs, leagues and fronts of the Depression decade. Newspapers and news magazines were soon leading their puzzled readers through a new organizational labyrinth on the left—FSM, SDS, PLP (Progressive Labor Party—Maoist), the May Second Movement (anti-war—pro-Viet Cong), the National Coordinating Committee to End the War in Vietnam, the National Conference for New Politics, the Peace and Freedom Party, and countless others. These groups held meetings and even national conventions, collected dues (when they could get them), and had acknowledged spokesmen (if not leaders). They kept mailing lists and knew how to run a mimeograph machine. In short, despite the New Left's early emphasis on freewheeling response, group decision-making, local autonomy, and minimal bureaucracy, this activist wing was a lot more organized than the anarchic black rioters and flower children of their generation.

They were also a good deal more self-consciously ideological—again, despite their best efforts to avoid the pitfalls of a rigid 1930's-style "party line." No single ideology sufficed for all groups, of course, and views sometimes changed from year to year. Nor were they much given to deep historical study: a poll of twenty-five SDS leaders, taken by a friendly observer, revealed that "less than five had ever read Lenin or Trotsky, and only a few more had ever read Marx." Only the PLP read Mao, and Che was still unmartyred and unheralded in Cuba. But almost all of them had at least browsed in C. Wright Mills and in Camus, and a good half were familiar with such political prophets of their generation as Herbert Marcuse and Frantz Fanon.[19]

Out of this welter of sources, the New Left did acquire certain general notions held in common—most of them already touched on above. Marked for destruction were white racism, capitalist exploitation, imperialist war, the "power structure" and the "military-industrial complex." Among the goals: participatory democracy, creative labor, socialist distribution of goods and services to all, and humane self-development of the individual. A radically new social framework, these new militants insisted, must be established before the specific ills that afflicted America could be truly healed.

Bull Horns and Nonnegotiable Demands

The road to the new society, however, lay through many more narrowly focused struggles and specific, concrete battles. New Leftists fought on many fronts through these restless, innovative years, probing for the issues, the weaknesses that might bring down the dehumanized, capitalist-imperialist Leviathan that to them was America.

In 1964, Mario Savio's demand for "Free Speech" at Berkeley launched the drive for university reform and gave the FSM generation its first sense of solidarity and strength. That same year, Tom Hayden and his friends at SDS went into "community organizing" in the slums—to put pressure on city hall. They soon had a dozen projects going, from JOIN (Jobs or Income Now, in Chicago) to Hayden's own NCUP (Newark Community Union Project).

In 1965, the Vietnamese War escalated rapidly, from 25,000 troops in the spring to 200,000 in the fall. The New Left and their growing number of liberal allies promptly launched a wave of dramatically staged college "teach-ins" on the war, sweeping still more disturbed young people into their dissenting camp. SDS led an anti-war march of seventy thousand to Washington—and promptly tripled the number of SDS chapters around the country, from thirty-five to over one hundred. The largest of the "free universities" was also organized that year (FUNY, in New York), as the student demand for humanity and relevance from their alma maters grew apace.

And so on through 1966 and 1967. The youthful leftists hurled a whole battery of attacks against the system, focusing increasingly on the war and its supporting institutions at home. Year after year, the radicals managed to come up with new tactics, new targets, new gimmicks to rekindle the enthusiasm of their restless young troops. There were draft-card burning, flag-burning, refusal to report for induction, efforts to stop troop trains and close down induction centers, demonstrations against Dow Chemical (manufacturers of napalm) and other war industries. There were countless rallies and marches, including one huge anti-war march that put 200,000 people into the streets of New York City, and a smaller but more celebrity-studded March on the Pentagon in 1967. For their black generational contemporaries, there was support for the Freedom

Ballot in Mississippi. For the burgeoning counter culture, there was sympathy for freaks and other students busted for dope by the police state, though the comparatively puritanical activists had little use for drugs themselves.

The long-haired young agitators seemed to be everywhere in the middle sixties, bullhorn at the ready, nonnegotiable demands in hand. And everywhere, the kids were listening. The hippies could generally be rounded up for a major demonstration: it was a sport with them, an afternoon's kick, like baseball. The black cadres still sometimes talked to their old allies from civil rights days—despite the Black Power purge of whites from SNCC—and SDS's community organizing projects kept grass-roots ties alive for awhile. Even the straightest students, carrying draft cards in their pockets or clutching draftable boy friends, began to pay some attention to the impassioned arguments of the hairy wildmen with the bull horns.

Thus the pressure mounted and the Youth Revolution grew through the middle sixties. Whenever interest flagged, the New Left militant dug into his bag and came up with new issues, new strategies to excite the imagination of the young. Their ingenuity seemed unending, their energy unflagging, and their middle-aged, middle-class elders grew angrier by the minute.

The FSM generation, the generation of the middle sixties, turned the corner: from nonviolence to black rage, from single-issue reformism to sweeping radicalism, from undiluted militance to a partial resurgence of Bohemian withdrawal. The next generation, the last of the cycle, would take it from there.

4. *THE LATER SIXTIES: THE GENERATION OF '68*

A Blaze of Pyrotechnics

The final generation of this cluster brought the decade to an end in a wild crescendo of youthful rebelliousness.

In some ways, the wave of youthful dissent that crested between 1968 and 1970 or 1971 was the biggest of the lot. Certainly their demonstrations were larger, their rhetoric more revolutionary, and their headlines more sensational than they had ever been. And more young people flocked to the motley banners of the Movement than ever before. Astonishing numbers of concerned young idealists turned out to oppose the war and support the radical victims of official repression. Hair, headbands, and dope flooded over campuses where perhaps a single, derided long hair had shuffled a few years earlier.

But there was a strident note to the rhetoric, a desperation behind the headline-catching violence of the young rebels, that did not bode well for the Movement. The gigantism that afflicted the festivals and demonstrations of the late 1960's gave little indication of the extent of true commitment. The tendency of the Movement to fragment, and of movements to spring up on every side—Women's Liberation, Gay Liberation, Chicanos, Indians, ecology and the rest—revealed a fundamental lack of health. And the rash of books *about* the youth crusade (as distinguished from tracts intended to advance its purposes) spread a Hellenistic fragrance of decay over the whole performance. When the fury of creation exhausts itself, the scholars move in for the post-mortem.[20]

This was a generation that had grown up, through the better part of a decade now, with a gathering surge of radical enthusiasm among the young. During the critical years when they themselves moved to the edge of adulthood—the middle sixties—they had witnessed an unparalleled outburst of activism and a massive generational withdrawal, both accompanied by a blare of journalistic hoop-la, legitimizing liberal admiration, and a sweeping radical critique of American society by all hands. Sheer generational momentum, if nothing else, would surely have carried the Movement through the end of the decade.

But there was something more, of course. Repression was rife in the land those last years. The result was a familiar pattern in the history of the Youth Revolution: a cycle of repression and revolution, each feeding on the other, creating between them a terrifying upward spiral of violence. From the Chicago Democratic Convention of 1968 to the Mayday bust in 1971, it was really all downhill for the youth revolt. But it did go out with a blaze of pyrotechnics seldom equaled in the genre.

The Incredible Year

The militant stream of the Movement—the New Left and the Black Power activists—had kindled resentment and repression well before 1968, of course. Rioting blacks had been stacked up like cordwood in their blazing ghettos—as many as ten blacks killed for every white. New Left leaders ran fewer fatal risks, but federal agencies and local-police "Red Squads" began to infiltrate and harass the radicals well before Chicago.

From 1968 on, however, repression was the increasingly visible order of the day. As in Russia in the 1870's, the young rebels responded with new extremism of their own. Indeed, if we read *"To the People!"* for *Civil Rights* and *People's Will* for *Weatherman,* we will have an almost perfect parallel for the evolution of the American youth revolt of the sixties. Under the growing weight of government repression, the drift from nonviolence to terrorism was as predictable as darkness after day.

Nineteen sixty-eight was the incredible year: the year that broke the Movement's back, for all the hullabaloo that followed.

The year began with a burst of hope. Senator McCarthy won his startling New Hampshire "moral victory" in February, and the improbable "children's crusade" quickly coalesced around his antiwar candidacy. Robert Kennedy made his "agonizing reappraisal" and announced *his* decision to run. And Lyndon Johnson amazed the nation in March with his abrupt withdrawal from national politics—an announcement widely hailed as a stunning victory for the Movement.

But there were few victories after that—only snowballing disaster for the left, from liberal to revolutionary. Martin Luther King was assassinated in April, and Bobby Kennedy in June. Senator McCarthy was steam-rollered with ease at the Democratic Convention in August, while Chicago police clubbed militants, hippies, Yippies, and other assorted young people on the streets. For the growing extremist wing of the youth revolt, there were plenty of catastrophes too: the Columbia occupation busted; a state of "civic disaster" called at Berkeley after four days of confrontations; eight blacks and three cops killed in a series of shoot-outs in Cleveland. In September, Black Panther leader Huey Newton was convicted of killing a policeman and sentenced to fifteen years in prison. In

November, Richard M. Nixon was elected President of the United States.

The activists responded with renewed efforts, increasing bitterness, and calculated violence.

The Score Is Four

The all-purpose *radical* tag was rapidly becoming as dated as *nonviolence* before it. People in the Movement talked about *the Revolution* now, and their enemies were *pigs* and *fascists*. The American flag no longer flew at rallies: it was the yellow-starred Viet Cong banner now—or the red flag of revolution—or the black flag of anarchy. Mark Rudd coined a slogan for his angry generation when he concluded an open letter to Columbia's president, Grayson Kirk, with the ringing ultimatum: *Up against the wall, motherfucker!* [21]

It was in 1968 that aggressive revolutionaries like Rudd began to foment the series of great university strikes and occupations of the late sixties, paralyzing Columbia, Harvard, Chicago, Berkeley, and many other major institutions of higher learning. In 1969, more moderate Movement-types organized the massive "Moratorium" demonstrations against the war, putting better than 350,000 people into the streets of Washington alone in November of that year. In the spring of 1970, following the killing of four Kent State students by National Guardsmen, the New Left provided what direction there was to the tidal wave of campus riots, strikes, and demonstrations that swept the country. As recently as May of 1971, the militant left managed to clog the jails of Washington with thousands of young anti-war demonstrators.

But the pressure mounted inexorably as, following the ancient pattern, public opinion turned against the activists and government felt free at last to move against them. There was a great liberal outcry, for instance, when "the kids" were routed from the streets and parks of Chicago in 1968. But the people of Chicago, and even of its posh liberal suburbs, felt that Mayor Daley had done just right. A pattern of growing public demand for "law and order," accompanied by shrinking liberal support for youthful militance, developed from that point on. The "radic-libs," as Vice-President Agnew called them, might sympathize with the Chicago Eight, brought to trial in 1969 for "conspiring" to start the Convention riots of the previous year. But most Americans blamed the defendants—old-time SDSers Tom Hayden and Rennie Davis, Panther leader Bobby Seale, and self-styled Yippies Abbie Hoffman and Jerry Rubin in particular—for turning the courtroom into a circus.

When the Berkeley street people built a "People's Park" on an unused piece of University of California land, and the police drove them out with gas, clubs, and volleys of birdshot that injured over one hundred and killed one young man—nobody much cared. A year later, liberal editors were still capable of lamenting the "tragedy" of Kent State; but the citizens of Kent, Ohio, declared angrily, even gleefully, that the damn kids had got just what they deserved. "Since when is rioting, looting, burning, assaulting a town called academic freedom?" they demanded. They shot four fingers in the air as long-haired students passed, half-whispering the savage jingle:

> The score is four
> And next time more . . .[22]

We'll Blow Up the World!

The revolutionary left battened on such persecution, of course. Within a year, the "V" peace sign of innocent McCarthy days had been replaced by the clenched fist, and the disciplined cadres of SDS's Weatherman faction were in the streets. These self-styled street fighters no longer waited passively for the pigs to bust them. They charged police lines, helmeted like their Japanese confreres, clad in thick jackets and heavy gloves, armed with sticks and bricks, shouting the hard, angry, "pig-fucking" chants of the late sixties:

> Ho Ho Ho Chi Minh
> NLF is gonna win!

And:

> One two three four
> We don't want your fuckin war—
> Five six seven eight
> Organize and smash the State—

And, like rolling thunder over the prairie:

One more war—*Reh-volution—*
One more war—REH-VOLUTION—
ONE MORE WAR—

The year after the Chicago Convention, the bombing and the shooting began in earnest. Every morning's paper brought more news of terrorist explosions attributed to the Weatherman Underground, or of shoot-outs between Panthers and police. Black revolutionaries lured policemen into traps and shot them down. Bombs went off in the offices of major corporations, police stations, even the Capitol at Washington. "We'll blow up the whole fucking world!" a nineteen-year-old, self-styled terrorist told a national news magazine. "And when the pig picks up arms this time, he won't get rocks and bottles back—he'll get rifle rounds." [23]

The polarization of the generations was complete. Older citizens grew red with anger as they watched the Viet Cong flag go by at the head of a surging column of ragtag young revolutionaries. They heard the chanting, watched the fists go up, listened to the things that were said about "Pig Amerika" at revolutionary rallies—and could not believe their ears.

Many of the young rebels, on the other hand, no longer saw or heard their elders at all. They saw only black churches burning in a Southern night—was it only five years ago? They heard only the endless deafening roar of bombs falling on Vietnam, day after day, month after month, year after year. That was Pig Amerika to them—the Leviathan State, the super-imperialist that must be destroyed for the safety of mankind.

It didn't work, of course.

Only a small minority was capable of such views, or at least of acting on them. If their cogenerationists would not turn the revolutionaries in, they would not march with them either. As the State proceeded on its majestic way in spite of the bombing and the shooting, as SDS fragmented and the Panthers split, a bewildered and unhappy generation turned its back on militance.

"What's the point?" said last year's Kent State demonstrators, the Moratorium marchers of the year before. "Everything has been tried—new politics, demonstrations, even blowing things up. Nothing works. You can't change the System."

The youth revolt had come full circle.

Crazies, Communes, and Woodstock Nation

The failure of activism has traditionally encouraged the rise of Bohemian withdrawal. For a time, the hippie tribes did, in fact, profit from the debacle of the New Left. But in the late sixties, the counter culture was in trouble too.

The flower children had had their troubles before, of course, and not always from the police. As early as 1967, "Haight Street . . . was a nightmare," thronged with "alcoholics, pickpockets, thieves, con men, drug addicts, sex degenerates, and knifers . . ." [24] The Mafia peddled bad dope to the kids. The police busted them for loitering, panhandling, violating curfews, disturbing the peace—and dope. The kids themselves, with their supreme contempt for bourgeois soap and water, were wracked by VD, hepatitis, bad teeth, bad trips, and increasing addiction to hard drugs.

In short, for many, the Age of Aquarius had never really come at all.

In the last years of the decade, however, the tribes rallied their forces for a determined stand against the impending victory of the straights. This was the age of the great festivals, of the "people-colored hill" in upper New York State where perhaps half a million long hairs gathered for a three-day secession from America. Abbie Hoffman called it "Woodstock Nation," the physical embodiment of "our energy, music, politics, school, religion, play, battleground and our sensuality . . . liberated land in which we can do whatever the fuck we decide." [25] Woodstock Nation—the kingdom of the young.

These years also saw the rise of what we might call the hard-core drop-outs—"the scragglies, the raggedy bunch, longhairs, the white niggers of American society . . ." The closest thing these "crazies" had to an organization was the Youth International Party —the Yippies—a bitter, Dada put-on that defined itself as "just an excuse to rebel," waved the black marijuana flag ("Means any damn thing you want it to") and assured potential converts that "There are no ideological requirements to be a yippie. . . . Protest your own issue. Each man his own yippie." [26]

Most of the dirty, hairy, denimed "raggedy bunch" never even got that close to structured living. For this was also the age of the wandering hordes of true street people, totally freaked out and cut off from the straight world. These compleat drop-outs were ugly, battered, beaten, and free, thumb-tripping back and forth across the country on a restless, aimless Easy Rider quest that made Kerouac's years On the Road and even Ken Kesey's famous psychedelic bus tour of 1964 seem quaint and old-fashioned.

This was the generation, finally, that began the mass exodus to the communes. Urban communal pads—families, tribes, collectives—had been common enough from the beginning, a natural part of the flower people's thrust toward a more total sense of community and oneness. In the later sixties, however, amazing numbers of city and suburban youth hit out for the back country to establish self-supporting little communities, communally owned and operated, in the tall timber, or the deserts of the Southwest. It was the last ditch, the final retreat for the counter culture, 1970 American style.

Sour-Out of the Sixties

But the Age of Aquarius seemed bent on self-destruction. As the decade turned, the bad vibes mounted and mounted, until they shook the fragile structure of the love generation to pieces.

After Woodstock, there was the Altamont festival in California, a Rolling Stones freebee, where the Hell's Angels hired to police the gathering turned on the flower children with pool cues and bike chains and ended by stabbing a man to death. In less than a year, two of the youth culture's superstars, Jimi Hendrix and Janis Joplin, died of drug overdoses. The Beatles broke up, with shocking revelations of cynical exploitation all through the years of their international suzerainty over the world of rock. Finally, there came the horrifying truth about the Manson case—and, by implication, about the subculture that produced it:

> There was no philosophy in the desert, no books. No church. . . . But music. . . . It was beautiful. Always beautiful music. We used to listen to Ravi Shankar from India. We had instruments, violin and flute and guitar Charlie and the girls played . . .

And then:

> . . . she picked up the fork and went over and left the fork in the man's stomach. . . .

She sat and watched it wobble, and she said she was fascinated by it.

Tex, she said, carved "War" on the man's chest. When Katie told me that, I flashed and said: "Wow. Pretty far out."

I thought it was pretty far out.[27]

It was the end of the great be-in, the sour-out of the sixties.

A large part of three generations had risen up against the richest and one of the most permissive of modern societies. This, the last of these generations in revolt, was not likely to have immediate successors. For the Movement no longer won spectacular victories in the streets, and the legitimizing support of politicians, the media, and liberals in general ebbed rapidly away. The heritage of the Southern sit-ins, the momentum built up through the creative middle years of the decade, were dissipated at last. The next generation would draw little inspiration from this one's bloody, futile confrontations with the inexorable System.

Despair was the legacy of the generation of 1968.

5. *BALANCE SHEET*

But that is surely not the whole story.

Time and again over the past century and a half, we have seen ideologically impelled young people rise up against—or withdraw from—the society that raised them. Repeatedly, the young rebels have been brought low. But that has not typically been the end of it. Rebellious younger generations have made a dent—and sometimes considerably more than that—in the history of their times.

What, then, have the insurrectionary youth of the sixties done to our own future history?

It was not the cataclysm they were banking on, of course—the apocalyptic upheaval described in the booming chant of *One More War—Revolution!* But few would deny the Civil Rights marchers of the early sixties a considerable share of the credit for the Civil Rights Acts of those years. Furthermore, in a less tangible but perhaps even more significant way, the young black militants of the entire decade have radically changed the image of black Americans. Liberals of older generations pitied and patronized the poor Negro—Uncle Tom, Old

Black Joe, the darky, the slave. But black men stood tall in the 1960's; and white generations that grew up then will seldom have to make that conscious effort at "toleration" that was the closest their most conscientious parents could come to color blindness.

The counter culture also would seem to have carried America closer to a new state of grace. Once the merely faddish has filtered out, something enduring is quite likely to remain of the new, gentler ethos of love, complete personal freedom, and deeper human community which the hippies built on the base of the beat generation and the 1920's. It is hard to imagine that these generations of the sixties, however involved they may become in the world's work, will ever be quite the driven, compulsive achievers their parents were. We are not on our way to the status of a fun-loving, richly human, banana republic: but the passion to be first does seem to be fading. We may well achieve less and enjoy it more in future decades.

And so on down quite a list.

American education, for instance, pressured by dissatisfied students and disgruntled parents, will almost certainly undergo significant changes as a result of the student revolts of the 1960's. American politics, especially after the current wave of repression has passed over, will undoubtedly feel the continuing demands of yesterday's activists for some action on the issues they raised in the last decade. A New Left political party, we are now told, is far from an impossibility. In foreign affairs, the generations of the sixties will find it very hard to fight a war in years to come—no matter how noble the purpose. Vietnam, like World War I, should make today's young Americans knee-jerk noninterventionists for some time.

All this, of course, is no more than vaguely informed guesswork at present. But it is inconceivable that once all the recriminations and disillusionments have faded, the tumultuous youth revolt of the 1960's will not have redirected the course of our future history at least as much as earlier generational rebellions shaped the histories of their own times.

Part IV

WHERE DO WE GO FROM HERE?

13

The Streets Belong to the People

We got up early that morning—not long after five o'clock. We washed the fumes of the night before out of our heads, shaved and dressed. Bill had the radio going in the other room while I was washing up. While I was scraping the stubble off my chin, he stuck his head into the bathroom to say: "There's a truck burning on Key Bridge already. And the radio says they're using gas."

So we didn't bother about breakfast, but simply stuck an apple in a bag, along with wet rags and some other essentials, and went out into the streets of Georgetown.

Out into the Youth Revolution.

1. *THE BIGGEST BUST IN HISTORY*

Mayday

Georgetown is a nice, residential part of Washington, full of Federal-period townhouses, narrow, steeply sloping streets, and old-fashioned, tree-shaded, brick sidewalks. Its main streets, however, are Wisconsin and M, both lined with artsy-craftsy shops, expensive restaurants, and various youth-culture joints. Long hair and peace symbols clog the sidewalks every weekend.

This was Monday morning, not yet six o'clock. But there they were, clogging not the sidewalks but the streets themselves, chanting, singing, clapping hands. Familiar, tattered words and phrases out of a vanished decade, already sounding oddly dated, like *twenty-three skiddoo* or some dust-bowl song about Okies:

One Two Three Four—
We Don't Want Your Fuckin War—

Powerrr
To the *PEE-PUL!*
Powerrr
To the *PEE-PUL!*

Hopping up and down, clapping out the rhythm, hair and fringes flying in the brisk, early-morning air. Jamming main intersections with their growing numbers. Drifting in restless, roving gangs down side streets, shaggy guerrilla bands in search of unlocked cars or loose garbage cans to roll out into the street. Talking, laughing nervously at their work, keeping a weather eye out for the police. There was, indeed, already a whiff of tear gas in the air.

It was the first Monday in May, 1971. Rennie Davis's Mayday Collective had sworn to shut down the capital of the United States that morning.

"If the Government of the United States won't stop this war," Rennie had told college audiences all across the country the preceding winter, "then we're going to stop the Government of the United States!" It always got a rolling cheer from the kids. Then he would get out his maps and start showing them how easy it would be to close key arteries, block the Potomac River bridges—and literally paralyze the government by monstrous traffic jams. All it would take would be enough street people, enough militants, freaks, and crazies willing to put their bodies on the line and determined to mess up the Man's machine at any cost.

That's what they were into that morning in May. Ten or fifteen thousand American kids who had come to put a stop to the American government.

We looked down a steeply sloping street onto Key Bridge. It was lined with troops in battle gear. A cordon of white-helmeted riot police sealed off the bottom of our own street from the bridge. When we were halfway down the hill, some kids behind and above us began to roll huge trash bins on wheels down the steep cobblestoned side street into the police lines below. The police shouted and charged up the hill, volleying a sudden cloud of burning, blinding, white gas.

A Movement medic swabbed out our eyes until the tears stopped coming and we could see again. As we headed back toward Wisconsin we saw that the long-haired kids in jeans and denims had got quite a number of cars into the intersections; they were letting the air out of the tires now. Here and there a car, a couple of garbage cans, a few large boxes and assorted junk approximated a skeletal barricade. According to my little transistor radio, Dr. Spock had led a charge across the Fourteenth Street Bridge—in an effort to reach the Pentagon—but had been stopped by the police. There was supposed to be some kind of running battle on the Mall downtown.

A small panel truck, painted in garish psychedelic colors, pulled up near the corner of Wisconsin and M, the handful of long hairs in the back yelling for more people. They were heading downtown, so we piled in.

The streets of Washington unrolled behind us, framed in shoulder-length hair and tie-dye shirts: people milling into the streets, knots of policemen moving after them, momentarily snarled traffic, people being busted, the sting of gas. Halfway downtown, two policemen roared up behind us on motorbikes, took one look at the motley horde jammed in the back, and pulled the truck over. We all spilled out and moved away fast. One officer had the driver spread-eagled against the hood. The other one couldn't do much about the spewing exodus from the back: he simply watched us go.

The two of us walked north, watching the wandering bands of kids, the clusters of policemen. The police had occupied all the key traffic circles. The kids had no chance there. If you ventured into the street, they grabbed you and hustled you into the waiting police vans. Some of these seemed to be full already. The radio in my pocket said that thousands of people were being swept off the streets, and that no bridges were closed yet.

We were on our way north to DuPont Circle, a traditional gathering place of the tribes, where the action was supposed to be heavy. Before we had gone more than a couple of blocks, Bill was busted. We had stopped to talk to some people on a street corner when a big green police bus, already crammed with prisoners, pulled up. Most of us moved away at once. Bill stood there on the corner, his hands in his pockets. His hair is somewhat long. A uniformed man jumped off the bus and grabbed him. "I haven't done anything," he said. "You have now," said the man in uniform, hustling him onto the bus.

He had indeed. He had been walking around with long hair—the sign and symbol of the youth revolt—in the middle of the biggest mass arrest in American history.

Mayday came as the climax to more than two weeks of youthful anti-war demonstrations in the capital. The kids had marched, rallied, sat in, and finally commenced the aggressive civil disobedience designed to stop the city of Washington in its tracks. Over the same period, the forces of law and order arrested more than twelve thousand of them—the vast majority during the Mayday attacks on Monday and Tuesday. Thousands of troops had also been mobilized—Georgetown was occupied by the First Army, troopers every ten feet along the main streets, by the time I got back Monday morning. Even the Marines had been called in: four Chinook helicopters full landed at the Washington Monument at mid-morning. Late Monday, Rennie Davis himself was scooped up by the FBI. And through it all, traffic flowed almost unimpeded into the city.

It was a total debacle for the Movement—for the last desperate effort to revive the spirit of the sixties in 1971.

Guns and Grass United

Or was it?

In some ways, Mayday was clearly not an end, but a beginning. From the generational point of view, in fact, it represented a significant new level of insight and determination on the part of the revolutionary left. It represented an explicit recognition of the fact that the real power behind the new radicalism of the sixties had not been the blue-collar workers of traditional Marxism, nor the oppressed Third World racial minorities in America—but the youth. The literate, clearly alienated sons and daughters of middle-class America itself.

This was a hard thing for ideological radicals to accept. Marx and Lenin, Che Guevara and Frantz Fanon had hardly made youth the cornerstone of their theories.

A few Movement leaders had seen the disturbing truth earlier on. There had even been some moves toward a coalition between the two main streams of the Youth Revolution. This did not look too difficult from a purely pragmatic point of view: many rank-and-file militants turned on, and many hippie types considered themselves political radicals, whenever they bothered to think about such things. It was just that—if you were a street person—activists were so organization minded, so big for meetings and steering committees. Or—if you were into the revolution—hippies were so totally lacking in seriousness and long-term commitment. And, of course, if you were into anything at all, the rest of the kids on campus—let alone off it—seemed so *apathetic*. And finally, the whole business *was* so much less impressive theoretically than the working classes united or the Third World up in arms.

Nevertheless, there were those who had begun to grope toward a united youth front even before Mayday.

The Youth International Party had been a half-serious thrust in that direction. The yippie, Jerry Rubin had said, is "the Marxist acidhead, the psychedelic Bolshevik . . . a hybrid mixture of New Left and hippie coming out something different." [1] A half-serious attempt—but no more than that.

On the militant side, the fabled Weatherman Underground had begun its first taped communiqué to the nation with a ringing assertion that: "All over the world, people fighting Amerikan imperialism look to Amerika's youth to use that strategic position behind enemy lines to join forces in the destruction of the empire." Bernardine Dohrn and her fellow revolutionaries boasted that they "move freely in and out of every . . . youth scene in this country." They declared that "guns and grass are united in the youth underground." [2] But for Weathermen, blacks and Third World people generally were the big battalions of the revolution: they themselves were mere skirmishers, and "the youth" in general were really little more than a peasant sea for them to swim in.

Rennie Davis himself, the most articulate nonleader in the Mayday Tribe, had repeatedly recognized the generational nature of the conflict. "Judge," he said during his trial for conspiring to start the Chicago Convention riots, "you represent all that is old . . . and repressive in this country . . . the spirit at this defense table is going to devour your sickness in the next generation." And, more specifically still, to Mr. Foran, the prosecutor: "I am going to be the boy next door to Tom Foran and the boy next door . . . is . . . going to organize his kids into the revolution. We are going to turn the sons and daughters of the ruling class in this country into Viet Cong." [3]

In the winter of 1970–71, Rennie Davis and the radicals of the Mayday Collective had apparently decided to gamble massively on the youth; not only on the college activists, but on the "unserious" counter-culture people, and on as many straight kids as could be lured to the scene by the prospect of rock, dope, and resolute non-violence. Mayday literature appealed particularly to the tribes, the freaks and street people, by emphasizing individual freedom, small-group decision-making, and no steering-committee bossism. The Mayday demonstrations proper were preceded by a week of camping out, music and drugs in West Potomac Park and by a full-scale rock festival the preceding Saturday. Routed from the park on Sunday by the police, the people had gathered at area universities that night for a bizarre mixture of old-fashioned Martin Luther King-sytle inspirational oratory and wild tribal circle dancing: "We know why we are here now," Hoseah Williams of King's old Southern Christian Leadership Conference intoned. "We will go out *into the streets* tomorrow, and we will put our *bodies on the line.* We will *fill the jails* of this city—"

One Two Three Four—
We Don't Want Your Fuckin War—

the laughing circle-dancers shouted, leaping and clapping to a thunder of drums.

"There's one person in our group who has a rheumatic heart," a serious-looking young girl said, as we sat in a litter of sleeping bags, rucksacks, sandwich papers and drowsy people late that night, the night before the action. "And one guy who's actually blind. And I had a miscarriage last night. So we want to be sure we have the medic and bust numbers . . ."

And a husky, black guitar player struck up one of the syncopated message things that hundreds of kids can join in at once:

Gonna change this coun-try
OH YEAH
Gonna build some hou-ses
OH YEAH
Gonna feed some pee-pul
OH YEAH

Gonna *change* this coun-try
OH YEAH
Sing NAA NA-NA-NA NAA
Sing NAA NA-NA-NA NAA

And then, hardening the beat, leaning into it:

Tired of mar-chin
OH YEAH
Tired of plea-din
OH YEAH
Ready for *figh-tin*
OH YEAH
SING NAA NA-NA-NA NAA . . .

They did very little fighting the next day—their harassing tactics were, in fact, almost universally nonviolent. But they did fill the jails of Washington. Ten thousand nice WASP kids saw the inside of an American jail for the first time, and went home with the startling, proud, disturbing knowledge that they had been part of the biggest mass bust in American history.

It will not be the last.

2. *A POWER IN THE LAND*

A Sense of Identification

Movement leaders may have been consciously slow to recognize their real source of strength; but practically speaking, they had always been well aware where their troops were coming from.

All campus-based demonstrations have, of course, aimed at arousing the apathetic or middle-of-the-road student to action for the cause. Often, especially where the apparent persecution of fellow students by the authorities was involved, the nonradical majority has, in fact, been effectively mobilized, at least on a short-term basis. The Moratorium demonstrations of 1969 were particularly successful at bringing normally nondemonstrating college kids into the streets. And, as we have seen, the Kent State shootings moved perhaps half the campus populations of the country to some sort of response. By 1970, according to one authority, "a clear majority" of American college and university students "had joined in one or more protests against the status quo." [4]

Noncollege youth had also been brought to support some aspects of the Movement. The Black Panthers inspired ghetto youth to dream of revolutionary glory, and occasionally to take a shot at a policeman themselves. Marxist-oriented Movement literature was full of hopeful enthusiasm for "revolutionary grease," the admittedly small radicalized minority of the offspring of blue-collar, inner-city workers who could be brought out for demonstrations. And hundreds of high schools in the later sixties did have their underground presses, their local-issue protests, their teen-age militants.

The hippie subculture, of course, made even deeper inroads into the kingdom of the straights. The music, costumes, and hair styles of the drop-outs swept over college campuses in the later sixties. Youths' demands for the right to dress and cut their hair as they pleased fired bitter disputes over "dress codes" in countless high schools across the country. On this superficial level, at least, there was no question of the impact of the counter culture on the nation's youth.

The trend of the tribes toward freer sexual mores and widespread experimentation with drugs also reached well beyond the rather arbitrarily defined limits of hippiedom. Greater change was perhaps visible among university populations, but there were significant changes among other groups as well. The drug problem, which had first manifested itself on the campus, spread steadily down the age and educational ladder to high-school and even junior-high and grammar-school children. The so-called sexual revolution apparently took another great leap forward in the 1960's, the first quantum jump toward sexual anarchy since the 1920's. And all this among young people who had no intention of tuning in and dropping out—young Americans who simply saw no fundamental difference between marijuana and alcohol, or who had come to believe that sex was a legitimate expression of human affection—and no business at all of a blue-nosed society.

A number of polls attempted to measure the extent to which a larger generational consensus was developing around the views and values of the New Left and the hippie subculture. When asked about hazy abstractions, like morality, social restraints, and even family ties, the younger generation often piously echoed its parents' views for the pollster. On specific contemporary issues, however, startling generational discrepancies cropped up. This was, understandably, particularly so among the college youth, the vast, ideologically aware middle ground between the conforming masses and the small revolutionary minority. But it was also true to a surprising extent of the nation's youth as a whole.

On one such poll, for instance, a *majority* of university students felt that such well-known vices as homosexuality, abortion, and premarital sexual relations were simply "not moral issue[s]." A majority of *all* young Americans either strongly or partially agreed that "economic wellbeing in this country is unjustly and unfairly distributed," that "our foreign policy is based on our own narrow economic and power interests," and that "basically, we are a racist nation." [5] No do-your-own-thing street freak, no New Left activist could have asked for more.

Most revealing of all, when they were asked to indicate with which social groupings they themselves felt "a sense of identification, forty-one per cent of *all* American youth expressed a strong identification with their fellow countrymen; forty-two per cent with members of their own religion; fifty-one per cent with people of their own race; sixty per cent with "the middle class"; and seventy-one per cent of the young felt a strong sense of identification with *"other people of* [*their*] *own generation."* [6] Generational differences are so clearly marked and widely recognized in our time that it is not, perhaps, surprising that generational consciousness has so rapidly outstripped all others. Nevertheless, it is a striking fact that no other center of loyalty—not social class, not race, not religion or nationality—can match the growing realization of the younger generation that it is precisely that: that they are members of an age group, shaped by history within this framework, and closer to their own generational contemporaries than to any other group of people on earth.

Power-Seeking in the New Generation

The younger generation, then, is a real and significant social subgroup. It is also a group with a growing thrust toward power—a group that can make, and has made, a difference in history.

Frederick G. Dutton, analyzing the *Changing Sources of Power* in 1970's America, cites an informed educator to the effect that "the American university student of today is involved, he cares, and he has left the sandbox of student activities for good." In his thoughtful analysis of the youth of the early seventies, Dutton offers a provocative comparison between the insurgent younger generation and the rise of other social subgroups in this country:

> The power-seeking in the new generation . . . is as real and determined as that of earlier social groups who pushed their way into the country's political structure, from the unpropertied freemen early in the nation's history to the offspring of the 1900-to-1914 immigration wave that provided the generation base on which Roosevelt built.

"The new group," he pointedly adds, "is proportionately larger compared to the rest of the population than were either of those earlier historical waves, and it already has a stronger beachhead within this society than those earlier groups initially had." [7]

On the face of it, anything so fickle, fun-oriented, and ephemeral as the younger generation—here today and gone tomorrow, quite literally—may seem a weak reed for sober political analysts (and serious revolutionaries) to lean on. But then, as Dutton emphasizes, many other groups that subsequently loomed very large indeed in history seemed at first wholly incapable—indeed, undesirous—of playing such a role.

The working classes of the West, for instance, were once regarded as obviously too overworked, ignorant, and unconcerned with public affairs—beyond their own narrow bread-and-butter interests—to merit a share of political power. They themselves, furthermore, demonstrated a hopeless lack of politically focused "class consciousness" that drove socialists up the wall through much of the nineteenth century.

The American Negro was also well known at one time for his shiftlessness, his fun-loving irresponsibility, and, of course, his intellectual inferiority. His "Uncle Tom" humility—subsequently defined as a "colonial mentality"—was once so strong that liberal politicians put blacks at the bottom of their list of reform priorities throughout the first half of the twentieth century.

Women also, it was once believed, were disqualified from playing a part in politics by their emotional nature, their underdeveloped rational faculties, their physiological handicaps, their "natural" family responsibilities—and the fact that a majority of women evinced no particular interest in voting or running for office.

The same charges were repeatedly hurled at them all—blacks, immigrants, women in this century, proletarians and landless freemen in the last: they were disqualified *by their very nature* from exercising power—and they *didn't want it anyway.* These same points are endlessly made about the young today. They are too emotional, too fickle and faddish, too transitory as a social subgroup—and once the fun and games are over, too lacking in real social and political concern to be taken seriously as a force in the land.

If an undemocratic generalization may be offered, it seems probable that large numbers of peasant freemen, proletarians, immigrants, blacks, women, young people, *and* solid, middle-aged, middle-class citizens are really too emotional, too uninformed, too busy with their own concerns, and in other ways *naturally* disqualified from exercising political power. Yet all of them—to speak now in plain historical terms—have, in fact, made important contributions to the course of modern history. All of them—however ignorantly, emotionally, and intermittently—are already power blocs in our society. And of them all—as this book has tried to show—youth has not played the least significant part in shaping our world these past two centuries.

3. THEY WILL BE BACK

An Unslakable Discontent

The kids will be back. They always have come back. This book has been the story of that eternal return, of modern youth's unslakable discontent with modernity and of his lemming-like longing for the streets.

In 1819, they broke the German youth movement—smashed it flat all across the German states. The Student Unions were dissolved or driven underground, their leaders arrested or harried across the Rhine. The movement was shattered beyond repair.

But German youth was marching again in the early 1830's . . . in 1848 . . . in the later 1890s and the early 1900's . . . in the 1920's and 1930's . . . in the later 1960's . . . and just yesterday, surging across my TV screen with signs and banners, songs and shouting. The issues have changed, of course, from generation to generation and decade to decade—but the youth has gone on marching.

The solid bourgeois citizens of the France of Louis Philippe laughed off the first Bohemia, the first withdrawal of alienated youth to a private, cheerfully antisocial subculture of their own. A bunch of bums who couldn't make it in straight society—or frivolous kids using romantic idealism as an excuse for a good time. By 1835, most of the first Bohemians were gone from the Latin Quarter, driven from Paris by sheer poverty, driven sometimes even to seeking employment in bourgeois society itself.

But the *quartier* has never really been empty from that day to this. Murger popularized the *vie de bohème* in the 1840's; the Realists followed the Romantics in after the middle of the century; and then the Symbolists and *décadents;* the gaslit street life of the *Moulin Rouge* and *Ubu Roi;* the Paris of Picasso and the Cubists; of Hemingway and the Lost Generation; and on and on, Bohemia forever, with all its incessantly multiplying stepchildren around the world.

We have seen the birth of the Youth Revolution, with all its principal forms and key characteristics, in the nineteenth century. We have seen its rapid growth and spread in the twentieth. We have also seen that whatever specific issues and contemporary pressures may shape any given generation in revolt, the disaffection of modern youth in general is deeply rooted in two inescapable realities of modern history: the accelerating pace of change and the wide dissemination of ideas in the modern world. Accelerated *social change* cuts the young man off from his elders, making their wisdom and many of their institutions irrelevant to his life—and his life experience almost incomprehensible to them. The easy availability of *new ideas* of all sorts—through vastly expanded educational institutions, cheap books, and an avalanche of popularization in the mass media —offers young people many criticisms of the world their elders run, and many theoretical alternatives to it. Result: intellectual disaffiliation, the revolt or withdrawal of significant segments of the younger generation.

A movement so deeply rooted in history is not likely to evaporate overnight. The Youth Revolution, in fact, seems likely to be with us as long as rapid change makes yesterday's conventional wisdom untenable today—and as long as alternative truths are made available for youthful exploration.

The Youth Revolution is not fading away. It is, in fact, a growing force in history.

Between 1815 and the present, the sheer numbers of disaffected youth have grown spectacularly, both in absolute terms and relative to the growth of the general population. Let us look, for example, at the generational base, the numbers of educated young people, a certain percentage of whom may be expected to rebel. The total university population of the German states in the years after Waterloo numbered no more than ten thousand—only one out of every three thousand Germans. The population of our own colleges and universities in the late 1960's, by contrast, ran to nearly seven million. One out of every thirty Americans was a college student.[8]

The same picture emerges if we focus more precisely on the numbers of young dissidents themselves, insofar as these can be measured. The famous Wartburg Festival of 1817, for example, involved less than five hundred young German-nationalist crusaders. A century and a half later, the November, 1969, Moratorium march on Washington put at least a third of a million young anti-war demonstrators into the streets of the nation's capital. And one final comparison, this from the Bohemian stream of the youth revolt. In the 1830's, the wild-haired young French poet Philothée O'Neddy boasted publicly that at least six thousand romantic Bohemians were committed to the struggle against bourgeois morality, conformity, and materialism. In the summer of 1969, perhaps half a million hippies and countercultural fellow travelers gathered for a single celebrated rock festival in upper New York State.[9]

If a few hundred young German nationalists 150 years ago could start a snowball rolling that would create a new great power in the heart of Europe; if a few thousand French aesthetic drop-outs could forge a subculture that would spread around the world—what effect will the restless young millions of today have upon all our futures?

Pathbreakers for the Human Spirit

They will be back—and they will make a difference.

This book has attempted to illustrate, not only the reality of generational rebellion, but its importance as a causal force in history. That importance, to boil it down to a single phrase, would seem to consist in the younger generation's special role as a carrier of new ideas and a promoter of social change.

Youth rebellions, as we have seen, typically fail in the short run. Their long-term impact, however, has generally been considerably greater than their contemporaries could well imagine. Most frequently, younger generations in revolt seem to perform a unique function. Congenitally more open to the winds of ideology than their more settled elders, disaffected youth may provide a crucial *first constituency* for radical new ideas whose time has *almost* come. Their noisy, violent rebellions, their ostentatious withdrawals, may fail of their immediate objectives, but they leave an indelible mark upon society at large. They serve as an essential *middle term* between yesterday's subversive notions and tomorrow's new majorities.

Whether it is nationalism in Germany in 1815, socialism in Russia in the 1870's, or Freudianism in America in the 1920's; whether it is an artistic revolution in turn-of-the-century Paris, or a sexual revolution in mid-century America—the basic pattern remains the same. The kids try it first.

Kids will try almost anything once, of course, and many such generational experiments—if we may so term them—simply do not pan out. There is always a large admixture of chaff in with the grain—much that is impractical, utopian, or just plain silly. But a significant percentage of the ideas the young periodically impose upon us with so much sound and fury do prove out. They become the world views, the ethical imperatives, the institutions, and the styles of life of generations yet unborn.

Modern societies may yet devise ingenious strategies to channel the very real power of the continuing Youth Revolution. Some efforts have already been made along these lines—too often by totalitarian states, and not infrequently without successfully sublimating youth's unfortunate capacities for arrogance, extremism, and pure violence. All such efforts, however, will have to bear in mind one crucial truth above all about the ongoing Youth Revolution: the simple fact that rebellious younger generations are, by their very nature, forces for change.

Whether they are generating counter-cultural havens to be human in, or are projecting new social systems for mankind at large, this ideologically oriented minority of the young has, historically, always been the pathbreaker, the seeker of new ways for man to live. It is seldom creative, in the way that a great leader or a man of genius can be creative. But these insurrectionary young people can experiment with, adapt, and propagate new ideas more effectively than any other group in society. It is these special talents of the young true believer in revolt which any effort to channel their ardor and their energies must focus on.

For the conforming majority of each generation—those upon whom the continuity of society depends—there are already any number of organizations and institutional outlets for youthful vigor and more orthodox idealism. For the few who have found it impossible to mesh with the system, who will rebel against or withdraw from the *status quo* if society itself does not find some use for their insurrectionary energies, other socially acceptable forms must be found.

The world needs trail-blazers and experimenters with change as much as it does bastions of the established order. Surely we can devise means whereby the natural pioneers may be charged with the pioneering missions—whether it be opening up virgin lands or conducting reconnaissance probes into the inner space of the human spirit—that will always be necessary if mankind is to survive in a changing world of his own inadvertent making.

One thing *is* sure, however: whether or not we learn to canalize their nonnegotiable demands, tomorrow's youth *will* be up in arms against today's realities. And in the long run, far more often than his elders like to admit, he will have his way with history.

Notes

PREFACE

1. Michael Rossmann, "Barefoot in a Marshmallow World," *Ramparts,* January, 1966.

CHAPTER 1

1. Bill Warren, ed., *The Middle of the Country: The Events of May 4 as Seen by Students & Faculty at Kent State University* (New York, 1970).
2. *Newsweek,* May 18, 1970, p. 29. Seymour Martin Lipset and Gerald Schaflander, *They'd Rather Be Left: The Past, Present, and Future of Student Activism in America,* to be published by Little, Brown, and Company in the fall of 1971, suggest that "close to half the undergraduate campus population was involved" in the post-Kent State upheaval. I am indebted to Professor Lipset for letting me see the manuscript of this illuminating volume prior to publication.

CHAPTER 2

1. Bibliographical guides to the varying roles of dissident youth in history are not easy to come by. For key works on students as rebels, however, see Philip Altbach, *A Select Bibliography on Students, Politics, and Higher Education* (Cambridge, 1967), and the updated bibliography appended to Altbach and S. M. Lipset, *Students in Revolt* (Boston, 1969). For studies of youth movements—student and nonstudent—see the voluminous notes appended to S. N. Eisenstadt, *From Generation to Generation: Age Groups and Social Structure* (Glencoe, Ill., and London, 1956). On social generations, the specific approach adopted here, see note 3 below.

2. Much of the pioneer work on youth in history has been done by non-historians—sociologists like S. M. Lipset, political scientists like Marvin Rintala, psychologists like Kenneth Keniston, and scholars of a social-psychological bent like Lewis S. Feuer (all cited in the pages that follow). Historians are, however, taking a greater interest in youth as a force in history—witness the work of Stuart Hughes on the intellectual generations of the 1890's and early 1900's, Douglas Hale's papers on the German Student Unionists, Fritz Redlich's early work on the generational factor in American business history, Peter Loewenberg's paper on the German Nazi generation, Alan B. Spitzer's upcoming paper on the French generation of the 1820's, and Robert L. Tyler's coming study of the theory of social generations as a historiographical tool.
3. An up-to-date introduction to the subject of social generations may be found in the pair of articles in the most recent edition of the *Encyclopedia of the Social Sciences,* edited by David L. Sills (New York, 1968): Julian Marías, "Generations—the Concept," (VI, 88–92) and Marvin Rintala, "Political Generations," VI, 92–95. For the uses of the notion of social generations for the historian, see Marías, *Generations: A Historical Method,* recently translated by Harold C. Raley, (University, Ala., 1970); Karl Mannheim, "The Problem of Generations," translated in *Essays in the Sociology of Knowledge,* Paul Kecskemeti, ed. (New York, 1952), pp. 276–320; and the present author's paper on "Rebellious Younger Generations as a Force in Modern History," read at the American Historical Association in December, 1970.
4. Henry Smith, "The Young Man's Task," *Sermons of Master Henry Smith,* edited by Thomas Man (London, 1611), p. 228.
5. On the Reformation, see Herbert Moller, "Youth as a Force in the Modern World," *Comparative Studies in Society and History,* X (1968), 237–241; on the American Revolution, see the controversial article by Stanley Elkins and Eric McKitrick, "The Founding Fathers: Young Men of the Revolution," *Political Science Quarterly,* LXXVI (1961), 181–216.
6. Kingsley Davis, "The Sociology of Parent-Youth Conflict," *American Sociological Review,* V (1940), 523.
7. *Future Shock,* New York, London, and Toronto, 1971, p. 1.
8. Hans Richter, *Dada: Art and Anti-Art* (London, 1965), p. 48.
9. J. E. Downey, "Is Modern Youth Going to the Devil?" *Sunset,* No. 52 (November, 1925), p. 19; A. M. Royden, "The Destructive Younger Generation," *Ladies Home Journal,* No. 41 (March, 1924), p. 31; I. Bacheler, "The Unspanked Generation," *Century,* No. 112 (July, 1926), pp. 348–355; "Keeping Up With Susanna, by the Mother of a Radical Daughter," *Woman's Home Companion,* No. 52 (November, 1925), p. 19.
10. David Thompson, *Europe Since Napoleon* (New York, 1957), p. 122.

CHAPTER 3

1. Harold Nicolson, *The Congress of Vienna* (New York, 1961), p. 244.
2. Henry E. Dwight, *Travels in the North of Germany in the Years 1825 to 1826* (New York, 1829), p. 203.
3. Heinrich Bünsen and Georg Heer, "Die alte Göttinger Burschenschaft 1815–1834," in Herman Haupt and Paul Wentzke, eds., *Quellen und Darstellungen zur Geschichte der Burschenschaft und der deutschen Einheitsbewegung* (Heidelberg, 1910–1940), XII, 211.
4. Herman Haupt, "Aus F. J. Fromanns Aufzeichnungen über seine Studentenzeit," in Haupt, ed., *Quellen und Darstellungen zur Geschichte der Burschenschaft und der deutschen Einheitsbewegung* (Heidelberg, 1955——), IV, 41; Johannes Ferdinand Wit, genannt von Dörring, *Fragmente aus meinem Leben und meiner Zeit* (Leipzig, 1830), I, 5–6.
5. Lewis S. Feuer, *The Conflict of Generations* (New York, 1969), p. 64.
6. Karl Hoffman, in Adolf Follen, ed., *Freye Stimmen frischer Jugend* (Jena, 1819), No. 13.
7. George W. Spindler, *The Life of Karl Follen* (Chicago, 1917), p. 14.
8. Elizabeth Follen, *Life of Charles Follen,* in Karl Follen, *The Works of Charles Follen, with a Memoir of His Life* (Boston, 1841–1842), I, 44.
9. Spindler, p. 23; Elizabeth Follen, I, 46.
10. Friedrich Münch, *Aus Deutschlands trübster Zeit,* in *Gesammelte Werke* (St. Louis, Mo., 1902), pp. 59, 49.
11. Martin Luther, "Der 46. Psalm," in *Werke für das christliche Haus,* edited by Dr. Buchwald *et al.* (Braunschweig, 1892), VIII, 68–69. Translation based on the most common English version of the well-known hymn.
12. Bülau, pp. 422–423.
13. Edward Dietz, *Neue Beiträge zur Geschichte des Heidelberger Studentenlebens* (Heidelberg, 1903), p. 35.
14. Heinrich von Treitschke, *History of Germany in the Nineteenth Century,* translated by Eden and Cedar Paul (New York, 1917), III, 56; Bülau, p. 436.
15. Guillaume de Bertier de Sauvigny, *Metternich et son temps* (Paris, 1959), pp. 161–162.
16. Twentieth-century interpretations of the first *Burschenschaft* generation have suffered from the tendency to see the Student Unionists of 1815 as precursors of the Nazi youth of the 1930's, particularly in their anti-Semitism. See, for instance, Peter Viereck's chapter on Father Jahn as "the first Storm Trooper" in his *Metapolitics: From the Romantics to Hitler* (New York, 1941), and Feuer's chapter on the *Burschenschaft*

in his *Conflict of Generations.* The Student Unionists and gymnasts of 1815 were often—like many other nineteenth-century Europeans—anti-Semitic; but it is impossible to imagine this romantic, puritanically pious youth stoking Hitler's ovens.

17. Karl Biedermann, *25 Jahre deutschen Geschichte* (Leipzig, 1889), I, 188, 190; Treitschke, III, 611; Karl Follen, "Bundeslied der Schweizer auf dem Rütli," in Elizabeth Follen, I, 606–607.
18. Josephine Blesch, *Studien über Johannes Wit, genannt von Dörring . . . nebst einem Exkurs über die liberalen Strömungen von 1815–1819* (Berlin and Leipzig, 1917), p. 51.
19. Münch, p. 15.
20. Edith J. Morley, ed., *Crabb Robinson in Germany 1800–1805: Extracts from His Correspondence* (London, 1929), p. 102.
21. *A Memoir of Charles Lewis Sand: Including a Narrative of the Circumstances Attending the Death of Augustus von Kotzebue* (London, 1819), pp. 57, 70.
22. C. E. Jarcke, *Karl Ludwig Sand und sein an dem Kaiserliche russischen Staatsrat von Kotzebue verübter Mord* (Berlin, 1831), p. 150.
23. Karl Alexander von Müller, *Karl Ludwig Sand* (Munich, 1925), p. 102; Spindler, pp. 62–63.
24. Herman Haupt, "Die Jenaische Burschenschaft von der Zeit ihrer Gründung bis zum Wartburgfeste," in Haupt, *Quellen und Darstellungen* (1955——), I, 111.
25. Müller, pp. 163–164.
26. Richard Metternich, ed., *Memoirs of Prince Metternich,* translated by Gerard W. Smith (New York, 1881–1882), III, 268.
27. *Memoir of Charles Lewis Sand,* p. xxiv; J. R. Seeley, *Life and Times of Stein* (Boston, 1879), II, 446.
28. The Karlsbad Decrees are here cited from the version printed in James Harvey Robinson, *The Restoration and the European Policy of Metternich (1814–20)* (Philadelphia, 1894), pp. 14–19.

CHAPTER 4

1. See Kenneth Keniston, "The Sources of Student Dissent," *Journal of Social Issues,* XXIII (1967), 109–115.
2. Théophile Gautier, *Histoire du romantisme* (Paris, 1927), p. 102.
3. *Ibid.*
4. Victor Hugo, *Hernani* (Boston, 1900), lines 1–2.
5. Adèle Hugo, *Victor Hugo raconté par un témoin de sa vie,* (Paris, n.d.), II, 342–349; Gautier, *Histoire du romantisme,* pp. 2, 97 ff; and

Alexandre Dumas, *My Memoirs,* translated by E. M. Waller (London, 1908), IV, 23–26.

6. Adèle Hugo, II, 341.
7. John E. Matzke, Introduction to Victor Hugo, *Hernani,* p. xxvii.
8. Gérard de Nerval to Victor Hugo, quoted in Adèle Hugo, II, 349.
9. Gautier, *Histoire du romantisme,* pp. 93, 101, 117–119.
10. Malcolm Easton, *Artists and Writers in Paris: The Bohemian Idea, 1803–1867* (New York, 1964), p. 57.
11. Jouffroy, loc. cit.
12. Augustin Challamel, *Souvenirs d'un Hugolâtre: la génération de 1830* (Paris, 1885), p. 9.
13. Theodore Roszak, *The Making of a Counter Culture: Reflections on the Technocratic Society and Its Youthful Opposition* (New York, 1969), p. 42.
14. Théophile Gautier, *Les Jeune-France: romans goguenards* (Paris, 1875), p. 87.
15. *Ibid.*
16. Charles Baudelaire, *L'art romantique* (Paris, n.d.) p. 152.
17. Cartoon from *Charivari,* reproduced in John Garber Palache, *Gautier and the Romantics* (New York, 1926), facing p. 38.
18. Gautier, *Histoire du romantisme,* p. 87.
19. René Jasinski, *Histoire de la littérature française* (Paris, 1947), II, 426.
20. Cesar Graña, *Modernity and Its Discontents: French Society and the French Man of Letters in the Nineteenth Century* (New York, 1964), p. 79.
21. Théophile Dondey, *Lettre inédite de Philothée O'Neddy, auteur de Feu et flamme, sur le groupe littéraire romantique dit les bousingos* (Paris, 1875). "Philothée O'Neddy" was Dondey's typically exotic pen name.
22. A. D. Vandam, *An Englishman in Paris, Notes and Recollections* (New York, 1892), I, 127–128.
23. Théophile Dondey, *Feu et flamme* (Paris, 1926), pp. 3, 19.
24. Gautier, *Les Jeune-France,* p. 1.
25. Théophile Gautier, Preface to *Mademoiselle de Maupin* (Vienne, n.d.), p. xxxv.
26. *Feu et flamme,* p. 3.
27. Gautier, *Histoire du romantisme,* p. 21.
28. Gautier, *Les Jeune-France,* pp. 1-2.
29. Critique of O'Neddy's *Feu et flamme* in *Revue encyclopedique,* LIX (1833), 270.
30. The celebrated Chapter Two of *La confession d'un enfant du siècle,* probing the essential nature of the *mal du siècle,* first appeared sepa-

rately as an article in the *Revue des Deux Mondes,* September 15, 1835.

31. Ochs' "Crucifixion," quoted in J. Marks, "The Dream Is Over," *Second Supplement to the Whole Earth Catalogue,* p. 1.
32. Enid Starkie, *Petrus Borel the Lycanthrope: His Life and Times* (London, 1954), p. 14.
33. Murger's original collection of Bohemian tales was entitled simply *Scènes de la vie de bohème* (1849). The Puccini opera, first performed in 1896, is of course *La Bohème.*
34. Erik H. Erikson, *Identity: Youth and Crisis* (New York, 1968), pp. 156–157.

CHAPTER 5

1. Frederick B. Artz, *Reaction and Revolution, 1814–1832* (New York, 1934), p. 238.
2. Arthur J. May, *Vienna in the Age of Franz Joseph* (Norman, Oklahoma), 1966, p. 25.
3. Frances Trollope, *Vienna and the Austrians* (Paris, 1838), I, 257–259.
4. Robertson, p. 211.
5. Josephine Goldmark, *Pilgrims of '48: One Man's Part in the Austrian Revolution of 1848 . . .* (New Haven, 1930), p. 42.
6. Heinrich Reschauer, *Das Jahr 1848: Geschichte der Wiener Revolution* (Vienna, 1872), p. 186.
7. James Granville Legge, *Rhyme and Revolution in Germany . . . 1813–1850* (New York, 1970), pp. 261–262; Henri de Weindel, *The Real Francis-Joseph* (London, 1909), pp. 47–48.
8. Robertson, p. 211.
9. Diary of Count C. Fr. Vitzthum von Eckstädt, in Legge, p. 268.
10. Grillparzer, in Legge, p. 264.
11. Vitzthum von Eckstädt, in Legge, p. 269.
12. Robertson, p. 215.
12. See, for instance, Günter Böhmer's chapter on the family in *Die Welt des Biedermeier* (Munich, 1968), pp. 65–116.
14. Rolland R. Lutz, "Fathers and Sons in the Vienna Revolution of 1848," *Journal of Central European Affairs,* XXII (1962), 167.
15. Lutz, p. 165.
16. See especially the work of Richard Flacks—e.g., "Student Activists: Result, not Revolt," *Psychology Today,* I (1967), 18–23.
17. Ludwig August Frankl, *Erinnerungen* (Prague, 1910), p. 317.

18. Jerome Blum, Rondo Cameron, and Thomas G. Barnes, *The European World Since 1815: Triumph and Transition* (Boston, 1970), p. 107.
19. P. H. Noyes, *Organization and Revolution: Working-Class Associations in the German Revolutions of 1848–1849* (Princeton, 1966), p. 57.
20. Goldmark, pp. 32–33.
21. William H. Stiles, *Austria in 1848–49:* (New York, 1852), I, 104.
22. *Ibid.,* I, 138–139.
23. Ludwig Frankl, "The University," in A. E. Zucker, ed., *The Forty-Eighters: Political Refugees of the German Revolution of 1848* (New York, 1950), p. 86.
24. Stiles, I, 159.
25. Joseph Redlich, *Emperor Francis Joseph of Austria* (New York, 1929), p. 14.
26. Stiles, I, 133.
27. A. J. P. Taylor, *The Habsburg Monarchy, 1809–1918* (New York, 1965), p. 58.
28. Berthold Auerbach, *A Narrative of Events in Vienna from Latour to Windischgrätz,* translated by J. E. Taylor (London, 1849).
29. Adolf Pichler, *Das Sturmjahr,* in Legge, p. 495.

CHAPTER 6

1. Custine, *Lettres de Russie,* edited by Henri Massis, (n.p., n.d.), p. 167; Herzen, *From the Other Shore and the Russian People and Socialism* (Cleveland and New York, 1956), p. 13.
2. Ivan Turgenev, *Fathers and Sons,* translated by Barbara Makanowitzky (New York, 1959), p. 20.
3. *Ibid.,* p. 52.
4. Daniel R. Browser, "Fathers, Sons, and Grandfathers: Social Origins of Radical Intellectuals in Nineteenth-Century Russia," *Journal of Social History,* II (1968–1969), 353.
5. I. A. Goncharov to E. P. Majkova, April, 1869, and January, 1870, in Charles A. Moser, *Antinihilism in the Russian Novel of the 1860's,* The Hague, 1964, p. 91; Fyodor Dostoyevsky to N. N. Strachov, 5 April 1870, in *Gesammelte Briefe 1833–1881* (Munich, 1966), p. 343.
6. Moser, p. 43.
7. V. Sorokin, *Vospominaniya starogo studenta,* in Franco Venturi, *Roots of Revolution: A History of the Populist and Socialist Movements in Nineteenth Century Russia,* translated by Francis Haskell (New York, 1960), p. 227.

8. London *Times,* October 15, 1861, p. 10.
9. "Studencheskie istorii kontsa 1861 goda," *Moskovskii Universitet v vospominaniakh sovremennikov,* p. 269.
10. London *Times,* October 16, 1861, p. 7.
11. Avrahm Yarmolinsky, *Road to Revolution: A Century of Russian Radicalism* (New York, 1962), pp. 114–115; Donald Mackenzie Wallace, *Russia on the Eve of War and Revolution,* revised edition (New York, 1961), p. 453.
12. *Literary Reminiscences,* p. 174.
13. W. E. Mosse, *Alexander II and the Modernization of Russia,* revised edition (New York, 1962), p. 113.
14. Yarmolinsky, p. 156.
15. Peter Kropotkin, *Memoirs of a Revolutionist,* James Allen Rogers, ed. (New York, 1962), p. 165.
16. Georg Brandes, *Impressions of Russia* (New York, 1966), p. 100.
17. Nicolas Berdiaev, "Psychologie du nihilisme et de l'athéisme russes," *Problèmes du communisme* (Paris, 1936), p. 75.
18. Geoffrey Gorer and John Rickman, *The People of Great Russia: A Psychological Study* (New York, 1962), p. 135.
19. Kropotkin, *Memoirs,* p. 157.
20. James H. Billington, *Mikhailovsky and Russian Populism* (Oxford, 1958), p. 91.
21. Bernard Pares, *A History of Russia,* fifth edition (New York, 1952), p. 371; Kropotkin, *Memoirs,* p. 198; Peter Kropotkin, "An Appeal to the Young," in *Kropotkin's Revolutionary Pamphlets,* Roger N. Baldwin, ed. (New York, 1927), p. 274.
22. Sergei Mikhailovich Kravchinsky, *Underground Russia: Revolutionary Profiles and Sketches from Life* (New York, 1883), pp. 21, 23.
23. Ekaterina Breshko-Breshkovskaia, *Hidden Springs of the Russian Revolution: Personal Memoirs of Katerina Breshkovskaia,* Lincoln Hutchinson, ed. (Stanford, California), 1931, p. 19.
24. Ekaterina Breshko-Breshkovskaia, *The Little Grandmother of the Russian Revolution: Reminiscences and Letters of Catherine Breshkovsky,* Alice Stone Blackwell, ed. (Boston, 1917), pp. 34–35.
25. *Ibid.*
26. *Ibid.* p. 42.
27. *Ibid.,* pp. 46–47.
28. *Ibid.*
29. *Ibid.,* p. 51.
30. Breshko-Breshkovskaia, *Hidden Springs,* p. 35.

31. Yarmolinsky, p. 91.
32. An estimate of two to three thousand is generally given. See Venturi, p. 740; Yarmolinsky, p. 186.
33. Michael T. Florinsky, *Russia: A History and an Interpretation* (New York, 1958), II, 1077; Yarmolinsky, p. 201.
34. Ronald Seth, *The Russian Terrorists: The Story of the Narodniki* (London, 1966), p. 40; Yarmolinsky, p. 201; Brandes, p. 48.
35. Yarmolinsky, p. 201; Brandes, p. 43.
36. The parallel with the 1969 SDS split into Weatherman and Progressive Labor factions is quite exact. The Weathermen even referred to themselves as *narodniks* for a while—referring of course to the later, terrorist phase of the career of the Russian *narodnik* generation.
37. Léon Tikhomirov, *La Russie politique et sociale* (Paris, 1888), p. 442; Henrietta M. Chester, *Russia, Past and Present* (London, 1881), p. 196.
38. David Footman, *Red Prelude: A Life of A. I. Zhelyabov* (London, 1944), pp. 106–107; Kravchinsky, p. 38.
39. Kropotkin, "The Spirit of Revolt," in *Revolutionary Pamphlets,* p. 38.
40. Fyodor Dostoyevsky, *Memoirs from the House of the Dead,* translated by Jessie Coulson (London, 1965), p. 7.
41. George Kennan, *Siberia and the Exile System* (New York, 1891), II, 160.
42. A. Maylan, *À travers les Russies* (Paris, 1880), pp. 124–128. The government executed more than two dozen terrorists and other revolutionaries between 1878 and the hanging of the tsar's assassins in 1881. The terrorists succeeded in killing less than half a dozen high officials, though they made attempts on others. The killing and injuring of a number of policemen, soldiers, suspected traitors to the movement, and innocent bystanders raised the terrorists' score considerably, however.
43. Yarmolinsky, p. 288.
44. Footman, epigraph, title page.
45. Robert Payne, *The Terrorists: The Story of the Forerunners of Stalin* (New York, 1957), p. 166.
46. *Ibid.,* p. 173.
47. E. M. Almedingen, *The Emperor Alexander II* (London, 1962), p. 344; Mosse, p. 173.
48. Vera Figner, *Memoirs of a Revolutionist* (New York, 1927), p. 103.
49. Constantin Pobiedonostsev, *L'autocratie russe: mémoires politiques, correspondance officielle et documents inédits . . .* (Paris, 1927), pp. 422, 424; Baron Rosen, *Forty Years of Diplomacy* (New York, 1922), I, 43.

50. N. V. Charykov, *Glimpses of High Politics through War and Peace, 1855–1929* (New York, 1931), p. 155.

CHAPTER 7

1. Barbara Tuchman, *The Proud Tower: A Portrait of the World Before the War 1890–1914* (New York, 1967), p. xv.
2. The immense popularity of books, films, and songs conjuring up a similarly romantic vision of "1900 yesterday" indicates that the need to believe in a golden age before the wars remains as strong today as fifty years ago.
3. *Beneath the Wheel,* translated by Michael Roloff (New York, 1969), p. 3.
4. The play had originated as a sketchy schoolboy farce, a collaborative effort in which Jarry's hand had been only one of several. Jarry was subsequently charged with plagiarism. None of his former schoolmates, however, contested the honor of authorship.
5. Roger Shattuck, *The Banquet Years: The Arts in France, 1885–1918* (New York, 1961), p. 205.
6. *Ubu Roi,* Act I, Scene I, line 1. *Merdre* is often translated by such quaint Olde-Englishe equivalents as *shite* or *shitte. Merdre* is, however, as close an approximation of *merde (shit)* as Norman Mailer's famous *fug* is of *fuck.* The audience at *Ubu Roi,* like the readers of *The Naked and the Dead,* undoubtedly understood precisely the word the author intended.
7. William Butler Yeats, *Autobiography* (New York, 1965), p. 233.
8. André Fontainas, *Mes souvenirs du symbolisme* (Paris, 1928), pp. 167–168; Jacques-Henry Levesque, *Alfred Jarry* (Paris, 1963), p. 47; Yeats, p. 234.
9. Arnold Hauser, *The Social History of Art* (New York, 1958), IV, 192.
10. Hans Jeschki, *La generación de 1898 en España,* translated by Pino Saavedra (Santiago de Chile, 1946), p. 54.
11. Pedro Salinas, "El concepto de generación literaria aplicado a la del 98," *Literatura española siglo xx* (Mexico, D. F.), p. 55.
12. Howard Becker, *German Youth: Bond or Free?* (London, 1946), p. 51.
13. *Ibid.,* p. 18, and Chapter 1 *passim.*
14. Carl Robert Schmid, "German Youth Movements: A Typological Study," *Summaries of Doctoral Dissertations, University of Wisconsin,* VII (Madison, Wisconsin, 1942), p. 168.
15. Poultney Bigelow, "From the Black Forest to the Black Sea," *Harper's Magazine,* LXXXIV (1892), 335.

16. Walter Z. Laqueur, *Young Germany: A History of the German Youth Movement* (New York, 1962), p. 19; Hans Blüher, "Die deutsche Wandervogelbewegung als erotische Phänomen: Die weibliche Gesellschaft," *Die Rolle der Erotik in der männlichen Gesellschaft* (Stuttgart, 1962), pp. 253–268.
17. Lucien Aressy, *Verlaine et la dernière bohème* (Paris, 1947), pp. 214–249.
18. H. Stuart Hughes, *Consciousness and Society: The Reorientation of European Social Thought 1890–1930* (New York, 1958), p. 35.
19. *Ibid.,* Chapter 2.
20. Isaac Deutscher, *Stalin: A Political Biography* (New York, 1960), p. 18.
21. Leon Trotsky, *Stalin: An Appraisal of the Man and His Influence* (New York, 1941), p. 14.
22. Deutscher, pp. 23–24.
23. Alexander Petrosov, in David Shub, *Lenin: A Biography* (New York, 1948) p. 23.
24. Krupskaya's *Memoirs,* in Bertram D. Wolfe, *Three Who Made a Revolution* (Boston, 1948), p. 100.
25. Krupskaya, in John A. Reshetar, Jr., *A Concise History of the Communist Party of the Soviet Union* (New York, 1960), p. 17.
26. V. I. Lenin, *What Is To Be Done?* in *Selected Works* (New York), 1967, I, 123.
27. Ethel Smyth, in Josephine Kamm, *The Story of Emmeline Pankhurst* (New York, 1961), p. 133.
28. W. L. George, "The Story of Women," *The Fortnightly Review,* CXVI (1924), 851; Ray Strachey, *"The Cause": A History of the Women's Movement in Great Britain* (Port Washington, New York), 1928, pp. 304, 305.
29. *The Subjection of Women* (Philadelphia, 1869), p. 153. In the battered library copy I have been using, a more recent convert to the cause has written "Right on!"
30. Constance Rouer, *Women's Suffrage and Party Politics in Britain 1866–1914* (London and Toronto), 1967, p. 74; Kamm, p. 164.
31. E. Sylvia Pankhurst, *The Life of Emmeline Pankhurst: The Suffragette Struggle for Women's Citizenship* (New York, 1969), p. 66.
32. Pankhurst, p. 83.
33. *Ibid.,* p. 75.
34. Pankhurst, p. 92; Kamm, p. 160.
35. Millicent Garrett Fawcett, *Women's Suffrage: A Short History of a Great Movement* (London, n.d.), p. 86.
36. Kamm, p. 142; Pankhurst, p. 103.
37. Vladimir Didijer, *The Road to Sarajevo* (New York, 1966), p. 197.

38. Martin Pappenheim, "Conversations with Princip," translated by Hamilton Fish Armstrong, *Current History,* August, 1927, pp. 702 ff; Sidney Bradshaw Fay, *The Origins of the World War,* revised edition (New York, 1947), II, 95.
39. "To Those Who Are Coming," in Didijer, p. 239; Lewis S. Feuer, *The Conflict of Generations* (New York, 1969), p. 79.
40. Feuer, pp. 83–84.
41. Didijer, p. 321.

CHAPTER 8

1. Philip Gibbs, "The Social Revolution in English Life," *Harper's Magazine,* CXLII (1921), 561; Robert Graves, *Goodbye to All That* (Harmondsworth, England), 1960, p. 54.
2. Ernest Hemingway, *A Farewell to Arms* (New York, 1957), pp. 184–185.
3. Mark Sullivan, *Our Times: The United States 1900–1925,* Volume 6, *The Twenties* (New York, 1937), p. 116, note 4.
4. *The American Mercury,* Volume I (1924), number 1, p. 75.
5. Richard Le Gallienne, "What's Wrong with the Eighteen-Nineties?" *The Bookman,* LIV (1921), 2; Carl Zuckmayer, in Peter Gay, *Weimar Culture* (New York, 1968), p. 114.
6. Ernest Hemingway, *A Moveable Feast* (New York, 1964), pp. 29–31.
7. Frederick Lewis Allen, *Only Yesterday: An Informal History of the Nineteen-Twenties* (New York and London, 1931), p. 88; Calvin B. T. Lee, *The Campus Scene, 1900–1970: Changing Styles in Undergraduate Life* (New York, 1970), p. 23; Sullivan, pp. 384–385.
8. Allen, p. 90.
9. Magazine articles on "Youth" listed in the *Reader's Guide to Periodical Literature,* for instance, expanded from a dozen entries in the 1910–14 volume to two solid pages of fine print in the 1925–28 volume.
10. Allen, p. 105. My wife, by contrast, says she can dress herself quite comfortably in a mere three yards of cloth in the early 1970's.
11. *Op. cit.,* p. 115.
12. Sullivan, VI, 393.
13. "Professional Youth," *The Saturday Evening Post,* April 28, 1923, pp. 156–157.
14. *This Side of Paradise* (New York, 1948), p. 287.
15. John F. Carter, " 'These Wild Young People,' by One of Them," *The Atlantic Monthly,* CXXVI (September, 1920), 302.

16. *Exile's Return: A Literary Odyssey of the 1920's* (New York, 1956), pp. 60–61.
17. Allen, pp. 393–395.
18. *Ibid.,* p. 175.
19. Tristan Tzara, "Memoirs of Dadaism," Appendix to Edmund Wilson, *Axel's Castle: A Study of the Imaginative Literature of 1870–1930* (New York, 1931), p. 243; André Breton, in Elmer Peterson, *Tristan Tzara: Dada and Surrational Theorist* (New Brunswick, N. J.), 1971, p. 29; Tzara, "Seven Deadly Manifestos," in Robert Motherwell, ed., *The Dada Painters and Poets: An Anthology* (New York, 1951), p. 75.
20. Tzara in Wilson, p. 241.
21. René Lacôte, *Tristan Tzara* (Paris, 1948), p. 18.
22. Hans Richter, *Dada: Art and Anti-Art* (London, 1965), p. 37.
23. *All Quiet on the Western Front,* translated by A. W. Wheen (London, 1929), pp. 286–287.
24. Arp, Janco, and Richter, in Richter, pp. 25, 122; Richard Huelsenbeck, *En Avant Dada,* in Motherwell, p. 23.
25. Richter, pp. 37, 48.
26. Richter, p. 38; Wilson, p. 242.
27. Hans Arp, "The Guest Expulsed 5," Richter, p. 52.
28. *The Waste Land and Other Poems* (New York, 1934), pp. 39, 34.
29. Mary Agnes Hamilton, "Where Are You Going, My Pretty Maid?" *Atlantic Monthly,* September, 1926, p. 301.

CHAPTER 9

1. Van Wyck Brooks, *Days of the Phoenix* (London, 1957), p. 183.
2. *Life,* July 11, 1930, p. 18.
3. Sidney Pollard, *The Development of the British Economy 1911–1950* (London, 1962), p. 243; Koppel S. Pinson, *Modern Germany,* second edition (New York and London, 1966), p. 453; Arthur S. Link, *American Epoch: A History of the United States since the 1890's* (New York, 1955), p. 359.
4. *Life,* Christmas issue, December, 1930, p. 41.
5. Maxine Davis, *The Lost Generation: A Portrait of American Youth Today* (New York, 1936), pp. 32, 27.
6. Calvin B. T. Lee, *The Campus Scene, 1900–1970: Changing Styles in Undergraduate Life* (New York, 1970), pp. 65–66.
7. Hal Draper, "The Student Movement of the Thirties; A Political History," in Rita James Simon, ed., *As We Saw the Thirties* (Urbana, Chicago and London), 1967, p. 176.

8. Again I am indebted to Seymour Martin Lipset and Gerald Schaflander for a look at the manuscript of *They'd Rather Be Left: The Past, Present, and Future of Student Activism in America,* to be published in the fall of 1971. I draw here upon Chapters 4 and 5 of this work.
9. Irving Kristol, "Ten Years in a Tunnel: Reflections on the 1930's," in Morton J. Frisch and Martin Diamond, *The Thirties: A Reconsideration in the Light of the American Political Tradition* (De Kalb, Ill.), 1968, p. 12.
10. Davis, pp. 3–4.
11. Lee, p. 48.
12. Murray Kempton, *Part of Our Time: Some Ruins and Monuments of the Thirties* (New York, 1955), p. 305.
13. Draper, p. 169; Lee, p. 63. Some estimates for 1936 run as high as 500,000.
14. Alfred Kazin, *Starting Out in the Thirties* (Boston and Toronto, 1962), pp. 82–83.
15. Kempton, pp. 1–11.
16. *Ibid.,* p. 5.
17. Ralph de Toledano, *Lament for a Generation* (New York, 1960), p. 25.
18. Richard Crossman, ed., *The God that Failed* (New York, 1952), p. 146.
19. Kempton, p. 303.
20. Draper, pp. 183–184.
21. Laqueur, p. 191.
22. I am indebted, here and below as noted, to Professor Peter Loewenberg's paper on "The Psycho-Historical Origins of the Nazi Youth Cohort: 1928–1933," read at the American Historical Association meetings in Boston, December, 1970.
23. Alice Hamilton, "The Youth Who Are Hitler's Strength," reprinted in John Weiss, ed., *Nazis and Fascists in Europe, 1918–1945* (Chicago, 1969), p. 87.
24. *Goodbye to Berlin* (Harmondsworth, England), 1945, p. 60.
25. Loewenberg, *op. cit.*
26. *Hitler's Table Talk, 1941–44,* London, 1953, pp. 698–699; Adolf Hitler, *Mein Kampf,* John Chamberlain *et al.,* eds., pp. 19–20.
27. Bradley F. Smith, *Adolf Hitler: His Family, Childhood and Youth* (Stanford, California), 1967, p. 137.
28. David Schoenbaum, *Hitler's Social Revolution: Class and Status in Nazi Germany, 1933–1939* (Garden City, New York), 1966, p. 69.
29. May Day Address to the German Youth, Berlin, 1 May 1936, in *The Speeches of Adolf Hitler, April 1922–August 1939,* Norman H. Baynes, ed. (New York, 1969), pp. 545 ff.

30. Hermann Führbach's autobiographical narrative from the Hoover Institution's Abel File, in Joachim Remak, ed., *The Nazi Years: A Documentary History* (Englewood Cliffs, N. J.), 1969, p. 46.
31. Hamilton, p. 88.
32. *The Rise and Fall of the Third Reich* (Greenwich, Conn.), 1962, p. 349.
33. Laqueur, p. 215, note 1.
34. *Op. cit.*, p. 354.

CHAPTER 10

1. Radio Budapest, Tuesday, 23 October 1956, in Richard Lettis and William E. Morris, *The Hungarian Revolt* (New York, 1961), p. 11.
2. UNESCO, *World Survey of Education,* I (1955), 19; IV (1966), 15; Basil Fletcher, *Universities in the Modern World* (London, 1968), pp. 28, 5.
3. Herbert Gold, "The Beat Mystique," in Seymour Krim, ed., *The Beats* (Greenwich, Conn.), 1960, pp. 155–156; Jack Kerouac, *The Subterraneans* (New York, 1958), p. 32.
4. John Clellon Holmes, "The Philosophy of the Beat Generation," in Krim, p. 14; Norman Mailer, "The White Negro," in Gene Feldman and Max Gartenberg, eds., *The Beat Generation and the Angry Young Men* (New York, 1959), pp. 372–373; "Howl," in Allen, pp. 182–184.
5. Feldman and Gartenberg, Introduction, p. 11; David McReynolds, "Hipsters Unleashed," in Krim, p. 209.
6. M. Stanton Evans, *Revolt on Campus* (Chicago, 1961), p. 217; Kenneth Keniston, *The Uncommitted: Alienated Youth in American Society* (New York, 1965), pp. 27, 58.
7. Lawrence Ferlinghetti, "Junkman's Obbligato," *A Coney Island of the Mind* (New York, 1958), pp. 54, 57.
8. "Upon My Refusal To Herald Cuba," *Long Live Man* (New York, 1962), p. 57.
9. Walter Allen, "Review of Lucky Jim," in Feldman and Gartenberg, p. 368.
10. Allen Sillitoe, *The Loneliness of the Long Distance Runner* (London, 1959), p. 8.
11. Feldman and Gartenberg, p. 17 note.
12. John Osborne, *Look Back in Anger* (New York, 1959), p. 82.
13. Giuseppe Boffa, *Inside the Khrushchev Era,* translated by Carl Marzani (New York, 1959), pp. 207, 209.
14. Yevgeny Yevtushenko, *A Precocious Autobiography,* translated by

Andrew R. MacAndrew (New York, 1964), p. 102; Robert Rozhdestvensky, "Morning," in Hugh McLean and Walter N. Vickery, eds. and translators, *The Year of Protest, 1956: An Anthology of Soviet Literary Materials* (New York, 1961), p. 150.

15. A ZR, "The Conscience of a Generation—A Commentary," in Abraham Brumberg, *Russia Under Khrushchev: An Anthology from Problems of Communism* (New York, 1962), p. 427.
16. Francis Sejersted, *Moscow Diary* (London, 1961), p. 76.
17. *Inside Russia Today,* revised edition (New York, 1962), p. 73.
18. *Ibid.,* p. 72.

CHAPTER 11

1. *Time,* volume LXXV, No. 1, January 4, 1960, pp. 11–13, 35, 45.
2. *Ibid.,* volume LXXVI, No. 26, December 26, 1960, pp. 6, 16–18.
3. Inaugural Address, 20 January 1961, quoted in *Time,* volume LXXVII, No. 5, January 27, 1961, p. 8.
4. Gregory Henderson, *Korea: The Politics of the Vortex* (Cambridge, Mass., 1968), p. 140.
5. C. I. Eugene Kim and Ke-soo Kim, "The April 1960 Korean Student Movement," *Western Political Quarterly,* XVII (1964), 94.
6. Henderson, p. 175.
7. Walter F. Weiker, *The Turkish Revolution 1960–1961* (Washington, D. C., 1963), p. 16.
8. Leslie L. Roos, Jr., Noralou P. Roos, and Gary R. Field, "Students and Politics in Contemporary Turkey," in Seymour Martin Lipset and Philip G. Altbach, *Students in Revolt* (Boston, 1969), p. 257.
9. Weiker, p. 17.
10. David R. Gordon, *The Passing of French Algeria* (London, 1966), p. 61.
11. Paul Henissart, *Wolves in the City: The Death of French Algeria* (New York, 1970), p. 45; *Time,* volume LXXVI, No. 26, December 26, 1960, p. 17.
12. Gordon, p. 62; Henissart, p. 46.
13. *Sartre on Cuba* (New York, 1961), pp. 88, 89.
14. Georges Friedmann, *Signal d'un troisième voie?* (Paris, 1961).
15. *Time,* volume LXXVI, No. 7, August 15, 1960, p. 28.
16. Lewis S. Feuer, *The Conflict of Generations: The Character and Significance of Student Movements* (New York and London), 1969, p. 205.
17. Fukuji Taguchi, "Japan in Transition," in Bernard Crick and William

A. Robson, *Protest and Discontent* (Harmondsworth, England, 1970), pp. 174–175; Charlotte Nassim, "Notes on the Revolutionary Students in Japan," in Tariq Ali, *The New Revolutionaries: A Handbook of the International Radical Left* (New York, 1969), p. 256.

18. Joseph A. Califano, *The Student Revolution: A Global Confrontation* (New York, 1970), pp. 31–32.
19. Tarzie Vittachi, *The Fall of Sukarno* (New York and Washington, D.C., 1967), p. 163; Robert S. Elegant, "Indonesia's Slaughtered Reds," San Francisco *Chronicle,* 5 May 1966, p. 2E, in Feuer, p. 216.
20. John Hughes, *Indonesian Upheaval* (New York, 1967), p. 217; Seth S. King, "Students Emerge as Jakarta Force," *The New York Times,* April 2, 1966.
21. Victor Nee, *The Cultural Revolution at Peking University* (New York and London, 1969), p. 71.
22. Feuer, p. 193.
23. "The Sixteen Points," in Joan Robinson, *The Cultural Revolution in China* (Baltimore, Md., 1969), p. 24; "Red Guards Destroy the Old and Establish the New," *Peking Review,* No. 36, September 2, 1966, in K. H. Fan, *The Chinese Cultural Revolution: Selected Documents* (New York, 1968), pp. 186–187.
24. Stephen Spender, *The Year of the Young Rebels* (New York, 1969).
25. A. H. Hanson, "Some Literature on Student Revolt," in Crick and Robson, p. 142, note 15.
26. Trevor Fisk, "The Nature and Causes of Student Unrest," in Crick and Robson, pp. 82–83; Califano, pp. 18–19.
27. Barbara and John Ehrenreich, *Long March, Short Spring: The Student Uprising at Home and Abroad* (New York and London, 1969), pp. 56–58.
28. *Ibid.,* p. 38.
29. *Ibid.,* p. 40.
30. Spender, p. 94.
31. Ehrenreich, p. 42.
32. F. C. Hunnius, "The New Left in West Germany," *Our Generation,* Volume VI, Nos. 1–2, p. 34.
33. Patrick Seale and Maureen McConville, *Red Flag / Black Flag: French Revolution 1968* (New York, 1968), p. 83.
34. *Ibid.,* p. 72.
35. *Ibid.,* p. 84.
36. Spender, p. 39.
37. Seale and McConville, pp. 87, 86.
38. Ehrenreich, pp. 82–83.

39. Seale and McConville, p. 92.
40. Reprinted in Peggy Duff, "The French Revolution: 1968," *Our Generation,* Volume 6, Nos. 1–2, p. 72; Spender, p. 42.

CHAPTER 12

1. See Chapter 2 above.
2. Theodore H. White, *The Making of the President 1960* (New York, 1961), pp. 395–396.
3. The following extracts are cited from "The Port Huron Statement," in Paul Jacobs and Saul Landau, *The New Radicals: A Report with Documents* (New York, 1966), pp. 149–162.
4. Martin Luther King, Jr., *Stride Toward Freedom: The Montgomery Story* (New York, 1964), pp. 192–193, 200.
5. Claude Sitton, in *The New York Times,* May 7, 1963, in Anthony Lewis, *Portrait of a Decade: The Second American Revolution* (New York, 1965), p. 159.
6. Max Heirich, *The Beginning: Berkeley, 1964* (New York and London, 1968), pp. 199–200.
7. *Ibid.,* p. 256.
8. See Chapters 4 and 6 above, and Anthony Esler, "Youth in Revolt: The French Generation of 1830," in Robert J. Bezucha, ed., *Modern European Social History: A Collection of Original Essays,* to be published in the spring of 1972.
9. Karl Mannheim, "The Problem of Generations," in *Essays in the Sociology of Knowledge,* Paul Kecskemeti, ed. (New York, 1952), pp. 302 ff.
10. Hugh Davis Graham and Ted Robert Gurr, *Violence in America: Historical and Comparative Perspectives (Report to the National Commission on the Causes and Prevention of Violence)* (New York, 1969), p. 576; *Report of the National Commission on Civil Disorders* (New York, 1968), p. 38.
11. Tom Hayden, *Rebellion in Newark: Official Violence and Ghetto Response* (New York, 1967), p. 17.
12. *Commission on Civil Disorders,* pp. 128–129; Stokely Carmichael, "Black Power," in David Cooper, ed., *To Free a Generation: The Dialectics of Liberation* (New York, 1969), pp. 166, 169.
13. Robert Conot, *Rivers of Blood, Years of Darkness* (New York, 1967), p. 42.
14. Henry Gross, *The Flower People* (New York, 1968), p. 58.
15. Tom Wolfe, *The Electric Kool-Aid Acid Test* (New York, 1969), p. 68; Burton H. Wolfe, *The Hippies* (New York, 1968), p. 187;

William Braden, *The Private Sea: LSD and the Search for God* (New York, 1968), pp. 190 ff; Gross, p. 3.

16. Burton Wolfe, p. 103.
17. Theodore Roszak, *The Making of a Counter Culture: Reflections on the Technocratic Society and Its Youthful Opposition* (Garden City, New York), 1969, p. 66; Gerome Ragni and James Rado, *Hair* (New York, 1969), p. 3.
18. "America and the New Era," in Massimo Teodori, *The New Left: A Documentary History* (New York, 1969), p. 180; Jack Newfield, *A Prophetic Minority* (New York, 1967), pp. 155, 158.
19. Newfield, pp. 87–88.
20. The present author pleads guilty in advance, adding by way of mitigating circumstance only that he at least began to concern himself with the Movement when it was still in its salad days.
21. Mark Rudd to Grayson Kirk, April 12, 1968, in Jerry L. Avorn *et al., Up Against the Ivy Wall* (New York, 1969), p. 27. The phrase is a quote from the angry young black writer LeRoi Jones.
22. James A. Michener, *Kent State: What Happened and Why* (New York, 1971), pp. 438, 447.
23. Karl Fleming, "We'll Blow Up the World," *Newsweek,* October 17, 1970, p. 49.
24. Burton Wolfe, p. 189.
25. *Woodstock Nation* (New York, 1969), pp. 10, 8.
26. Jerry Rubin, *Do It!* (New York, 1970), pp. 80, 84.
27. "Susan Atkins' Complete Story," in Lawrence Schiller, *The Killing of Sharon Tate* (New York, 1969), pp. 94, 116.

CHAPTER 13

1. *Do It!* (New York, 1970), p. 82.
2. "Communiqué No. 1. From the Weatherman Underground," in Harold Jacobs, ed., *Weatherman* (n.p., 1970), pp. 509–510.
3. Harry Kalven, Jr., ed., *Contempt: Transcript of the Contempt Citations, Sentences, and Responses of the Chicago Conspiracy 10* (Chicago, 1970), p. 90; Mark L. Levine, *et al., The Tales of Hoffman, Edited from the Official Transcript* (New York, 1970), p. 280.
4. Frederick G. Dutton, *Changing Sources of Power: American Politics in the 1970's* (New York, 1971), p. 38.
5. Daniel Yankelovich, Inc., *Generations Apart: A Study of the Generation Gap Conducted for CBS News* (n.p., 1969), pp. 17, 24, 25.
6. *Ibid.,* p. 32.

7. Dutton, pp. 38, 40.
8. Henry E. Dwight, *Travels in the North of Germany in the Years 1825 to 1826* (New York, 1829), p. 203; "Class of 69: The Violent Years," *Newsweek,* June 23, 1969, p. 69.
9. Franz von Schnabel, *Deutsche Geschichte im neunzehnten Jahrhundert* (Freiburg im Breisgau, 1933), II, 246; "Parades for Peace and Patriotism," *Time,* November 21, 1969, p. 24; Albert Joseph George, *The Development of French Romanticism: The Impact of the Industrial Revolution on Literature* (Syracuse, New York, 1955), p. 79; *Life:* special issue, *Woodstock Music Festival,* 1969, p .1.

Index